THE THADOU KUKIS

THE THADOU KUKIS

BY
William Shaw

with an Introduction by
J. H. Hutton

GYAN

Published by

Gyan Publishing House
5, Ansari Road
Daryaganj, New Delhi-110002
Phone: 011-47034999, 9811692060
E-mail: books@gyanbooks.com

Distribution Network
gyanbooks.com
India, USA, Canada, UK, Australia, France

ISBN : 978-81-212-1998-3 (HB)
First Published, 1929

2nd Impression 2021

Printed at: Gyan Press, Delhi.

The Thadou Kukis
Author: William Shaw

INTRODUCTION.

Mr. Shaw, the author of these notes on the Thado is qualified to write of them by seven years residence as Subdivisional Officer of the North-west area of the Manipur State, which is there inhabited by scattered groups of Thado Kukis living among Kabui and Kachha Naga communities who were established in those hills long before the Thado intruded there. He was also in intermittent contact with Thado Kukis during five years service in the Naga Hills district. Of the Thado groups in these areas the Shitlho clan is the most important and claims to be the senior clan of the descendants of Thado, the ancestor of the raee. There is an appreciable degree of divergence between details of custom in different areas and in different clans, and Mr. Shaw's account must be taken to refer primarily to the Shitlho practice. In other respects also his account has perhaps some bias towards the Shitlho point of view. Thus he describes the house of Dongngel, which is senior in origin to that of the Shitlho, as *ingam* or extinct in the male line, and represented only by the descendant of a slave. This is the Shitlho view and is so stated by them with some emphasis, but it is so far from being universally accepted, that Chengjapao, the present head of the Dongngel clan, is accepted as the legitimate descendant of Dongngel by collaterals of unimpugnable pedigree who would be able to substantiate their own claims to represent Dongngel if Chengjapao's were rejected.

I suspect, moreover, that Mr. Shaw's estimate of the Thado has been coloured by the fact that he has had to deal with a society in the process of reconstruction on a new basis. Before the Kuki rising of 1918-1919 the administration in the hill areas of the Manipur State was not very close, and the Thado, ruled as they were by their own well-recognized chiefs, and treated, as they had been in the past at any rate, by the Manipur State as allies almost as much as subjects, managed their own affairs in their own way and had recourse to the courts only in exceptional cases.

With the suppression of the Kuki rebellion the confiscation of all guns and the punishment of several of the leading chiefs, an era of much closer administration set in, and the Thado have had to put up with a great deal more administrative interference. In addition to this, American and Welsh Missionaries have been allowed to extend their work among them and considerable numbers have been converted to the new faith. The result of all this must have been to loosen old ties and to weaken tribal sanctions so that the Thado society is at present in the process of adapting itself to greatly changed conditions, and social disturbance of this sort is inevitably bound to cause a good deal of discomfort, litigation and general friction. This, I think, has caused the Thado to appear to Mr. Shaw in an unduly unfavourable light. It has also, perhaps, affected his report on them in other ways for they have had little chance of recovering the condition of prosperity which they had in many cases attained before 1918. Thus at any rate the Hôlthang Thado and a good many of the Shitlho had built for themselves fine and permanent villages and were living in a much higher condition of comfort than they are now. Had Mr. Shaw been able to see such villages as Santing and Chongjang before they were destroyed during the rebellion he would hardly have described the Thado dwelling as he does without qualification.

A word is needed on the question of transliteration. Mr. Shaw has followed the Manipur convention of writing *OU* for *Ō*. This has its advantages in getting rid of a diacritical mark, but to my ear the sound represented is a simple vowel and not a dipthong and I have therefore generally thought it unnecessary myself to use more than a simple *O*. Similarly, in one or two other respects it will be observed that Mr. Shaw's spelling and mine do not always agree, but I have not thought fit to alter his nor necessary to change my own. *J*, *Y* and *Z* have presented some difficulty, being interchangeable, and *Y* and *Z* have been discarded in favour of J as the best to represent all three values, of which a hard *Z* is probably the rarest and the French value of *J* the commonest. *Zh* is preferred by some, but there is not really any perceptible aspirate. *Y* may occassionally be found with a purely euphonic significance separating *i* from another *i* following. The language is at present being written down and taught in Schools by the American Baptist Mission, and it is to be hoped that their labours will result in the formation of a scientific and logical system of transliteration, but the difficulties are many.

The Thado are a scattered tribe inhabiting parts of the North Cachar Hills, the Naga Hills, the Manipur State and spreading east into Burma in the Chin Hills and Somra Tract. Their total numbers probably amount to about 50,000 souls, the females exceeding the males by about 5%, and the great bulk of the tribe being found in the hills of Manipur. The northern origin of the Kuki race in general will be found discussed in the first chapter, but it is obvious that though no doubt nearly related to the Kachins by origin the race has absorbed many—alien elements, probably including Shan, Mon-Khmer and Negrito. The latter is often suggested by the appearance of many of the Thado, and by a tradition of war with little, dark and bitter men. The history of Burma is one horrid catalogue of the smashing of kingdoms and the massacre, dispersal and transportation of populations and it would be surprising if a tribe that had migrated down the Chindwin Valley and sojourned on the west bank of that river had not absorbed Shan elements from the break up of the kingdom of Pong and Mon elements from the inhuman destruction of the Talaing kingdom of Pegu by the Burmese. Indeed Peter Heylin's description of the people of Pegu (quoted below, p. 20 n.[1]) would well fit the Thado, and some customs, such as the ordeal by diving, seem definitely associated with the Mon culture. Pinto speaks of "auburn" hair in Pegu, and rusty brown is common among Thado. Many Thado customs are suggestive of the Khasis and of the Hos, both of Indonesian affinity, and anyhow we may be sure that there was no lack of actual contact with the races of Burma as Pinto mentions Tipperas [1] as serving in the Burmese armies, in which case we may be sure there were Kukis too, if "Tuperaas" may not actually be taken to include them. There are however many points of Kuki culture which are vividly suggestive of the culture of the pagan Malays of the Indian Archipelago and the Philippines. For instance the Thado custom of burying the dead in what must be a troublesome excavation leading out of a simple pit grave reappears in Sumatra and in the Philippine Islands, where the Tinguian and the Mandaya follow it, and also share with the Lushei and probably some tribes of Borneo the practice of eating part of the liver of a slain foe.[2] In particular all Kukis, and the Thado is no exception, are or have been slave-hunters, as well as brigands in general, professions to which the Malay Tribes of Indonesia were notoriously given. Other points of contact will be found mentioned in the notes or appendix. The migratory condition of the Thado is probably to be ascribed in part at any rate to their having been unable to find vacant land on which to settle as proprietors. Their migrations since they were driven north out of what is now the Lushai Hills by the Lushei have been almost entirely in country already fully populated, a fact which has probably perpetuated their migratory inclinations beyond their natural term. They are by no means nomads but they lack the restraint of proprietorship. Where they have succeeded in acquiring suitable land of their own they seem ready and content to settle down permanently, and some are even taking to wet cultivation. Change, however, is likely to be rapid, and as the invariable effect of Mission enterprise seems to be to cause converts to forget all they can of the traditions of their fore-fathers, it is well that Mr. Shaw has recorded what he could before the opportunity has passed for ever.

---

1 *Voyages of Fernando Mendez Pinto*, tr. H. Cogan, 1663, pp. 200,204.

2 The *Melanesian* of Florida, like the Lushei, licks from his spear-blade the blood of the first foe he kills (Codrington, *The Melanesians*, 305, Lewin, *Wild Races of S. E. India*, 269).

I have to acknowledge here the kindness of Col. J. Shakespear and of Messrs. Macmillan & Co. in permitting the reproduction of the map published by them in Col. Shakespear's *Lushei-Kuki Clans*, also the help of Mr. S. J. Duncan of Tamenlong in making drawings of a number of objects specimens of which I was unable to find in this district, but a few of which exist in the Manipur State.

KOHIMA,
July, 1928.

J. H. H.

CONTENTS.

ILLUSTRATIONS.

FOREWORD.

These notes on the Thados are not to be taken as exhaustive, but include all important peculiarities and customs of a very important tribe on the eastern frontier of Assam, among whom I have had the fortune of working for many years. In particular I have to thank Jamkithang, a Thado of the Shitlho clan, second clerk Tamenlong Sub-division, Manipur State, Kopsat, Dongpu and many chiefs of the various clans in helping me to get at customs and beliefs. I am indebted to Dr. Hutton for editing my MS.

Before missionary influence should make their customs and beliefs things of the past it was my desire to place on record what was still remembered, and existed, for those who might be interested to read.

W. Shaw.

Hailakandi,
August 1928.

CHAPTER I.

General Description.

General Habitat.

The Thadou Kukis[1] live in a large area of hilly country bounded by the Angami Nagas of the Naga Hills District in the north, the Province of Burma in the east, the Chin Hills and Lushai Hills in the south and the District of Cachar in the west. Mainly, it may be said, they occupy the hills of the State of Manipur on all sides of the Imphal valley. The Shitlhous, whose chief is Khotinthang alias Kilkong living in the village of Jampi, reside to the northwest of the valley. The Dongngels, chief Chenjapao, are in the northeast. The Haokips, chief Lhokhumang, border the valley on all sides but are mostly on the northeast. The Kipgens are mainly to the west. The Shingshons, chief Mangpu, are to the southwest of the valley. The Chonglois, Hangshings, Phohils, etc. are all promiscuously mixed up in the villages whose chiefs are one or the other of the clans given above and have no recognised chiefs of their own. They have become absorbed gradually for various reasons by the more powerful clans. The Hangshings, however, have recently formed a village under Vumpu, alias Kapjavum, who is the head of their branch, in the Tamenlong Subdivision at Vongjang; but he is unquestionably under the thumb, politically, of the Shitlhous in whose midst he has started his village.

---

[1] *Kuki.* The origin of this word is not known, but it first appears in Bengal, Rawlins writing of the "Cucis or Mountaineers of Tipra" in *Asiatick Researches* (II, xii.) in 1792. *Klongshai* is the name used in Aracan for the Lakher tribe (Shakespear, *Lushai Kuki Clans*, p. 213) and some of the Thado—Haokips, I think—are said to use a word *Khongshai* for Kukis in general, which reappears in the Meithei *Khonjai* and probably in the Angami Naga *Kotso-ma.* They speak of themselves as Thado, and though this term may be taken to cover only the descendants of that eponymous ancestor, it is generally used to cover also dependent clans now intermingled with and closely associated with those descendants, though not actually claiming Thado as an ancestor, such, in particular, are the descendants of Lenthang and Lunkim (*v. infra* pp. 24, 26 and 29 n.a.) for whom, if they are not to be called Thados, there is no other distinctive term. Thado, it may be noted, seems to be a Burmese title, apparently denoting courage or ability (*vide* Scott and Hardiman, *Gazetteer of Upper Burma and the Shan States* I, ii, 147), and MacRae, writing in 1799 mentions a then existing individual chief called Thandon (*Asiatic Researches* VII, 188). Soppitt, nearly a century later (*Short account of the Kuki-Lushai Tribes*) derives Kuki thus :—*Kuki* .. *Kukai* .. *Lukai* .. *Luahai* (=*Lushai*), and translates *Luahai* as the "Lua people" of *Lua* he says "In some accounts of Burma mention is made of traces having been found of a people ruled over by the Lua kings or king in days gone by." A little fanciful, perhaps. Anyhow I cannot trace these *Lua* unless they are *Lawa*, a synonym for *Wa* (Harvey, *Burma*, p. 354). Lewin (*Exercises in the Lushai Dialect*, p. 1) suggests a derivation for 'Kuki' from the Dzo (Lushei) word, *Tui-Kuk*, for the Tippera (Sakchip) Tribe.—(Ed.

The total number of houses which could be classified as Thadou would roughly be about 5,500; and placing an average of 5 persons per house this would give a total of 27,500 souls spread over an area of about 10,000 square miles. This would appear a small proportion for the area envolved, but it must be remembered that there are Kacha Nagas, Kabuis, Tangkhuls, Koms, Chirus, Aimols, Marings, Manipuris and others who also inhabit the same area. In the area given is included the Mauza of Henima in the Naga Hills District under Palal Mauzadar where there are some Thadou villages. In addition a few odd villages are to be found in the North Cachar Hills, in the hills bordering the Cachar valley, in Sylhet on the southern hills and in the hills in Burma on the Manipur State frontier.

Appearance and physical Characteristics.

All the Thadous resemble each other very closely in appearance and have, generally speaking, a Mongolian type of countenance. The Haokips and Kipgens are fairer than the others and have a yellow-olive complexion. The same may be said of the Dongngels. The Shitlhous, Lhouvum, Shingshon[1] etc., are certainly of a darker shade and some of a distinct copper colour. The chiefs are usually fairer and the reason for this is not far to see as they do not expose themselves to climatic influences to the same extent as their villagers, yet they are not as fair as those of the Haokips and Kipgens even when compared with the ordinary villagers.

Miscegenation with captives and neighbouring tribes exists at the present day among the Thadous. There are examples at Kandung village in the Naga Hills and in many Thadou villages where Naga slaves have been absorbed. There are admitted instances of Manipuris becoming Thadous. But chiefs lose their position by such marriages, and they occur mainly among the ordinary villagers.

Beards and whiskers are uncommon but there is a distinct liking for a few hairs at the corners of the mouth on the upper lips. It is not uncommon to see men picking out the other

---

[1] The fairest Thados I ever saw were Shingshuans and Mr. J. C. Higgins tells me his experience is the same, but I think it would probably be correct to say that the Thado living in the north-west of Manipur and in the adjacent area of the Naga Hills are darker and shorter than those living further south and west, and I fancy the reason is to be found in a greater admixture of non-Thado blood. The Old Kuki tribes, Aimol, Kom, Anal, Bete, Hrankol and others (see Shakespear, *Lushei Kuki Clans*, pt. II, ch. III) were probably the advance guard of the Kuki group in its migration, the Thado coming next, and the later the arrival the less the need or the opportunity would be for miscegenation. I am inclined to give a similar reason for the fairer complexions of the Thado chiefs. Mr. Shaw's explanation does not satisfy me, as though the chief does not work in the fields in the same way as his villagers, I do not think that the difference in the extent to which he exposes himself is enough to make any appreciable difference in the colour of his skin.—(Ed.)

hairs on their upper lips with tweezers. The old men, however, appear to appreciate a few hairs on their chins and some have cultivated a distinct "Imperial." The hair on the head, when a boy, is regularly shaved off leaving a tuft at the back end of the head. When the boy grows up to the age of puberty he is then allowed to grow the rest. It is never cut again and, when long enough, is tied up in a knot at the back of the head. It is combed back from the forehead and greased with pig's fat at frequent intervals. So it remains to the end of his life. Unfortunately they have taken to cutting their hair short, perhaps owing to Mission influence, and say it is cooler and less troublesome to manage. The old folk naturally view this attitude with grave displeasure and vow those who do so will never reach MITHI KHU (The village of the departed souls).

The girls are also shaven[1] except for a small patch at the back of the head which is allowed to grow unhampered. When they reach maturity—sometimes a little before—their hair is allowed to grow. Here again plenty of pig's fat is used. When long enough it is divided down the centre of the head and plaited into two strands on each side of the head. When this grows longer the strands are crossed and brought round the head and tied in front above the forehead. The plait on the right side is taken around the back of the head and over the left ear, while the plait on the left goes round the back of the head and over the right ear. A piece of cotton or combings of hair are interplaited at the ends of these two strands so as to facilitate the tying of them at the front of the head. A husband may use his wife's hair oil (pig's fat) or vice versa, but it is "taboo" for another person to do so other than of that household. The reason given being that it would cause the hair to fall out and some awful ailment would be the consequences to the culprit.[2] Now-a-days, cheap and smelly bazar hair oil is

---

[1] This practice of shaving the heads of unmarried girls is prevalent throughout the hill area that divides Assam and Bengal from Burma and occurs also in the Nicobars (Hamilton, *Account of the East Indies* II, 71). In some tribes the shaving is continued even after marriage and throughout life, and supplemented by actually plucking out the hair in places. Westermarck, *History of Human Marriage*, p. 175-6, points out that short hair is often symbolical of chastity. The fact that the hair is allowed to grow just before or after marriage seems to support this, but probably in this particular area some weight must be attached to the consideration that shaven heads are much the easiest to keep free of vermin, a very good reason for forgoing the sexual attraction of long hair as long as possible.—(Ed.)

[2] This tabu on alien hair-grease is to be associated no doubt with the world-wide view that the hair is a particular seat of the soul or life-force (cf. Shakespear, *Lushei-Kuki Clans*, page 109). The story of Samson is a familiar example, and the theory is common in the Indonesian area. Thus the Karens of Burma appear to have the idea (Marshall, *Karen people of Burma*, page 287) in that the father of an expected child may not cut his hair for fear of shortening the life of the child; in Malaya a warrior on an

becoming daily commoner and there does not appear to be any objection to sharing a bottle. As men and women reach a ripe age they pay less attention to their coiffure and it becomes an untidy lump tied anyhow. A good many seem to lose most of their hair and the top of the head becomes caked with dirt. Curly hair or waved[1] is rare, but isolated cases are seen. The hair generally is black with a copper tint in many. Hair, as a secondary male characteristic, is generally absent from the chest and armpits.

The Shitlhous are more squat than the Haokips and Kipgens. The others may safely be placed in the same category as the Shitlhous. They have disproportionately large thighs and calves and the appearance of being heavy and slow, which they undoubtedly are both physically and mentally. The Haokips and Kipgens differ as they are taller built and are not so heavy about the lower limbs. They are generally more agile and energetic both mentally and physically than clans of other bloods.[2]

---

expedition may not have his hair cut, nor may his wife or child during his absence (Skeat, *Malay Magic*). In Nias a chief kept his life in a hair on his head that was as hard as copper wire (Frazer, *Golden Bough*, XI, 148,) and in Amboyna and in Ceram strength depends on not having the hair cut (*ibid.* 158). This idea appears again in Fiji (Brewster, *Hill Tribes of Fiji*, page 245), as apparently in Madagascar (Osborn, *Madagascar, etc.*, page 332), and in the Marquesas Islands, where the hair of the victim of a cannibal feast is made into armlets or necklets of great virtue, suggesting that this is the reason why the people of Borneo, like the Nagas, wear the hair of their dead enemies. In America the Jivaros of the Amazon have the same belief about the hair (Karsten, *Blood Revenge, War, etc., among the Jibaro Indians* pp. 31,32,87), as well as the North American Indians, who took the scalps of their enemies. The same idea doubtless underlies the view held in India about the hair (*vide* Moses, *Sancity of hair in South India* in '*Man in India*' September, 1927), as it certainly does in Europe, where the hair is the seat of the external soul. (Frazer *loc. cit.* 104, 158.)

McCulloch (*Account of the Valley of Munnipore*, p. 63) mentions that Kukis are very particular as to who is entitled to use whose comb, and that social precedence among the Thado may be tested by this. Dalton (*Descriptive Ethnology of Bengal*, p. 47), drawing on Stewart (*Notes on N. Cachar*) mentions that the *thempu* presents a newly married couple with a comb each; that man and wife only may use the same comb; that it is most unlucky to lose a comb, and that when a man dies his comb is buried with him, while his relations break their combs and wear their hair dishevelled as a sign of mourning.—(Ed.)

[1] I fancy curly and wavy hair would be a good deal more noticeable than they are, if it were not for the use of grease and the practice of plaiting the hair. Characteristics suggesting a negroid strain are fairly frequent among Thado women, and I fancy that somewhere in their wanderings they have absorbed some of the Negrito stock, which seems to have been the indigenous element in the Naga Hills, and which, according to traditions collected by Mr. J. H. Crace, seems to have survived as a separate race in the North Cachar Hills to as late a date as the Dimapur Kingdom, a Kachari King of which exterminated the survivors. (See *Negrito Substratum in Assam*, '*Man in India*' December, 1927.)—(Ed.)

[2] I doubt the advisability of laying down any such rule other than that of locality and environment, which does not always go by clans.—(Ed.)

The women are mostly prolific but child mortality is heavy owing to their want of knowledge in matters medical concerning children and their upbringing. Sometimes there are two and three children being breast fed at ages varying from infancy to three years. They are very uncleanly and hardly ever think of having a wash. After dyeing cloths and cotton with indigenous indigo, which is boiled in a pot and the material or cotton steeped in it with their fingers, they never think of taking off the stains or washing. They just go on with their daily work and eat their food with their fingers as if nothing had happened. The same applies, no matter what they have been doing, generally to both men and women. They wash their dishes and plates after meals (even this not always) but usually do not wash their hands before taking their meals.[1] There is a Kuki story that when they had to cross the Imphal river by wading the fish died all the way down to the sea because of the dirt of ages on their bodies.

They are all good walkers and do not walk on their toes when going uphill. They plant the whole of their foot down pressing upwards with their thighs and calves for the forward step. Even on the level the same action is noticeable and they do not straighten out their legs for the next step but assume a kind of bent knee action of their own. I have noticed this among most hillmen.

Abortion and infanticide are not uncommon when the pregnancy is attended by any circumstances causing shame to the woman. Suicide happens occasionally and is usually by poison. The cause is generally some incurable illness or poverty. A case is known where a woman poisoned her husband so that she might marry her paramour, but this one may class as exceptional. Divorce is easy and frequent owing to the fact that in many marriages the two persons have not ever seen each other before, because marriages are arranged by parents generally. This, however, is dying out and the sons and daughters are insisting on having more say in the matter.

---

[1] I should have said, as far as my own experience goes, that the practice of washing the hands before eating was, on the whole, commoner than its absence. The wild Thado is, however, certainly no great advocate of ablution. I remember well the compulsory washing of one of my Thado carriers, who admitted without shame that his skin had not known water for two years, and he seemed to be a healthy enough young buck. Hodson (*Naga Tribes of Manipur*, p. 12) gives a Memi story of how the Thado, the Naga and the Manipuri had a jumping match across a watery valley. The Thado entirely cleared it, and bathes not at all, the Naga very nearly did, and washes in moderation, while the Manipuri fell in and has been given to excessive cleanliness ever since. The Thado tell what is virtually the same story, omitting the Naga, to explain why the Manipuri washes himself after evacuation like any other Hindu of India, while the Kuki, like all Nagas also, follows the Burmese custom.—(Ed.)

Comparatively few Thadous can swim but a good many are fairly expert with bamboo rafts which they use for crossing rivers. The Chura Chandpur Subdivision Thadous of Manipur State are more expert in the water and on rafts than the others.

All Thadous are exceedingly expert in making all kinds of traps for animals, birds and fish. Hunting plays an important part in their lives and customs, as will be seen further on. They are good trackers and are never happier than when on the trail. Their next joy is the *ju* jar and lastly, but not least, a quarrel over marriage price or the like of some relative dating back three or more generations.

The Thadou is migratory and moves from village to village on the slightest pretext. Sometimes whole villages vanish to be absorbed in others just because they have had enough of the place and the wander-lust has got hold of them.

The chiefs have great power among them but this is being shaken by the advance of administration—or should it be called civilisation? Persons who are not related to chiefs are to be seen as heads of villages just because they have some wealth behind them and are, in consequence, able to get ready followers. The chiefs naturally do not appreciate such persons setting up as such, especially when they become next door neighbours. Yet the chiefs have often themselves to blame as they become too exacting on their villagers.

Affinities.

The Koms, Aimols, Khotlhangs, Thadous, Lusheis, Chins, Pois, Suktes, Paites, Gangtes, etc. are undoubtedly all connected. The language alone has many similarities and the syntax is not dissimilar. Again there are their customs which have a common principle running through them all. The Thadous admit coming from the south where all the other tribes mentioned are now residing. Wars and want of land for cultivation were certainly the main causes for the northward movement, and I suggest that this movement, which had to be repeated so frequently, might have been a cause of the development of the wander-lust.

The traditions of the Thadous all point to the south and they admit having come northwards. I shall deal with this at length when giving the history of the Thadous as given by them from various sources which I have condensed. Also the pedigrees and genealogical trees which will follow in later chapters will go to prove the contentions put forward now. However I must differ with Lt.-Col. Shakespear (*Lushei-Kuki Clans* p. 8) in his contention that the Kabuis—or more correctly Songpus—are related to the Thadous through the Lusheis. First because of their customs, secondly because of their mode of living and the type of houses, and thirdly because of their language. The Songpus are unquestionably allied to the Kacha Nagas who in turn are connected with the Angamis.[1]

The village of Toushem, a Zemi Kacha Naga village on the western border of the Tamenlong Subdivision of Manipur State, claim that they were originally Lenthang Kukis and on reaching Maram village, which is a little more than half-way between Imphal and Kohima on the west of the cart road on the top of a hill about 3 miles away, on their forward or rather northward movement were absorbed into the Naga community and then spread south-westernly down to their present site. The village of Liyangmai, which is north-east of Tamenlong, a long day's march, give me a story of coming up from the south until they reached Maram village and from there they came southward to their present site. They do not say they were Lenthangs or any other kind of Kukis. They are Liyangmei Kacha Nagas and apparently were the last to leave Maram village since they have remained the nearest to it while the

---

1 The affinity of the Thado with the other branches of the Kuki race mentioned by Mr. Shaw is unquestionable, I think, but there is no doubt whatever in my mind that there has been an infiltration, often a very strong one, of the same stock, into most of the Naga tribes. Major Fryer (*On the Khyeng People of the Sandoway District*, Arakan, *J.A.S.B.*, No. 1 of 1878) convincingly traces the Chin migration to the upper sources of the Chindwin, in which case the Kuki race has first migrated from north to south down the valley of that river, and then, stopped by the Bay of Bengal, turned north again up the ranges forming the watershed to the west of it (*cf.* Lewin, *Wild Races of South-Eastern India*, pp. 138, 73.) Thrown off during the long course of the southward migration, offshoots of the Kuki stock undoubtedly penetrated the western watershed of the Chindwin valley long before the Thado came up the watershed from the south again. Thus the Maring tribe includes a village, Khoibu, which will not intermarry with other villages, and which has a tradition of a common origin with the Poi of Falam, having migrated to the Manipur valley from the Kabaw Valley (near the Chindwin) apparently with the genuine Maring villages ("*Man in India*" VI, No. 4, *Notes on the Marings*, by Mr. Gimson). The Tangkhuls have one origin legend associating them with the Marings (Hodson, *Naga Tribes of Manipur*, p. 10), and the Angami, still further north west, have a legend of origin from the Tangkhul country. On the other hand there are many traditions which show that the last imigrants into the Angami country speak a language classified by Grierson (*Linguistic Survey of India* III, ii) as Naga-Kuki. "Relationship with the Kukis," says Hodson (*op. cit.*, p. 17) "is directly claimed by the people of Yang," *i.e.*, the Kachha Naga village of Yang-Khulen or Chekwema. The Ao tribe, in the north of the Naga Hills district shows entirely unexpected traces of Kuki influences, and the Sema tribe in whom the dominant element is derived from a migration from the south-west in the Manipur State, has its whole social and political system clearly modelled on a Kuki pattern.

To return to Fryer, the Chin tradition, quoted by him from a Chin ballad, of the brick walled city of their forefathers, suggests that the Kukis may have once possessed a higher culture than they have now. If so, this would perhaps account for the exceptional readiness with which he adopts the strange culture offered to him by the American Missionaries, a characteristic in which he differs from all Nagas that I know, except the Ao, and possibly the Sema.—(Ed.)

Zemi Kacha Nagas and the Kabuis or Songpus are all further south and southwest of them.

No better idea of the clear differences between Kukis and Nagas can be had than by reading Lt-Col. Shakespear's book referred to above with that on the Angamis by Mr. J. H. Hutton.[1]

There is one point that makes me suppose that they must have been previously either ocean-shore, creek, river or lake-bank dwellers. They build their houses on piles and do not live on the ground like Nagas, (excepting the Aos).[2]

Dress.

The men wear a loin-cloth[3] worn somewhat like a "Dhoti" and have one or more clothes to wrap around themselves over one shoulder or both. They also wear a cloth as a "Pugri" about a yard or just a little longer. It is tied round the head with the ends or one end sticking up in front. The women wear a loin cloth which is wrapped round their waists and reaches a little over half-way down their thighs. Attached to the cloth, sometimes separately, is a string which is passed round the waist and so holds it up. In addition they wear a breast cloth which is wrapped tight round the torso, the outer corner being tucked in at the top at a spot between the left breast and the armpit. Sometimes an additional wrapper is used thrown over the shoulders thus completing their wardrobe.[4] Although the

---

[1] The differences are usefully summarised by Mills in an article on the Hill Tribes of Assam in the *Assam Review* for March, 1928.—(Ed.)

[2] Many Naga tribes build their houses on platforms also, and if Dixon ("*Racial History of Man*") is right in assigning the brachycephalic element in the population of Burma and Assam to an immigration of the Alpine race, it is just possible that the practice of building on piles in Assam, and the remains of prehistoric lake villages in Europe are to be derived from a common source, though the actual lake dwellers appear to have been dolichocephalic themselves. But see p. 84, n. 2.

[3] It can only be short time since the Thado male went naked. Men are still to be seen naked in the Chin Hills occasionally, though the women wear clothes, and I have heard of Old Kukis being seen naked in their houses in Cachar during the last few years, and the memory of the time when the men wore no clothes is still fresh. Indeed Surgeon MacRae writing of the Kukis of the Chittagong Hill Tracts in 1799 describes the men as going naked (*Asiatic Researches*, VII, 184), while Damant, writing of *The North Cachar Hills and their Inhabitants* (*Calcutta Review*, 1875), says "The proper dress of a Kookie is a large square sheet, which is thrown loosely over the shoulders; this is still the dress worn in remote villages, but most of the Kookies in the plains have taken to wearing a *dhuti* as well."—(Ed.)

[4] Thado women are careful to cover the breasts until they have borne a child, after which it does not matter exposing them. The same rule is observed by the Lusheis, the Toungtha and the Tipperas of the Hill Tracts of Chittagong (Lewin, *Wild Races of S.E. India*, pp. 192, 207), the Aos, the Santals (Bodding, in *J.A.S.B.*, LXVII, iii, 6), the Hos of Singbhum, the Dusun of Borneo, the Negritos of Zambales in the Philippine Islands. The reverse, curiously enough, is reported of the Khyengs (Chins) of the Chittagong Hill Tracts (Hutchinson, *Account of the Chittagong Hill Tracts*, p. 170). Similarly in some tribes of Australia the

method of fastening seems inadequate, strenuous action does not seem to make their clothes work loose, or fall off.

All these clothes are woven from cotton which is grown on their lands and spun by the women. Now-a-days quite a number of Manchester goods are gaining sway among them such as shirts, shorts, etc. owing to Missionary influence and advancement of civilisation among them. The villages not near the valley of Imphal have not got as far yet and seem to be the happier for it. Both men and women have also a kind of jumper which is very crudely made. It consists of two strips of cloth about 4 ft. by 9 inches. These are stitched together leaving an unstitched gap in the middle about a foot long. Through this gap the head goes. The sides of this chest and back protector are again stitched together leaving a gap in the centre of each for the arms.

There is another coat-shirt with short sleeves and a collar and a few buttons down the front, but this is most certainly not of Thadou origin but is a copy from the fashions of the foreigner.

The wrappers used by the men and women may be white or dark indigo blue. The white ones usually have one black band at the extremities while the blue ones have some embroidery work in place of those bands. The indigo dye is obtained from the plant *Strobilanthes flaccidifolius* grown by them. The pattern of embroidery that may be worn on a man's or woman's black cloth is varied according to his or her achievements. The shade of blue is varied by steeping the cloth or cotton twice or oftener in the dye. There are other dyes of various shades all from plants of different kinds.

For the rainy season a sort of tray, oval shaped, rather like a tortoise's shell made out of palm or bamboo leaves on a bamboo frame is used as a covering by both sexes. This is large enough to cover the whole body when stooping down during field work. It has a plaited strap of cane or bamboo inside, which goes over the shoulders and thus keeps it in position, while arms are free. The leaves are dried and then smoked before they are used for the manufacture of these rainshields.

Both sexes have usually a small or larger haversack slung over one shoulder in which odds and ends, tobacco, etc. are kept.

Young men and the marriageable girls wear a piece of thread tied just above the ankle. It is supposed to make the feet attractive in their eyes. Similarly around the wrist sometimes a piece of wire is used, but this by the men mostly.

The men also have strings around their necks. Some of these have a tiger's tooth or a few fowl's feathers attached—

---

women discard their aprons after the birth of their first child (Westermarck, *History of Human marriage*, 3rd edit., p. 197).—(Ed.)

occasionally a pair of tweezers and a thorn-pick.[1] The tiger's tooth and feathers are to ward off the evil eye and keep them well on a journey, in addition to preventing them from suffering any misfortune.

The women, if unmarried, wear a spiral brass fore-armlet which starts at the wrist and goes up within 4 inches or so of the elbow. The spirals are flat internally on the flesh and are convex outside with a breadth of half an inch roughly. Just above the elbow an armlet of bellmetal is worn which is about 1½ lbs in weight and 1½ inches in diameter, the section being circular. Necklaces of blue or red beads are worn and a hollow ring about 2 inches in diameter in the lobe of her ear. This latter is very like a napkin-ring, but has an out-turned rim in front about ¼ inch wide. To make the ear capable of carrying these rings they pierce their lobes and extend them by putting in rolled leaves of gradually increasing dimensions. The ring is of bright metal or silver. The idea of having them silver is to my mind of recent formation.

The men wear a cornelian bead in each ear tied with a piece of cotton to the lobe of the ear which is pierced to admit it. The bead hangs about an inch from the end of the lobe. These beads are much treasured by them and often form an item in prices paid for brides.

Both sexes have almost always got a small bamboo tube or gourd which contains tobacco juice. They take a pull at it and keep the fluid in their mouths until its invigorative properties have been absorbed and then they spit it out again. Pipes are smoked by both. These are either wooden, bamboo, earthenware, brass or metal. There is a distinct pipe for producing the juice they use as a drug. It has a large bowl and receptacle of bamboo or wood for the juice. The bowl is earthenware and slants towards the smoker.[2] The tobacco is wetted before placing in the bowl and a red hot cinder is placed on top and then the operation begins. Dried tobacco leaves are also chewed by both sexes and spat out when all the juice has been extracted. The juice is not swallowed either.

Tied round a man's waist is the knife called "Chempong."

---

[1] Neck and ankle strings are sometimes worn as love tokens, I think. Round the neck a shell, made I fancy from the kernel of a wild mango or something similar, is hung as a receptacle into which the partly chewed quid of tobacco can be placed when removed from the mouth for any reason. Iron prickers for extracting thorns, and tweezers for that and for depilation are carried by almost all Kuki men, generally on a string round the neck. *Cf.* Fitch's account of the Burmese :—"These people weare no beards : they pull out the haire on their faces with little pinsons made for that purpose....for he carieth his pinsons alwayes with him to pull the haires out assoone as they appeare." Heylin, *Cosmographie* (1665) p. 890, describes the people of Pegu as "of a mean stature, somewhat corpulent, and naturally beardless. If any stragling hair thrust forth, they alwayes carry Pinsers with them, to pull them out."—(Ed.)

[2] See plate 4, fig. 3.

In his hand he has a spear called "Tengcha" or a muzzle-loading gun, licensed or unlicensed, and that completes his kit.

The youth of today in villages affected by "civilising" influences wears his hair cropped short, has a shirt and coat, wears shorts, stockings and boots. Often capping it all with a soft felt hat or even a "topee", and tries to converse with one in very bad English with an American twang. He has not the manly appearance of his jungly brothers or their open countenance. He appears to be carrying the whole weight of the world on those weary looking shoulders of his and in that worried expression on his face. He does not appear to be any the happier for the change.

The Thadou chiefs do not dress differently to others, except for Khotinthang (alias Kilkong), head of the Shitlhou branch, who has invested in a "Topee" since his release from his exile at Sadiya after the Kuki Punitive Measures of 1918-19.

Those who have performed certain rites are allowed to wear a blue-black cloth with a special embroidery but this will be dealt with further on. Most of the chiefs having performed those rites naturally wear those clothes on auspicious occasions when there are sure to be many people gathered together, as a mark of distinction.

Tattooing.

This is not practiced as a distinctive mark or as a rite among the Thadous. Some of the young bucks and girls tattoo a small circle or dot, just for fun, between the thumb and first finger in middle of the soft part of the flesh which links the two. It is done with any sharp needle-like implement and any colouring matter which is handy, such as indigo juice or soot, is used. Except for this tattooing is rare [1] among them.

Mentality.

The Thadou is a slow but deep thinker for the average wild man He is very obstinate and wilful It is to be expected from the way the children are brought up. Once the children can run about they are left very much to themselves and no form of disciplinary education is given them. In fact the parents seem to thoroughly appreciate the quality in their children if they see them bounce others or dupe them. They are left to

---

[1] A circle is sometimes tattooed on the forearm usually in a line with the back of the hand and a little above the wrist, but sometimes in the corresponding place in a line with the palm. The pattern is made by pricking the arm with thorns of the cane plant and applying the circular end of a small bamboo tube which has been rubbed on the sooty bottom of a cooking-pot. Carbon is the usual tattoo pigment from central India to the Philippines, but the Mundas are also reported to use a vegetable dye (Roy, *The Mundas and their Country*, p. 370) and also to mark their arms with a circular mark, made in this case with a heated iron tube. Waddell (*Tribes of the Brahmaputra Valley*, *J.A.S.B.*, pt. III, 1900, p. 51) says that this tattooing with a circle on the forearm seemed universal, but he was apparently writing of the Hrankol Kukis.—(Ed.)

improve their minds in the best way they can with no help. If they ask questions they are told to shut up—and this not even politely—as there are more important matters for consideration than answering childish queries. This may be to cover ignorance, because there is nothing the Thadou dislikes more than being proved to be wrong and ridiculed. He loves to be important and air his knowledge. Drink generally makes him become quarrelsome and look out for a scrap. He is truculent and has a tremendous idea of his own importance. I have often seen Thadous and Nagas pass each other on the paths and in nearly every instance the Thadou has kept the path while the Naga moves aside to let him pass. In Naga villages when some dancing is on and there happen to be some Thadous present they will almost always push aside the Naga lookers-on and get in front so as to have the best position without the slightest compunction. He has the appearance of being the dominant partner in his household, yet, he is very often led by his wife, more especially if she happens to be well connected. Grief does not affect him much but the women have long memories and will be often heard weeping aloud in a village one is visiting, because some one has turned up who looks like or has the same name as a long departed child, relation or friend, or some conversation has recalled some sad day in her life. When deserting a village the men will walk gaily off with anticipatory feelings of new ventures while the women will stay behind a while to shed a tear over the graves of their children and relatives, before catching up the men, because they may never see them again. Life is of very little value since murders are compromised for one or two mithuns (*Bos frontalis*), but the murderer usually becomes the "servant"—I prefer it to "slave"—of some powerful chief in return for protection. Murders are not common among the Thadous, as they look on it as a great sin to take life in cold blood. A very good reason has to be shown before they view it as justifiable. An example of this would be the taking of heads to be buried with the chief, but this is carried out by means of a raid against some village where a score has to be wiped out. The heads are to represent slaves in the next world for the chief, as the souls or spirits of the decapitated work for the Chief at "Mithi Khu." Both sexes like a joke, more so if it is vulgar, and are always ready for a laugh.

The older folk have generally very long faces since they have to remember the long line of pedigrees and genealogies dated back many, many generations in addition to all the marriage prices, etc. due and to be paid by their line, plus all the feuds. These persons are the reference books for the younger generations whenever ill feeling gives rise to quarrels or litigation.

They specially pride themselves on genealogical trees which play a part of importance in some of their rituals and festivities

The memories they possess for these matters are wonderful, as often far distant persons unknown to each other go through the same long list of names without an error.

The prevailing trait of self-importance and self-exaltation among the Thadous is understood when it is remembered that for long years they composed the levies of the Manipur State and were allowed to do very much as they pleased with all among whom they took up their abode. At times their ambitions have got the better of them and they broke out in open rebellion in 1918-19. Their tails are not down and I have heard it said that they hope to become a "Raj" some day.

The Thadous' developed, or perhaps natural, arrogance and truculence [1] has not abated much since that rebellion.

He is very litigious and his inclination to form small villages anywhere and everywhere with no respect of others' lands is a source of trouble administratively.

---

[1] When I first made the Thado's acquaintance and for years after, I regarded him merely as an administrative nuisance. His habit of splitting up his villages into scattered hamlets of two or three houses in the jungle, so that this year's village is never where you expected to find it, and his irritating way of making a fuss about the unpaid price of his defunct second cousin's great-grandfather's sister's bones are not calculated to endear him to a district officer. The operations against the rebellious Thado of the Manipur State in 1918 and 1919 led to a very much better acquaintance with him, and from then onwards the more I have seen of the Thado, the more I have respected him and the better I have liked him. For pluck, intelligence, straight-forwardness and cheerfulness he stands high among his neighbours. I cannot say so much for his industry or his sobriety. He is a bad cultivator, and much behind the surrounding tribes in agriculture, though as much ahead of them in such domestic arts as weaving or working in metal. When there is any killing afoot, he is bloodthirsty. Little game survives where the Thado settles. A few small villages, located for a few years in the Ti-Ho valley in the east of the Naga Hills, destroyed all the rhinoceros, almost all the wild mithun (*Bos gaurus*), all the elephant which did not escape back to Burma, and a very large proportion of the previously numerous sambhar (*Rusa Aristotelis*) there. In war the Thado, when he gets the chance, often carries out massacres on a fairly large scale, partly perhaps because he enjoys killing, partly, at any rate, from deliberate "frightfulness," adopting that method of cowing the other side. Thus during the Thado rebellion referred to, Thongngam, brother of the Dongngel chief Chengjapao, and acting probably under his instructions, joined with one of the Haokip chiefs from Somra to punish the Tangkhul village of Kashom for failing to supply the rebels with rice. The visitors billeted themselves through the village from house to house and got food and shelter for the night. The next morning their hosts awoke to find their weapons impounded. The men were all tied up and laid out in rows, the Khullakpa's wife being tied to the post in front of his house. The men were then butchered by gun, spear or dao according to the fancy of the various executioners, the Khullakpa's wife being presented with her husband's head and her release, and the women and children, who had naturally run off to hide, were partially rounded up and added to the holocaust. Altogether about 40 were killed. Fortunately affairs of this sort were not very frequent but there is no doubt but the Thado is a brigand by disposition.—(Ed.)

CHAPTER II.

ORIGINS AND GENEALOGIES.

Origin.

Before going into the details regarding the Thadou village and customs I have thought it best to give their origin and pedigree so that the reasons for certain customs, etc. may be understood more fully.

It may be noted that the number seven appears to be invested with some particular significance, as it reappears repeatedly.

The story of their origin is that they used to live under the earth, or rather inside it. Noimangpa was the Chief of this subterranean region. One Chongthu, a relative of Noimangpa, went hunting porcupines in the jungle with his dog and discovered a large hole. He perceived through this that the upper earth was uninhabited and there was a great darkness. This darkness, which lasted for seven days and seven nights[1] is called "Thimzin" by the Thadous. Chongthu so rejoiced at his discovery that he gave up his hunt and went back to his house. He conjured up ideas of forming a village of his own on the earth and planned accordingly. Just about then, Noimangpa, the Chief of the under-world was performing the *Chon* festival which everyone had to attend including Chongja, elder brother of Chongthu. Noimangpa's son Chonkim was also present. During this feast Chongthu started waving his sharp sword about so vigorously that he injured some of the folk present, at which all became angered. This action of Chongthu was premeditated as he thought that by doing so he would be turned out from the under-world and thus have an excuse for going out to the upper-world and forming a village of his own. The news of Chongthu's behaviour became known to Noimangpa who said

---

[1] For the Thimzin *vide* Shakespear, *Lushei-Kuki Clans*, Chapter V, and *cf.* Mills, *The Ao Nagas*, page 314, *The Lhota Nagas*, pp. 176, 193. The Chang Nagas have the story likewise (*Molola*, '*Man in India*,' II, 100) and versions are found among the Hos and Santals of Bengal, the Shans, and the Ami of Formosa, while similar stories pervade the Indian Archipelago generally (*vide* Frazer, *Folk-lore in the Old Testament*, I, iv.). The Thado version that I am familiar with is that the great darkness was preceded by fire and accompanied by flood, and it was this flood which drove the ancestors of the Thado proper to take refuge in the hills, where they found Lenthang, whom they forbore to kill as he, and his, knew the gods of the country; accordingly it was Lenthang who caused a white cock to dance on a stone and thus lured the detainer of the sun to come and look, whereby the sun escaped and came out again restoring light to the darkened world. The story is obviously suggestive of a separate racial origin for the Thado proper and the Changsen and allied clans, who presumably were in occupation when the Thado arrived in the hills.—(Ed.)

"Chongthu had better live in Heaven" meaning thereby that he had better be killed. Chongthu hearing of Noimangpa's wrath at once prepared to migrate out of the hole in the earth which he saw and which is spoken of as *Khul* by the Thadous. So Chongja and Chongthu killed many pigs, fowls, etc. and feasted in preparation for their departure.

Somehow Chongja's party was delayed but Chongthu's party moved off followed by Chongthu himself. On reaching the Khul the leaders found that a great snake called Gullheipi was in possession of it and when they made endeavours to pass it the snake killed them with his tail. Chongthu, on reaching the spot, was not to be thwarted in his ambitions, so he tied his cloth around him and placed a *phoipi*, a thick cotton cloth, over his head and so attacked the great snake which was disputing the passage. He used the sword called "Joudichem" in this attack, was victorious and killed the snake which he cut into seven pieces. At the same time a *lhoh*, a lion, also attempted to retard Chongthu's egress but Chongthu got the better of the animal by saying "Are you not created by the Pathen (the Thadou name for the Creator) as the King of the animals? If so I have also been created as the King of men by Pathen and therefore we should be friends instead of enemies". So saying, the lion withdrew and Chongthu's party moved up to the "Khul". They found that it was covered with a stone and one of Chongthu's party called Vangalpa lifted it up.[1] While he was able to do so only seven persons were able to get out and then the stone was dropped and all further attempts to raise it were in vain. The seven persons who thus emerged were Chongthu, Vangalpa, the stone-lifter, Khupngam, the keeper of the dog, and four others. The names of the other four are not known but are said to include the progenitors of the Manipuri, the Naga, the foreigner and the Burmese, however they are not definite about the last two although they are quite emphatic about the number being seven.

Chongja's party, following on, found the stone blocking their passage out and after making many attempts gave up and returned to Noimangpa reporting the result.

Nemneh, wife of Chongja, cursed Chongthu and his party before they left the "Khul" saying that they should suffer from all kinds of sicknesses, deaths, troubles, evil spirits and bad luck. These cursings were heard by Chongthu's party and they made sacrifices in an endeavour to avoid the curse which the Thadous say still rests on them. So, in cases of serious illnesses, etc., sacrifices are always made in the name of Nemneh, wife of

---

[1] According to McCulloch he went back for some previous belongings, and the bird that was holding up the stone got tired and let it drop (*vide* McCulloch, *Account of the Valley of Munnipore*, p. 55) Later on the party of Chongthu were shown where to find water by a bird (*ibid.*, p. 56).—(Ed.)

Chongja, in hopes of appeasing her wrath. When such sacrifices are made the *thempu, i.e.*, the medicine man or soothsayer, always repeats the name of seven of the most important villages of Noimangpa under the earth in one of which Nemneh is sure to be at the time, so that she may hear his solicitations. The names of those villages are:—1. Noimang, 2. Kholoichal, 3. Khopalva, 4. Khothip, 5. Khomang, 6. Khokanglai and 7. Khokisupi.

On reaching the upper earth Chongthu, in his wanderings, found two persons called Lenthang and Lunkim who had survived the Thimzin by making a fire of the skulls and bones of all the game they had killed as they were great hunters. These two were captured by Chongthu and used as guides during his wanders on the earth. So to this day it will be found that those of the Lenthang and Lunkim tribe of Kukis are living in most of the Thadou villages and have no villages of their own, nor do they possess hereditary chiefs as the Thadous.[1]

From Chongthu to Thadou, in the genealogical tree the persons are mythical and so when festivities entailing repetition of the genealogical tree of the Thadous take place the *thempu* starts from Thadou and not from Chongthu.

From Chongthu to Thadou there were no different languages; and animals and spirits as well as the mythical ancestors all lived together in peace.

The hole in the earth called "Khul" is said to be at the source of the "Gun" river which I find to be definitely identified with the Imphal river in the Manipur State,[2] "Gun" being the Thadou for the "Imphal" river In all the old stories and legends of the Thadous the river "Gun" is frequently mentioned and is of great fame.

---

1 *V. Supra*, note 1 on p. 24.—(Ed.)

2 I cannot help suspecting that this *Gun-tui* was originally the Chin- or Khyeng-dwin River, into which, of course, the Imphal River runs. *Vide* note on p. 17 *supra*.—(Ed.)

The lineage from Chongthu to Thadou is as follows :—

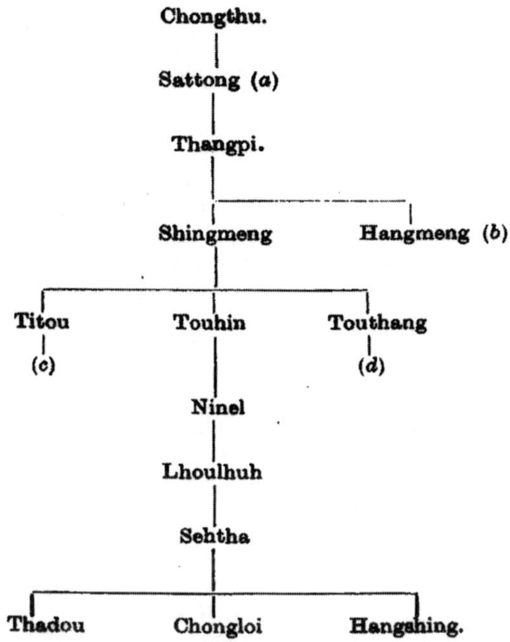

(*a*) Sattong married Sheichin, a woman of Vanlai village, which means the village in the heavens. There were two other brothers of Sattong but their names have been forgotten as they went east and west and have not been heard of since.

(*b*) Hangmeng is said to be the progenitor of the Kilongs, Koms, Waipheis, Chirus and other old Kukis. Some Koms and others have admitted this to me.

(*c*) Titou is the progenitor of the Dongngels whose seniority is not recognised by the Thadou of other clans now as the lineage has become extinct in the true line and is now represented by the descendant of a slave[1].

(*d*) Touthang is the progenitor of the Lamhao Kukis.

---

[1] I find it quite impossible to accept this view, which arises solely, I think, from the arrogant vapourings of Khutinthang (Khilkung), who as head of the Shitlho clan would be chief of all the Thado, if the Dongngel clan were really extinct. No doubt the fact that Thado himself, though a member of the cadet branch, has given his name to the whole tribe, has influenced the Shitlho in making this extravagant claim, but it is quite untenable. Even if the claim of the head of the Dongngel clan to an unblemished descent be rejected, there are plenty of cousins whose family tree is unquestioned, not to mention the Thomlhun and Haolai (Jongbe)

The mythical ancestors were known as Manmasinao while the Spirits were called Thilha.

The next point of interest is that there are two schools regarding the direction from which the Thadous had their origin. The first school support the contention that they come upwards from the south while the second school contend that they came from the north. I have gone into this in great detail and give below what information I have gathered, which leads me to support the latter view.

The Gun river plays a most important part in all Thadou songs and legends of the old days and this river is identified with the Imphal river. At the time of the flood the Thadous say they collected at Kholkipkholjang where every living thing took refuge. This has been located as above Kaithenmangpi in Manipur on the right bank of the Imphal river. The flood is spoken of as Tuitobin by the Thadous.[1] The upper portion of this place of refuge is known as Kholkip where all the animals are said to have congregated, while the lower portion is spoken of as Kholjang. They were then still in the condition of the mythical ancestors according to their traditions. When performing *shalhakou* to the wild animals, this place called Kholkipkholjang must be mentioned by the *thempu*, as never before were so many wild animals seen by the Thadous, nor since. Therefore they hope for its state of plenty to recur some day to satiate their unquenchable appetite for hunting.

This place, I am told, is also known to the Manipuris who

clans both senior in descent to the Shitlho and with unimpeachable pedigrees. It is unlikely, however, that there is any *bona fide* doubt about the legitimacy of Chengjapao's descent from Dongngel, as otherwise the cousins who reinstated Neingul's son Ngulchin would have claimed the chieftainship for themselves (*vide* Appendix B, 'The House of Dongngel.')—(Ed.)

1 This mythical flood is sometimes, at any rate, associated with the Thimzin (*V. supra* p. 24 n.). The story is common to many tribes in this area, and the Changs locate the mountain of refuge at a peak of some eight thousand odd feet high called Ngakushom a good deal further north, latitude 26°18', longitude 94° 48' (*vide Man in India*, II. page 100 sqq.). This name Ngakushom is distinctly suggestive of the name Noesakoe given to the mountain of refuge by the Alfurs of Ceram in the Indian archipelago. The Anals and the Lusheis have the same story (Shakespear, *op. cit.*, pp. 95, 176), the Lushei account being identical with the Chang Naga story, though of course the names are different and the peaks are located in different places. Obviously the identification of the Thado peak of refuge with a local mountain is much later than the widely distributed story on which it depends, and Mr. Shaw's theory that the Thados originally occupied the Manipur Valley and migrated down the Imphal Valley cannot be substantiated in this way. Even if it should happen to be the case, the event must be far more recent in the history of the race than the flood to which the tradition refers. Stories of this flood bearing a general and sometimes a particular similarity to the Kuki and the Naga versions are distributed all over south-eastern Asia and the Indian Archipelago and seem to extend even to Oceania and America. (*Vide* Frazer, *Folk-lore in the Old Testament*, I, iv.)—(Ed.)

speak of it as Khongjai Khunman which means the "Old site of the Kukis."

After the subsidence of the flood the Thadou found the plain unsafe for their occupation, since they had only just started living there when the flood took place. So they took to the hills on the east of the Imphal river and migrated down to the Tuihat river which I take to be the Chindwin. It was here that they first were initiated into cultivating rice. The story is that they found a grass growing on the right bank and a king of rats called Ju-thel used to collect the seed in the nests of his species and eat it.[1] The Thadou tried it and found it of excellent quality and so they became paddy growers. Chongthu came out of the earth with millet and Job's tears only to eat.[2] The mithun was found on the hill Sisep, the pig at Bonnol and the fowl at Molkoi.

On reaching the Tuihat river they followed it down some way but found that they came to a large expanse of water which could not possibly be crossed. So, as they were increasing in numbers rapidly they decided to retrace their steps on the left bank of the river and took up their abode at Lhanpelkot and Thijonbung which I am told lies in the country where

---

1 This story of the rat as the originator of the cultivation of rice, appears again in slightly different forms among the Angamis (*vide The Angami Nagas*, page 269), the Iban of Borneo (Hose and McDougall, *Pagan Tribes of Borneo*, II, 145), and the Toradjas of the Celebes (Frazer, *Folk-lore in the Old Testament*, I, 222).—(Ed.)

2 The cultivation of millet and sorghum seems to have preceded that of rice in the Naga Hills, and there are many villages across the frontier which still cultivate millet as their staple crop and grow little or no rice, even though the elevation is not too high for it. In most of them, however, the use of dry rice is increasing. Millet cultivation is to be associated with dry terraces and pollarded alders. Where the alder is carefully preserved and planted on terraces, it is possible to pollard the trees, and plant millet (but not rice) with excellent results once every four years, and this method of cultivation is still followed exclusively by Yonghong, Angfang and probably other transfrontier Konyak Naga villages. It also survives at Khonoma of the Angamis and probably in some of the bigger Nzemi (Kachha Naga) villages that adjoin it. It was no doubt the pre-existence of dry revetted millet terracing that enabled the wet rice terraces so typical of the Angami country to be started in the first place. In most, if not all Naga Tribes the millet crop has its own ceremonial officiants for planting and reaping, though they are now unimportant compared to those who preside over rice. In Formosa, where the culture of the hill tribes is nearly allied to that of the Naga Hills, millet preceded rice, which is still regarded as unclean food (McGovern, *Headhunters of Formosa*, p. 183).

Another Thado legend describes Lenthang (*vide supra* pp. 24 n., 26) as having taught the Thado rice cultivation, which, read with the legend of Chongthu's emergence from below to find Lenthang and Lunkim already inhabiting the upper world, looks as if the millet eating Kuki found his way up from the plains into a hilly country already acquainted with the growing of rice, or perhaps brought up with him rice cultivators from the plains who had been incorporated in the course of migration.—(Ed.)

the Pois are now living.[1] These two village sites are famous for the fact that the Thadou still believes that all the spirits of the dead have to pass through there on their way to their final resting place at "Mithikho". We hear that they next reached the junction of the Teo and Loh rivers. The names of these rivers come into the song called Langla which is sung only at the burial of persons who have performed the *Chon*. In survey sheet No. 84, E. Tiddim, I find the river Tyao rising in square B. 1 and flowing through squares B. 1, 2, 3, 4 and A. 4. From what will follow I have no hesitation in saying that this must be the river Teo they speak of in their songs. The Loh river is perhaps the Tuipui river shown on that map as flowing into the Tyao in square A. 1. At this stage they say there were four great clans of Kukis and they name them as Lushei, Suhte, Poi and Thadou.

They claim that the Changsan, Lhangum, Lenthang, Lunkim, Kom, Gangte, Waiphei, Kholhang, Chiru and those of inferior lineage were all under the wing of the Thadous and so were then included under that term.

For the elucidation of the list that follows of the names of the villages in which lived the ancestors of Khotinthang, the *Pipa*, or head of the clans descended from Thadou before they moved up to Jampi, his present site, reference may be made to the genealogical tree of the Shitlhous (*infra*, p. 33), which will give the approximate date, in terms of generations, for sites associated with particular chiefs. The total number of generations is twentythree, and taking the Thadou generation at thirty years (they do not marry as young as Nagas), we get the early XIIIth Century A.D. as the approximate date of Thadou's birth.

Tradition records the names of the former sites of what is now Jampi village as follows :—

1 Nanglengbung. In the time of Thadou. It was on this hill that Dongngel buried his *Chon Tul*, which is only used to kill mithun, when performing *Chon*. There was only one of its kind which was kept by the head of the Thadous who was of the Dongngel clan until it became "*ingam*" (extinct)[2]. This is supposed to be on the Gun river.

2. Molphei. Here they lived with the Lionmen and where their *Indoi* (House God [3]) was found. This was on the Tuihat river. Chief Munthom.

---

[1] *I.e.*, on the right bank of the Chindwin.—(Ed.)

[2] Chengjapao, Chief of the Dongngel clan is still the head cf the Thado Kukis. The Shitlho Chief, who contested the headship recently, used himself to pay *shathing* to Chengjapao till 1918, and on taking his case into court in Manipur in 1928 had his claim to priority laughed out of court.—(Ed.)

[3] "House Magic," rather.—(Ed)

3. **Lhungjang.** This was formed by Jelhao after the death of his two elder brothers. This was on the Teo river.
4. **Jampi.** This is said to be in the Lushei country and on the Loh or Tuipui river. Tongkhuthang was chief of it.
5. **Lunglen.** This shown on Survey map No. 83. H. Imphal square B. 4/d. The village taking its name from the hill marked 6,531 ft. This was in Thushong's time and it was while here that the Shitlhous and Shingshongs fought a great battle on Songchal Hill (No. 83. H. Sq: B. 4/middle).
6. **Lailenbung.** In North Cachar Hills. Used to be near Maibong (Assam Bengal Railway) Station in the time of the Cachari reign. This was in Thushong's time.
7. **Bollason.** Also in North Cachar Hills near Baladhan. This was in the time of Thushong.
8. **Saramba.** In Tamenlong Sub-division in the time of Khotinmang (No. 83. G/SW. Sq: 6/EF.).
9. **Insong.** In Naga Hills (No. 83 G/SE. Sq: A/3. b) at time of Khotinmang.
10. **Laloi.** In Naga Hills (No. 83 G/SE. Sq: A/3. b) at time of Khotinmang.
11. **Mechangbung.** In Naga Hills (No. 83 G/SE. Sq: A/3. b) at time of Thangchung, also called Thangchungmang.
12. **Langparam.** In Tamenlong Sub-division. (No. 83 G/SE. Sq: A/5. a) At time of Thangchung and the present head of the Thadous, his son, Khotinthang alias Kilkong.
13. **Jampi.**[1] Shown as Chongjang in Square B/4 of Survey sheet (No. 83 G/SE.) where Khotinthang was made to take up his residence after being exiled to Sadiya for three years as the result of the Kuki rebellion.

From all this it appears that the Thadous came down the Gun or Imphal river first. Thence down the Tuihat which I take to be the Chindwin till they came to the sea. Finding further progress barred they retraced their steps up the Tuihat river till its confluence with the Teo or Tyao river and thence

---

[1] There s also a Jampi in the Naga Hills; the Thado takes his place names with him wherever he goes and the older and more recent maps read together will show successions of Jampis, Aishans, Aithus, Kanjangs, etc. usually from south to north. It is the same with many Naga place names; the e are lots of Shipi, Shitz, Longsa, Lungkhung, etc., and the succession seems always to run south and north rather than east and west. —(Ed.)

up to that where they now are after varying their position on either side of it according to circumstances influenced by war and its economic effects.

The story of how the Haokips have become a distinct group also suggests that they lived then on the Gun or Imphal river. The story is that Thalhun, son of Thadou was fondling his wife who was somewhat careless with her garments. Hearing some people coming Thalhun told her to adjust her dress. As she did not do so at once he flew into a rage and threw a piece of wood at her which struck her in the abdomen resulting in her death. Being overcome with grief and shame, since he loved her much, Thalhun, leaving his son Elmun in his village, crossed the river Gun and lived in Pumtupa's house. There he remained for several years and becoming fascinated by one of Pumtupa's daughters married her. She gave birth to two sons Kipgen and Haokip. His second wife also died and then Thalhun took Kipgen with him back to his village and lived again with Elmun, his son by his first wife. Haokip was too young for the journey and so was left with Pumtupa who brought him up and so the Haokips to this day are almost a separate group of Thadous while the Kipgens for the most part live among the Shitlhous.[1]

All this satisfies me that the Kuki originally came from the north and reaching the sea and finding further progress impossible retraced his steps to where we now find him.

---

[1] But there are numbers of Kipgens in the north-east of Manipur and in the Somra tract, where they are mixed up with Haokips.—(Ed.)

[*The names which have become those of clans and sub-clans are printed in capitals.*]

- Sehtha
  - THADOU
    - Thalhun
      - Elmun (By 1st wife)
        - Ning-el
          - Ningshong
            - Songtong
              - Jakil
                - SHITLHOU
                  - Kiltong
                    - Lhoushing
                      - Tonglun
                        - Munthom
                          - Thomhil
                            - Luntong
                            - Khumang
                            - Jelhao
                              - Henmang
                                - Haotong (By 1st wife)
                                  - Manthu
                                    - Tongkhuthang
                                      - Thushung
                                        - Khutinmang
                                          - Thangchung (By 1st wife)
                                            - Khutinthang
                                            - Mangkhukai
                                          - Jamkhuthang (By 2nd wife)
                                      - Mangminthang
                                      - Letkhulun
                                    - Jallun
                                  - Tupshu
                                  - Kol-let
                                - Haokhutong
                                - Jemkai
                                - Hao-on
                                - Haokhup
                                - Kimkhup
                                - Neilet
                                - (These six sons are all by 2nd wife)
                              - Goulen
                        - MANGJEL
                  - Kilphung (LHOUJEM CLAN)
                  - Tongmang (LHOUVUM CLAN)
        - Hing-el
          - Shingshit
            - PHOHHIL (1st wife)
            - SHINGSHON
            - Shihkil (By 2nd wife)
            - Thonshong (By 2nd wife)
      - KIPGEN (By 2nd wife)
      - HAOKIP (By 2nd wife)
  - CHONGLOI
  - HANGSHING

Therefore Khutinthang (also known as Kilkong) is the senior living descendant of the Shitlhou branch of the Thadou clan. He lives at Jampi village in Tamenlong Sub-division of Manipur State. His brother Mangkhukai has enlisted as a sepoy in the 3rd Assam Rifles at Kohima, Naga Hills.

Goupi Kuki of Shongshang village of the Naga Hills is the senior living descendant of the Mangjel branch.

Vumkholal is the head of the Lhoujem branch and lives in Abong in North Cachar Hills.

Mangminlen of Aithu village of Tamenlong Sub-division is the head of the Lhouvum branch.

Lhunjapao of Leikot village of Chura Chandpur Sub-division of Manipur State is the living head of the Kipgen branch.

Lhukhomang of Chasat village in Ukhrul Sub-division of Manipur State is the head of the Haokip branch.

Tonkhohen of Bombal village, of Sadar Area of Manipur State, at present at Chongjang village of the Naga Hills District, is the living head of the Phoh-hil branch.

Mangpu of Tolbung village in Chura Chandpur Sub-division is the living head of the Shingshon branch.

Of the above those branches which have sub-clans as well are given hereafter with a genealogical tree to trace their positions.

GENEALOGICAL TREE OF CHONGLOI.

- CHONGLOI
  - LUTSONG
    - Chonghao
      - Gensei
        - Holkip
          - Manghil
            - Kimkhup
              - Holso
                - Khupkhopao (Extinct)
                - Khup-en
                  - Leolhun
                    - Vangdem
                      - Lhunpao
                        - Kip-hol
                          - Sehvung
                            - Chal-let
                              - Vungjakim
                                - Lunkhopao
                                - Vunglun
                              - Chungjam
                        - Kipchal
                    - Mangsei
                  - Leoman
            - Kimvuh
      - Genthang
    - Chongmang
    - Chongvuh
    - Chongvul
    - Chongton
    - Chongtong
  - SANDOU
  - HAOCHENG
  - LOISEI

The senior living descendant of the Chongloi clan is therefore Lunkhopao who is living in Jangnoi village of Sadar Area of Manipur State.

The senior living descendant of the Lutsong branch is Thangkot living in Thenjol village in the Naga Hills District.

The senior living descendant of the Sandou branch is Ngamjapao living in Ponlen Haohen village of Tamenlong Subdivision of the Manipur State.

The senior living descendant of the Haocheng branch is Sheijakhup of Shongshang village in the Naga Hills District.

GENEALOGICAL TREE OF THE HANGSHING CLAN.

- HANGSHING
  - HANGCHUNG
    - Shonsit
      - Phutngul
        - Kipnoh
          - Noh-hen
            - Nohkap
              - Nanglang
                - Kaplhun
                  - Kaptho
                    - Vumjakhup
                      - Kapjavum
                  - Vunghel
                  - Kapjatong
                - Shongmang
              - Shonghem
      - SHONLUNG
      - SHONLHOL
    - NINGTHIP
    - NINGLUN
    - HANGSON
  - SHONGTHANG
    - Haomang
    - MANGTONG
    - JASONG
    - TONGKIM

Therefore the senior living descendant of the Hangshing clan is Kapjavum of Vongjang village in Tamenlong Sub-division of Manipur State.

The senior descendant living of Shongthang sub-clan is Jamhao of Bongjol village in Sadar Area of Manipur State.

That of the Mangtong branch is Thangkhopao of Vongjang village in Tamenlong Sub-division of Manipur State.

Of the Jasong branch Shempu of Sinjol village in the Naga Hills is the present head.

Of the Tongkim branch Shehpu of Chunglal Chief's village in North Cachar Hills, is the senior living descendant.

Thangachong is the senior living descendant of the Ningthip branch, and lives in Molkon village in Sadar Area of Manipur State.

Of the Ninglun branch there is no heir as it became extinct.

Of the Hangson branch Onkhup of Mongken village of Chura Chandpur Sub-division of Manipur State is the head

Of the Shonlung branch Khuplen of Saheb Minai village of Tamenlong Sub-division of Manipur State, is the head.

Of the Shonlhol branch Tongcha of Jangnoi village in Sadar Area is the senior living representative.

GENEALOGICAL TREE OF PHOHHIL.

- PHOHHIL
  - Hilhao
    - Tonghil
      - Haohil
        - Haosong
          - Songhao
            - Songlheng
              - Koplet
                - Lhengtong
                  - Haopimang (Extinct)
                  - Palen
                    - Shongjakhup
                      - Tongkhohen
                - Tonlet
    - Vum-el
  - GOUNGOH
  - LHUHAO
  - DOUHONG
  - HANMANG

Therefore Tongkhohen is the senior living descendant of Phohhil. He lives at Chongjang village in the Naga Hills District.[1]

Khatseh of Songbem village of Sadar Area of Manipur State is the head of the Goungoh branch.

Shonthang of Songdop village in Tamenlong Sub-division of Manipur State is the head of the Lhuhao branch.

Pakeng of Tolbung village in the Naga Hills District is the head of the Douhong branch.

Shemjadou of Toloulong village in Tamenlong Area of Manipur State is the head of the Hangmang branch.

---

[1] Since migrated to Leijim, which he will probably rename Bombăl after the ancient family site.—(Ed.)

GENEALOGICAL TREE OF THE SHINGSHON.

Phohhil, Shingshon, Shihkil and Thonshong are all sons of Shingshit. Phohhil is by the first wife and all the others by the second.

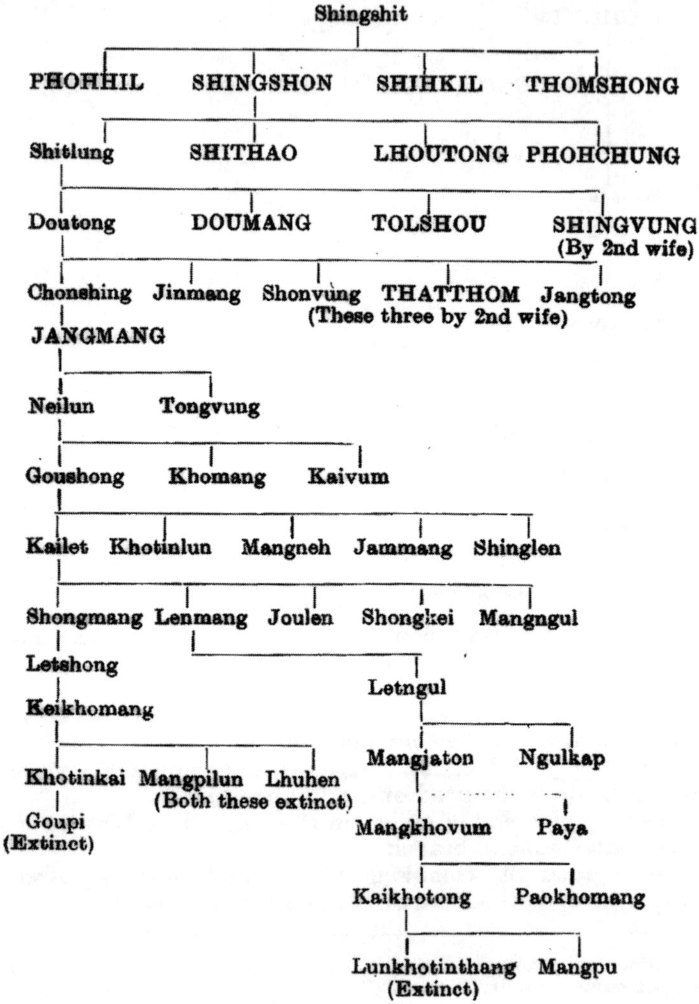

From this it will be seen that Mangpu of Tolbung village of Chura Chandpur Sub-division is the senior living descendant of the Shingshons and pays *shating* to Khutinthang the head of the Shitlhous.

Bungkhothang of Khopuibung village of Chura Chandpur Sub-division in Manipur State is the head of the Shihkil branch.

Of the Thomshong branch the senior living descendant is not known but is said to be in the Naga Hills.[1]

Of the Shithao branch Mangjashei of Leikul village in the North Cachar Hills is the senior living head.

Thongkhumang of Tolbung village in Chura Chandpur Sub-division in Manipur State is the senior living descendant of the Lhoutongs.

Ehkhothang of Nungthut village in Chura Chandpur Sub-division of Manipur State is the senior living descendant of the Phohchungs.

Of the Doumang branch Tongkai of Tolbung village of the Naga Hills is the senior living descendant.

Of the Tolshou branch Nguljamang of Vakot village in North Cachar Hills is the senior living head.

Of the Shingvung branch Lunmang of Bolbung village, Naga Hills is the head.

---

[1] Ngulkim of Teijang, I think.—(Ed.)

CHAPTER III.

HISTORICAL TRADITIONS.

The Thadou tradition runs that Chongthu came on to this earth with only millet and Job's tears. We are also told how he eventually discovered rice (*v. supra* p. 29), also that the Mithun was first caught at Sisep and domesticated. The fowl was found at Molkoi hill and the pig at Bonnol. We are also told that Nemneh, wife of Chongja, cursed Chongthu's party as she believed he purposely closed the Khul after passing through so that he might be King on the earth. That that was his real intention they say is proved from what the *lhoh* (lion)[1] was told by Chongthu when the former attempted to resist his egress.

Next Chongthu begat a son who married Sheichin of Vanlai (the sky) village. This goddess used to go regularly to her father's village and used to bring flesh of pigs to give to her husband. But her first three attempts were frustrated by Santhuh Kaoshe[2] her father-in-law's slave, who ate up the meat she brought. When she at last succeeded she told her husband of Santhuh Kaoshe's behaviour. Sattong became so enraged at this that he went and cut off Santhuh Kaoshe's head. However two *chil* (blindworms) ate up a piece of his neck and thereby brought Santhuh Kaoshe to life again but instead of being a mythical being as before he was transformed into a *guldu* (*Hylobates hoolock*) and so Thadous do not eat the flesh of the gibbon.[3]

The Thempu closely observed how the blindworms (*chil*) brought Santhuh Kaoshe to life again, and by studying it have developed the art of performing sacrifices in cases of wounds of all kinds where loss of blood results, and thereby save the lives of many.

Immediately after Sattong had cut off the head of Santhuh Kaoshe he became very ill with pains in his throat and nearly died. At that time his faithful dog having compassion on his sufferings licked his master's hand. At that Sattong became enraged with the dog and killed him instantly with his sword. The blood of the dog spurted out on Sattong's mouth and he became miraculously cured at once. So in cases of serious ill-

---

[1] It is interesting to find a genuine word for 'lion' and a tradition describing a lion as like a tiger but with shaggy hair about the neck and larger. A traditional lion, is of course, the common property of Manipuris, Shans and Burmese, but not Nagas, I think.—(Ed.)

[2] *I.e.*, Santhuh Vampire, *vide* Appendix G.—(Ed.)

[3] Cf. Mills, *The Ao Nagas*. pp. 16, 144; Hose, *Natural Man*, p. 223 (Kenyah).—(Ed.)

ness a dog is sacrificed to the Creator (Pathen) to relieve the sick of their sufferings.[1]

At that time the mythical ancestors were known as Manmasinao[2] and all spirits as Thilha They used to live together in peace until the following happened after which the Thilha and Manmasinao have always been at enmity.

There was a Manmasinao called Changkhatpu to play with whom a Thilha came one night. Changkhatpu lost his temper and wounded the Thilha with a dao on the hand. On this the Thilha said that the Manmasinao should suffer for it and went off to his cave in the jungle.

In revenge the Thilhas, during Changkhatpu's absence, killed his younger sister. In consequence of this the Manmasinaos gathered and pursued the Thilha killing all except a pregnant female Thilha who escaped. This Thilha went to Pathen in the skies. Pathen told her not to worry as the child in her womb would be a male child and that she must marry it and so revive the Thilhas. At the same time Pathen gave her a charm called Chollaivom[3] instructing her to place it in the water supply of the Manmasinaos and thereby they would not be able to see the Thilhas in future. So to this day the Thilhas cannot be seen by human beings who are the descendants of the Manmasinao. A male child was born to the pregnant Thilha and by marrying him the Thilhas multiplied to such large numbers that there were more Thilhas than Manmasinaos.

Later Japhal, the daughter of Kimchal the son of Hangshing younger brother of Thadou, got lost one day and all suspected the Thilhas of being responsible for this. Her parents wept bitterly and prayed to Pathen that they might be given back their daughter or might know where she had gone to. One night Pathen appeared in a dream to Kimchal and directed him to take the thing he (Pathen) had placed on the Shething tree near Kimchal's house and perform sacrifices to him (Pathen) and then Kimchal would be given many descendants instead of the lost one for whom he was crying. On waking up Kimchal did as he was told and so became the father of many children. This thing which the Pathen gave Kimchal is called *Indoi* (The House God). Thadous in consequence always have an *Indoi* hoping thereby that they may have large families. It is placed on the front verandah of the house to the right or left of the entrance door, up near the roof out of harm's way (for *Indoi*, *v. infra*, App. G.).

The next clear tradition is of the time when they used to

---

[1] *Cf.* McCulloch, *op. cit.*, 56; Shakespear, *op. cit.*, 75, 77, 102; Carey & Tuck, *The Chin Hills*, I, 200; *The Angami Nagas*, 204.

For the general belief in the efficacy of the dog in healing both in this area and elsewhere, see my note on p. 17 of *The Ao Nagas*.—(Ed.)

[2] That is "Mortals", *v.* Appendix A, vii.—(Ed.)

[3] *V. infra*, App. A, *Man and Spirit*.—(Ed.)

live at Lhanpelkot and Thijonbung, which is placed by them in the country at present occupied by the Pois, and through which place all the souls or spirits of the dead Thadous have to pass on their way to Mithikho (The village of the dead). At that time there was a famous man called Selleh who possessed a magical wand with which he could bring to life any corpse by touching it. He had done so many times. This wand was given him by a Thilha woman friend of his. Selleh's son was that wonderful person Galngam.

Selleh always lived in his jhum house (*lou buh*) and the people used frequently to come to call him to bring people to life. Finally he became much annoyed at their importunity and refused to go. The people thought that they could counter this by saying that Selleh's son had died, but when he went and found they were lying he decided he would never again comply with such requests, as his cultivation was much hampered by the frequency of these calls. Again they came and said Galngam was dead but he refused to go. They came however many times in haste and kept repeating it so that finally he decided to go, and on this occasion he found his són Galngam really dead, but owing to the delay Galngam's body had become much decomposed and in spite of many attempts to bring Galngam to life again with his wand he failed hopelessly. Not despairing he went to Lhanpelkot and Thijonbung in an attempt to arrest his soul there. He found Galngam's soul but it refused to return to the body as it had become decomposed. Galngam told his father that if he really loved his son then he (Galngam) would return to his mother's womb and that another male child would be born to him (Selleh). This child was to be given the same name and would become most famous. Selleh returned to his wife much saddened but did as he was bid and a male child was born to him. The child was called Galngam and is of much fame among the Thadous for all the supernatural things he is said to have done. Next come the happenings at Molphai in the time of Munthom.

Here the Human Beings lived as neighbours of the Lhohmi (Lion-men),[1] having a high fence between them. The latter gradually ate up the mithun, pigs, fowls, etc. of the Thadous and lastly asked them to supply them with human flesh, adding that if this request was not granted they (Lion-men) would attack the Thadous and eat them up.

The Thadous then told the Lion-men to wait as they would have to have a discussion over the matter among them regarding the granting of human flesh as food. When the *ju* (rice beer) was prepared the Thadous invited the strong young

---

[1] All Naga tribes believe in a village of cannibals, a village of tiger-men and a village of Amazons somewhere a little further East. It is interesting therefore to find Herodotus (IV, 102-110) associating as adjoining nations, head-hunters, cannibals, were wolves and Amazons.—(Ed.)

men into their village to talk the matter over. This the Lion-men did, and after much drinking and talking the Lion-men became drunk. The Thadous then rose up and killed them all. When the rest of the Lion-men heard of this they became much afraid and wanted to make peace. The Thadous agreed to this on condition that the remaining Lion-men took oath by throwing down *gahoh* (bean seeds) and cutting *moulthing* (a small plant) while swearing future friendship. This was done and so peace was declared. In consequence of this Thadous never discuss serious matters without drinking much ju, since it led to their salvation on this occasion. When peace is to be made between tribes and villages the above form of oath by throwing down *gahoh* and cutting of *moulthing* while taking the oath is resorted to in all serious matters of life and death. The Lion-men then moved off and are supposed to have taken up their abode in Kol[1] (Burma). Songs called *sala* are sung to commemorate that occasion at time of performing Sa-ai for killing game.

At that time there was a man called Chonsing who had an abnormally large mithun. The son of the Chief of the Lion-men who had migrated to Burma visited Chonsing's village and saw this mithun. The Chief of the Lion-men had already told his son not to visit the Human Beings and kill anything as they had taken an oath to the contrary, but the son did not obey his father. This son came to Chonsing's house with his *kolpelteng* (Burmese spear) and drove it into the ground in front of Chonsing's house. Then he jumped on top of this large mithun which he could not resist doing and sucked the mithun's blood from its neck killing it. Seeing this Chonsing shot at him with his bow and arrow but only wounded him in the leg though this was sufficient to make him run away into the jungle. Next morning when a woman of the village went to draw water she saw a strange man there at the spring with a wounded right leg. She asked what was the matter and was told that he had been cut by the *kengkou* (a kind of thorny plant) while passing through the jungle hunting deer and he gave her a leg of the deer and told her not to tell anyone and disappeared into the jungle again. When she returned to the village she told Chonsing about this and on searching the place they found a Lhohmi dead. So to this day when Thadous kill tigers they always blame the *kengkou* plant for it and ask the animal if it was blind.[2]

---

[1] The Thado word for the Burmese and Assamese is almost the same, and suggests a period when the only plainsmen known to the tribes were members of the Munda (Kol) race. The Talaings who belonged to it occupied Pegu until the Burmese conquered them in 1757, and a lineal descendant of the old Mon dynasty of Pegu still exists in the Bohmong of the Chittagong Hill Tracts.—(Ed.)

[2] No doubt attempting to evade the responsibility, for fear of the enmity of the tiger's ghost, *vide The Angami Nagas*, p. 262.—(Ed.)

Next we have a story of the time when the Thadous were at the river Teo or Tyao where it meets the Loh river. There was a man called Haophut who had cultivated at the junction of the rivers. One day a long log of wood with a *sajo* (kind of squirrel[1]) seated on it came floating down and being caught at the confluence in a large eddy could make no further progress down stream. There it kept going round and round. Haophut suspecting this as some bad omen returned to his house and found his son dead. He then made a song of what he saw and of what led him to go home to find his son dead. This song is called *langla* and is only sung at the burial of those who have performed the Chon festival.

On the way to Mithikho there sits a woman called Kulsamnu[2] who snatches all those on their way to Mithikho who have not performed *Gal-ai*,, *Sha-ai* or *Chang-ai* and makes them her slaves. So it is believed that only those who have performed these festivals have free passage to the village of the dead. Once a brave man called Ngambom, was captured by Kulsamnu but he got away by killing her by the aid given him by Khupting who loved him and had gone on ahead to Mithikho. She sent a wild cat to instruct him how to reach her. Kulsamnu only appeared dead but was not really so as she at once came to life again immediately Ngambom reached Mithikho. It is believed that Kalsamnu does not separate those who are really in love with each other and wishes them to live peacefully in Mithikho together.

At the period during which the Thadous lived in the present Chin and Lushei country, there was a small clan called Galte who were raided by the Lusheis and took refuge with the Thadous. They say the Galtes only had about 500 houses altogether then. After being given refuge one day the Galtes tried to murder a Thadou Chief but failed. For this treachery they

---

[1] I think *sajo* is the binturong, but it is a rare beast and I have never had a chance of identifying it.—(Ed.)

[2] Also called Kumsalnu and described as sitting weaving as she waits by the Path of the Death, and apparently a giantess. Men and boys are not afraid of her, but she makes women search her hair for lice—and eat them. Therefore women carry a tobacco-seed under their finger nails to cheat her. [Cf. *The Angami Nagas*, p. 226.] In some parts of the world there would be nothing outrageous in Kumsalnu's conduct. So near as Borneo lice are apparently often eaten by the Dusun of Tuaran [*vide* Evans, *Among Primitive Peoples in Borneo*, p. 123], while South American Indians of the Amazon regard a louse as a tit bit, and so also in Liberia, [*vide* Whiffen, *The North-west Amazons*, p. 130].

This fiend who bullies the souls of the dead, besides being known to all Naga and Kuki tribes [*vide*, *The Sema Nagas*, p. 212, 244] as well to Garos of Assam, is known throughout the Indian Ocean from the Andamans to Formosa, and from Malaya to New Zealand. For references see my note on page 227 of Mills' *The Ao Nagas*, and Moss, *Life after Death in Oceania, etc.*, Chapter X.—(Ed.)

were raided and many killed. They ran away to the Lusheis again who took them under their wing.

When the Hangshings were living at Khovong, the present village site of Haotinkhup Chief of the Suhtes,[1] they had a strong village at Lhungtin on the Salli range of hills. It was a very big village and harassed the Lusheis a great deal. The Lushei wished to make peace so they went to the chief of the Thadous, Jelhao, with one spear, one shield and one *khipichang* (ear bead) and requested him to influence the Hangshings not to raid them. Jelhao Chief of the Thadous told the Hangshings to stop and there was peace between the Lusheis and Thadous. About this time there was a great deal of internal trouble among the Thadous and inter-raiding among them. The Shingshons in particular were very anxious to reduce the power of the Shitlhous who claimed to be head of the Thadous. At this time some of the Lushei villages had also placed themselves under the protection of the Shingshon clan with the chief of Tuithang village who was the Pipa[2] of the Shingshon. This culminated in a great battle on Songchal Hill where the village of Jolpi was then. In this the Shingshons were defeated by the Shitlhous. It is said the Thilhas helped the latter in the battle. In the mind of the Shitlhous the Lusheis, Suhtes and Pois are all inferior to them according to the usual genealogical accounts, and it is said that the Lusheis actually call the Thadous *Lusong*, which is said to mean pride of birth. The Thadou is naturally a very self-important person and places a very high value on himself, and it may be doubted whether the Lusheis, Suhtes and Pois would admit their inferiority on the Shitlou claim.

The Pois next harassed the Thadous and it is admitted that the then large Thadou villages were destroyed by them *viz*:—Sailhem, Songbem, Songlhuh, Lasan, Tuithang, Chahsat and Lhuntin. Still the Thadous refused to submit to the Pois and so started the general move northwards again. Three main parties were agreed on and they moved as follows :—

Shitlhous with the Shingsons, Changsan, Lhangums and others moved up into the North Cachar Hills which was then in the hands of Tularam Senapati Kachari. The village of the Pipa of the Shitlhous took up their abode at a site called Lailenbung in the time of Thushong Chief, near what is now Maibong Station on the Hill Section of the Assam Bengal Railway.

Sangnao and Khaochangbung Chiefs of the Shitlhous and

[1] Spelt "Howchinkhup" and "Sokte" by Messrs. Carey and Tuck (*op. cit*, ch. X. *q. v.*) and (?) Sumtí or Suti by Brown (*Native State of Manipur*).—(Ed.)

[2] That is the genealogical head of the clan.—(Ed.)

their adherents moved up along the hills between the Barak river and the valley of Manipur.

The Chahsat Chief with his followers moved up along the hills on the east of the valley of Manipur and so came in due time to their present villages.

We next have the story of the Mutiny in Silchar. Many Thadous had been enlisted into a kind of armed levy and spread out in the North Cachar Hills in villages in an attempt to stop the Angamis from raiding those parts. The Indian troops in Sylhet and Silchar mutinied and after killing their officers gathered together with the intention of going to Manipur and settling there since they had heard that it was most fertile.[1] The Thadou levies said they would join them and fight their enemies with them be they even the Englishmen. So the Thadous were allowed to enter the fort in great numbers. Instead of helping the Indian Sepoys they killed them and capturing all their arms handed them over to the Sirkar. Mangjahu Kuki, the chief of Khodungsei village, was the head of this movement and led the Thadou Sepoys. In consequence more arms were supplied by the Sirkar to the Kukis and they were then used in greater numbers to keep off the raids of the Angami Nagas of the Naga Hills. This latter period seems to relate to the institution of Kuki Militia mentioned on page 148 of the *History of the North East Frontier* by Alexander Mackenzie, but I noticed that Thadou historians do not seem to know of the reasons for the abandonment of this Militia, or should I say that they prefer not to remember it.

The Thadous who moved up west of the Barak river were utilised by the Sirkar against the Angamis. Those who came up along the hills between the Barak river and the valley of Manipur were similarly used by the Raja of Manipur placing them among the Kacha Nagas, while those on the east were used as a barrier against the Burmese.

When Nehlam Kuki Chief of the Chahsat group went to pay his respects to the Raja he was well received. After the reception Nehlam Chief went to the then Political Agent and did likewise. The Raja hearing of this became much enraged and sent for Nehlam Chief. When he was produced he was murdered as the Manipuris thought he would become a follower of the British and not do what the Manipuris wanted done.

Soya Kuki Chief of Songchal village, a great warrior with a powerful following, established himself at the present site of

---

[1] These mutineers were not Indian troops of Sylhet and Cachar, but three companies of the 34th N.I. from Chittagong, who had reached Sylhet and Cachar through Hill Tippera, *vide* Gait, *History of Assam*, ch. XVII, who says that the mutineers heading for Manipur were repeatedly attacked by the regular troops and by Kuki Scouts, and that ultimately only three or four escaped death or capture.—(Ed.)

Lailong village of Chura Chandpur Sub-division of Manipur State. When the Raja heard of this he sent for Soya who appeared presenting a gong to the Raja, but he was also put to death because of his independence. Tungkhopao Chief of Laikot village hearing of this took all the Chahsat group with Soya's following over to the Raja of Alva (*i.e.* Ava—Burma) and requested that revenge may be taken for such a deed against the Raja of Manipur. The Raja of Alva said he would do so in three years' time and permitted Tungkhopao to take up his residence in the hills on the west of Alva. During this time Tungkhopao killed some people of the Raja of Alva's hill tribes and was sent for to answer for the deed. Tungkhopao feigned illness and was persuaded by the Shitlhous to submit to the Raja of Manipur who had the British to help them for safety's sake. And so Tungkhopao and the Chahsat group came back and were allowed to reside in the hills to the west of the Valley. This was in Sana Koireng's time.

The reason why the Manipuris call the Thadous "Khongjai" is, according to the Thadous, because the first village which came in contact with the State was Khongsai of the Lhungum clan and now living in Cachar District. It was destroyed by Chinthang and Toijam, who were great warriors, who put up the heads of those they killed on a tree with seven branches.[1] Each branch had seven stems with a head on each. Both of them died on that day also and were wearing *aimitjing*.[2] So it is said that if any one can repeat what those two did and count the heads correctly then he will die a *thilha* or spirit.

The place where Khongsai village cultivated is known as "Saite Loulen" and was again taken up by Khongson village of the Thanglhai sub-clan of the Lhouvum clan of the Thadous, after Khongsai village was driven out. Only the chili fields were not cultivated. These two villages are famous among the Thadous.

There was a girl by the name of Lenghoi or Nungmaidenga who fell in love with a large snake which resided near the village. She was of the Chothe tribe of Old Kukis.[3] To others the snake appeared as a snake but to the girl it was a very handsome young man. Eventually she became pregnant by

---

[1] When the Thado take heads otherwise than for a dead man's grave they are usually stuck up on stakes or on the branches of trees, a point being cut from the wood to go through a corresponding hole in the cranium of the skull.—(Ed.)

[2] *I.e.*, leaves of a magic plant which make the wearer invisible.—(Ed.)

[3] This association of the Manipuris with an Old Kuki origin is perhaps significant, in view of their many similarities both to Nagas, such as the Ao and the Tangkhul, and to Kukis, as in their language. The Old Kukis, generally speaking, are intermediate between the Naga and the Thado. The snake Pakhangba was the ancestor of the Ningthaja clan of Meitheis to which the Maharaja of Manipur belongs, v. Hodson, *The Meitheis*. p. 100.—(Ed.)

the snake and a male child was born to her. He grew up and all spoke of him as fatherless at which he used to be ashamed. His mother told him not to mind that but to go and make friends with his father the snake. The boy was not afraid and met the snake whom he caught by the neck and the snake told him many wonderful things that were to happen to the boy. The boy then went and told his mother of this and she gave eggs to perform the "Ahtuisan" when searching for a new site upon which he was to make a new village. He tried Langthabal first but the omen was not auspicious, so then he went to the middle of the valley where, on performing the *Ahtuisan*, the result was excellent; so he made a village there and thus the Manipuris were originated. At that time they lived like Kukis and Nagas but later a Brahman came from the south who so impressed them with his preachings that they took on their present religion.

At the time of the Burmese Invasion [1] the Raja of Manipur fled for protection to the house of Khongsat Kuki's father where he ate *ga* (beans) only for several months. When the Burmese left the Valley he returned home with Khongsat's father and Kaikholal Kuki. So the Manipuris have always treated the Kukis with respect since then.

When Ngameingam or Chandra Kirti Singh Raja was on the throne [2] he collected a great force to attack Molbem village (Kamhao Chief of the Suhte clan). Thangkhohen, Chief of Sangnao village, sent his cousin Pumjam, Chief of Bijang village, with some 1000 Kukis to help Ngameingam. The result was sad, as Kamhao Chief won the battle, inflicting great loss on the Manipuris and their Kuki levies. Pumjam, Jamkhupao and Langhel were the leaders of the Kukis. It came about as follows:—Just before the fight started the Suhtes shouted out that the Manipuris were attacking them because the Suhtes had revenged the death of Thangpao and Thanglam at the hands of Kaiap village of Kom Kukis. Also at that time the present village of Khongjang in the Chura-Chandpur Area was living with Kamhao. Thanglam was Pumjam Chief's father. Consequently the Kukis did not help and the force was defeated. The Raja was weeping on the banks of the Gun (Imphal) river at such disgrace when one Chongja Kuki taking pity on him fired off his gun before the Raja and said "The Raja shall not die until I, Chongja, am first killed by the Raja's enemies." This cheered up the Raja and the followers of Chongja having made a

---

1 The Burmese invaded Manipur in 1755, 1758, 1765, etc. repeatedly until the end of First Burmese War in 1826.—(Ed.)

2 Chandra Kirti Singh succeeded as a minor in 1834, but was taken by his mother in flight to Cachar. He returned after the death of Nur Singh in 1850 and died in 1886.—(Ed.)

vailang (cane suspension bridge) got the Raja safely across and into safety.

When Chandra Kirti Singh was about to die he directed that the custom of inheritance as among the Thadous was to be observed in the future and so elected his eldest son to be Raja after him in token of all the help the Kukis had given him.[1] However, Sena Koireng deposed the new Raja and sat himself on the throne. The ex-Raja fled to the British and appealed. In consequence of this the Chief Commisioner of Assam came to Imphal, the Capital of Manipur State, but Sena Koireng murdered him with 4 other sahebs also and drove out the remaining British force. Most of the Thadous fought for the Raja on that occasion. This resulted in the Manipur War of 1891 but the Kukis did not help the Manipuris then, as they knew that the latter had no chance. Sena Koireng fled to Tonglhu Chief of Chahsat and sought his protection. Tonglhu said he was seriously thinking of taking revenge for his father Nehlam's murder but as the Sirkar were in search of the Raja he told him to go away as he (Tonglhu) could not grant such protection. However in revenge for Nehlam's murder the Chahsat group attacked and destroyed a Burmese thana and implicated Manipuris thereby. For Soya Chief's murder the village of Chongjang in the Naga Hills attacked and destroyed a Manipuri Thana at Makui village. This was after Henima outpost had been established.[2]

At that time the Lusheis tried to enter the south-west hills of Manipur but the Shingshons drove them out. They then tried to persuade Goupi, Chief of Tuithang (Shingshon), to forsake the Shitlhous and come and live amongst them. He refused because of the agreement between him and the Jampi Chief, head of the Shitlhous, and so the Shingshons said they would take him by force even if the other Thadous helped him. On this the Shitlhous gathered all their folk and sent a message to Khongjang Chief saying that if they wanted to fight and not observe the previous agreement of peace then they were to come on. On this Khongjang Chief decided not to fight the Thadous to the north and so peace was declared again between them.

The agreement spoken off came about as follows: The Shingshons and Shitlhous fought a great battle on Songchal Hill in which the Shingshons were badly beaten and so the Shingshons became submissive to the Shitlhous. Jangvum Chief of the Shingshons was killed and Thushong Chief of

---

[1] The Meithei custom seemed formerly to have been for the throne to pass from the elder to the youngest brother, and then to the eldest son of the latter and so on, and not, as one would expect, back to the eldest brother's children.—(Ed.)

[2] The Henima outpost was established early in 1881.—(Ed.)

the Shitlhous was much grieved and punished the murderer, a man of the Lhoujem clan. It is not the custom to kill Chiefs in war [1] but only to capture them and keep them as hostages.

Since the Shingshons were a branch of the Thadous this sin of revolt was realised when Khotinkai Chief of the Shingshons could get no male issue although he had many daughters. In consequence he went to the Pipa of the Shitlhous who was Khotinmang and asked for his blessing and forgiveness of the sins of his ancestors in their rebellion against the Shitlhous. Khotinkai promised he would never permit such a thing to happen agein so Khotinmang gave Khotinkai his blessing and a son was born called Goupi and thus the lineage did not become *ingam* [2] (extinct).

The Thadous believe that they are destined to be rulers of their earth and not to be submissive to any one and so they are sometimes carried away by their ambitions and swayed by this belief in their destiny into illconsidered action, a process which culminated in the Kuki Rebellion of 1918-19. They do not consider themselves beaten yet and still brood over the future ahead of them which to their sorrow, is not developing as fast as they would like. In fact by the establishment of three subdivisions in the hills of Manipur State their prestige among other hill tribes has been much shaken. Also many who went to France in the Manipur Labour Corps are now convinced that the earth is not quite as small as they held it to be previously. However these are in the minority and ancient thoughts and traditions carry more weight among those still only slightly affected by contact with the outer world. Meanwhile conversion to Christianity is spreading rapidly among them and ere long these old thoughts of their destiny are likely gradually to fade and to lead no doubt to a better understanding between the Thadou and other hill tribes among whom they reside. Yet they still think they own the country they inhabit and regard the other tribes as their underlings, a point of view which they frequently evince to those engaged in their administration. Respect of others' property, moveable, and immoveable, they have practically none,[3] but it is slowly dawning upon them that times are changing only too rapidly.

---

[1] So too Shakespear (*op. cit.*, p. 58) but Lewin, (*Wild Races of S.E. India*, p. 251) says that a chief may be killed in the heat of battle. Both state that in theory anyhow all chiefs are blood relations, and that this is the reason for the prohibition.—(Ed.)

[2] *Ingam*, cf. the Khasi *iapduh* which has the same significance. Like the Naga, the Kuki and the Khasi have horror of the family line or still more the clan becoming extinct. The trait is natural in people like the Khasi and Naga tribes which are ancestor worshippers at heart, and no doubt the Kuki has absorbed some of the sentiment with the blood of his neighbours.—(Ed.)

[3] According to Lewin, in Kuki custom everything in a village belongs to the chief, who can demand anything he requires (*op. cit.*, p. 251). At

CHAPTER IV.

CUSTOMS.

Thadou Customs.

Childbirth.

Among the Thadous birth is given by the woman kneeling on some cloths, while in front of her her husband, sitting on a stool, holds her round the chest. She in turn putting her arms around him. Sometimes a relation or friend also kneels behind the woman and placing his arms above the child gently helps it into light by a slow light pressure downwards.

When the child is born a piece of cotton is tied immediately about an inch or so from the child's navel and then the umbilical cord is cut with the edge of a piece of split bamboo or a clean knife.[1]

The mother usually stands leaning against something or still in the position described above until the placenta comes away. After which she is given *ju* to drink and allowed to put the child to her breasts.

The placenta and umbilical cord are placed in a gourd and hung up at the top of the outside of the back wall of the house, where they remain until the receptacle decays and falls of itself.

The child should be named [2] at once on birth as soon as it is known whether it is a male or female. The name to be given is always previously decided upon and usually contains part of the compound name of grandfather or father, or grandmother or mother of the child according to whether it be

---

the same time presents given to the chief are, he says, common property and may be taken by any one (*ibid.*, p. 250). The claim of the Kuki chief to take what he pleases is probably to be associated with the Oceanic custom known in Fiji, for instance, as *Kérékéré*, under which a chief has a perfect right to confiscate an object if the transaction be ostensibly for the good of the community, this right entailing, of course, a compensatory privilege on the part of the owner of the confiscated property to come to his chief at some later date with a request for a favour (Deane, '*Fijian Society*, p. 119). The Thado disrespect of property alluded to by Mr. Shaw has to be considered in the light of the history of the tribe, who have spread themselves over a large area in very small bands dominating much larger communities of alien race, as qualified by some pre-existing custom of the nature of *Kérékéré* so that what is mere robbery from another point of view may be a very correct and proper action from that of the Thado, or even a compliment to the person robbed.—(Ed.)

[1] If a knife is used at all it is a very recent change indeed; most Thado regard the use of iron for this purpose as taboo like most Nagas, as well as many other tribes, *e.g.*, the Moi of Annam, the Kayan of Borneo and the Tinguian of Luzon.—(Ed.)

[2] Most Thado find a real difficulty in saying their own name. They cannot explain why, and, I think really do not know why.—(Ed.)

a male or female.[1] Thus Kapjavum is the son of Vumjakhup, and his grandfather's name was Kaptho, whose father was Kaplhun whose grandfather was Nohkap.

Naodopju is the name of the *ju* prepared for the occasion and is drunk by all participating in the ceremony.

Naodop an is the food prepared for the affair and eaten by all present.

The mother of the child is not supposed to go out of the house for 5 days in the case of a son and 3 days in the case of a daughter from the day of birth. This is called *Naolaichan*.

Kilhalho is performed for the child usually on the day after birth, but there seems no fixed day, and a string with some feathers is put around its neck implying that it is free from any evil or illness. The *Thempu* (Medicine man or priest) is called who kills a fowl outside the house taking the child's name and calling on the *Thilhas* (Spirits) not to molest the child and may it grow up strong and famous.

There is an interesting story attached to the naming of the child.

Once upon a time there was a man who went out hunting and as it became night took up a place under a tree for the night. About midnight he was awoken by all the *thilhas* calling to the *thilha* of that tree saying "Let us go to the village of the Human Beings and cut the navel cord of the child who is to be born this night." The Thilha of the tree replied "I cannot go with you as I have a stranger in my house." So the other Thilhas went and after a very short time returned. The Thilha of the tree asked who cut the cord and the others told him it had already been cut by a tiger. The Thilha of the tree then asked when the tiger would kill the child and the others replied saying "When the child grows up he will marry two wives. These wives after a time will quarrel over a paddy mortar. So the husband, in order to make peace between them will go to the jungle and make another mortar so that the two wives may have one each. It is then that the tiger will kill him." The hunter in the morning went back to his village and found that his wife had given birth to a son, so he was determined to remember what he had heard the Thilhas say. When the son grew up he married two wives and they quarrelled over a mortar and so the son went to make another in the jungle. His father secretly followed him and while the son was making the mortar a tiger came but the father killed it with his bow and arrow. The son was much pleased and going up to the tiger got hold of its whiskers and said "If my father had not killed you I would have." When drawing away his hand the tiger's whiskers cut him and he died almost at once. So in

---

[1] A boy is always given a name from the side of his patrilineal ancestors, but there is no fixed rule as to girls.—(Ed.)

spite of the father's care what the Thilhas said came true. Consequently Thadous say when cutting the umbilical cord "I will cut the cord and no one else."

After the child is strong enough to be carried distances, it is taken to the house of the father-in-law[1] who performs *Naopui* by killing a pig or a fowl which is merely feasted on, no ceremonies being performed. Sometimes the father-in-law gives the child his blessing by performing *Kilhalho* to ward off the evil eye and any future illnesses.

Among the Thadous, since descent is reckoned in the male line only, great rejoicing and heavy drinking is indulged in when a son is born; although now-a-days the birth of a girl is becoming nearly as important owing to the comparative certainty of getting her marriage price since they can depend on the assistance of the courts, the help of which they did not have in the old days.

Death rites.

When a person is dying all the relations are summoned to the house and they call to him or her not to leave them. It is said that by this means persons almost dead are sometimes brought to life again, since the soul's attention has been attracted back to the house from its wanderings by the calling of the name.[2]

When the person breathes his last the men shout out "Where is the *Thilha* who has taken you away? Let it show itself and we will kill it" and words to that effect.[3] They usually snatch up a dao and hack near posts to show their temper and determination of what they would do to the *Thilha*. There is then much weeping and show of sorrow although it does not last long among the men.

The corpse is then washed and wrapped in a cloth and placed in a log of wood which has been hollowed out to make a rough coffin. It is covered with a rough plank at time of burial.[4]

---

[1] *I.e.*, the mother's father.—(Ed.)

[2] Cf. *the Sema Nagas*, p. 209, and Mills, *The Ao Nagas*, p. 278. The Khasis do the same (Gurdon, *The Khasis*, p. 132). So, too, the Maoris (*Old New Zealand*, ch. XIV, and note), and the natives of Yap (Frazer, *Belief in Immortality*. III, 165), in Madagascar (Osborn, *Madagascar*, p. 314), the Kayans of Borneo (Hose and McDougall, *Pagan Tribe of Borneo*, II, 32). See also Frazer, *Golden Bough*, III, ch. ii.—(Ed.)

[3] So the Angami (v. *The Angami Nagas*, p. 227, and Butler, *Travels in Assam*, p. 150, and some Konyak Nagas (Owen, *Naga Tribes in Communication with Assam*, p. 24), and so too the Samoans (Frazer, *Belief in Immortality*, II, 208).—(Ed.)

[4] Although the Thado practise burial at present there are indications that this method of disposing of the corpse may be comparatively recent. Apparently up to the last generation, at any rate, cases survived of the separate disposal of the head, which, in the case of important persons was placed in inaccessible holes or niches in the rock on the face of cliffs. I remember a Thado who happened to be with me on coming across a sequestered limestone cliff in previously unvisited country

If the death is in the morning or during the night the

remarking at once that it would be a splendid place to put a dead chief's head. The explanation given for such separate burial is the protection of the head from enemies. Shakespear, writing in 1912 speaks of a similar custom as then dying out, and gives the same explanation, but describes the practice as one of separate burial of the head in an earthen pot (*op. cit.*, page 204). Soppitt (*Account of the Kuki-Lushai Tribes*, pp. 13, 14) describes the process, and definitely attributes the practice to the Thado. The body is put on a platform near the house and visited by the deceased female relatives every three days, who "so fasten up the cloths (as decomposition sets in and is progressing) that none of the putrid matter falls to the ground." When "the corpse has throughly decomposed and nothing is left but the skeleton, the bones and cloths are then carefully gathered and buried in front of the house, but the skull....is bleached in the sun, any loose teeth being refastened in with gum, and then, being thoroughly cleaned, it is placed in a woven cane basket. Another feast is now held, at the conclusion of which this basket is carefully hidden away by the relatives." In any case very diverse methods are followed by the different branches of the Kuki race. The old Kuki tribes bury (Shakespear, *op. cit.*, 164 sq). The Banjogis and the Shendus of the Chittagong Hill Tracts bury persons of position in a sitting posture, the latter using a stone-lined grave (Lewin, *op. cit.*, 246, 286). The Lushei put the corpse in a wooden coffin, with a plank cover, elevated over a fire with a bamboo tube leading from a hole in the bottom to the ground as also among some Kachins (Scott and Hardiman, *op. cit.*, I, i, 410). When dry the skull is separated and by some preserved in a basket in the house, by others buried in a pot (Shakespear, *op. cit.*, 84 sq; Lewin *op. cit.*, 274). One Lushei clan wraps its dead in pith and buries them after smoke-drying them on a fire, and the "Howlong" clan hang the coffin containing the corpse to the house beams for 7 days during which the widow must spin underneath (Lewin, *loc. cit.*). Rawlins, describing the "Cucis of Tipra" in the XVIIIth century describes them as smoking their dead on a platform and then burying, after which the first fruits of crops are offered on the grave, *cf.* the Ao custom described by Mills (*The Ao Nagas*, p. 279), that of the Kacharis (Soppitt, *Kachari Tribes in North Cachar Hills*, p. 40), and of the Mundas (S. C. Roy, *The Mundas*, p. 465). In all these cases final disposal of the year's dead is associated with the harvest. Others, he adds, put their dead in trees while yet others wash the bones and keep them dry in a bowl, to be consulted for omens in times of emergency (*Asiatick Researches*, II, xii). McRae writing of the "Kookies or Lunctas" in 1799 (*ibid.*, VII, vi), describes the corpse as kept on the platform till the spring festival when the bodies of all the year's dead are burnt together. Probably this spring festival coincided with the sowing. The Nagas of Laruri keep the smoked corpses of their dead until the following crop is sown, when all the past year's dead are brought out and finally disposed of together, probably in order that the soul released from the mortal husk may enter the sown seed and fertilize the springing crop with fresh sources of life.

In the Chin Hills again the Siyin expose the corpse to the weather and ultimately bury the bones in an earthen pot; the Sokte dry the corpse and bury in a family vault where the bones can be inspected. Burial places are outside the village, but the Haka and Tashon Chins bury inside the village (Carey and Tuck, *op. cit.*, page 192 sqq.). The Old Kuki tribes of the Sakchip (Tippera) and the Hrangkol both burn their dead. (Waddell, *loc. cit.*) also the Biete.

Cave or cliff burial, as formerly practised by the Thado, is practised by several Naga tribes and by other races sporadically throughout the Indian Archipelago from Borneo to the Philippines, in New Guinea and Melan-

corpse is buried the following day in the evening.[1] It is buried outside the house.[2] The relations dig the grave and are helped by the young men and friends. On the grave a bamboo is erected which is notched to show the number of animals he has killed in his time if a man. If a woman some of her favourite things are hung up and left.

At time of death of a man or woman "*Khunsum*" is performed if they have performed *Sha-ai* or *Chang-ai* in their life. This consists in killing a mithun and in the recital by the

---

esia, in Fiji, the Marquesas, and in Polynesia, New Zealand and Easter Island. As well as with concealment from enemies, it is associated with a future life underground (*vide* Frazer, *Belief in Immortality*, Moss, *Life after Death in Oceania and the Malay Archipelago*).—(Ed.)

[1] When the corpse is carried out for burial the fire in the house is put out and the ashes are removed, and afterwards new fire is made. This new fire should strictly be made with flint and steel, but though admittedly tabu, matches are now commonly used for making this new fire.—(Ed.)

[2] Carey and Tuck state (*loc. cit.*) that the Thado buries outside the village. This is normal in the case of 'apodia' (bad) deaths, otherwise just outside the house is usual. I have, however, seen Shingshuan graves outside the village where death was not 'apodia', and it is possible that the practice is more frequent among Thado on the Burma side. On the Assam side however the usual practice is to make a square excavation just in front of the house to the north side. From this excavation a vault is hollowed running north again, and into this the coffin is placed foot first so that the top of the head is just inside the vault and adjoins the excavation. A bamboo tube is placed close to the head and gradually drawn up as the vault is filled in. The reason given is to afford a means of exit for the soul, and it is to be noted that in Madagascar a similar means of exit is provided, only there the bamboo tube is embedded in the grave so that the mouth is flush with the surface (Sibree, *Madagascar before the Conquest*, 305). According to Hose (*Natural Man*, p. 213) the similar custom of the Kayans of Borneo is for communication with the dead. So too with the Sea Dayaks who place the bamboo just over the root of the nose, the place where the Angami Naga locates his *rhopfü*, the soul that is conceived of as a diminutive manikin (*v.* Hose and McDougall, *op. cit.*, *II.* 50, and *The Angami Nagas*, 98, 183). The purpose of the bamboo tube mentioned by Shakespear (*vide* preceding note) as used by the Lushei is not quite clear, but it occurs to me that it might conceivably be a survival of a bamboo tube, used in burial, retained when exposure has been substituted by an immigrant culture. Burial seems to be the older form in some parts of this area, as exposure has apparently partially replaced burial in the Chang Naga tribe (*v. The Lhota Nagas*, p. xxv), though burial is now replacing exposure in the neighbouring Ao tribe, as it seems to have done, perhaps in the Angami tribe.

Brown writing in 1871 (*Native State of Manipur*, p. 51), states explicitly, and he is a reliable authority, that the Thado ("Khongjai") buries his dead in a sitting posture, the body having been strapped to a board and smoked in that position. I propounded this to a Thado exceptionally well versed in custom and interested in his own traditions, and he was immensely tickled at the novel idea of anyone at all burying their dead sitting. He affirmed that it was never done by Thado, who always bury the corpse lying at full length on its back. The pattern of the Thado grave is found used in Sumatra [Marsden, *History of Sumatra* (1783) p. 250] and among the Tinguian of Luzon (Cole, *op. cit.*, p. 287, n[1]).—(Ed.

Thempu of all the good deeds of the person who has died, and in his blessing the spirit on its journey to Mithikho (The village of the dead). Now-a-days any rich person has a mithun killed on such occasions, but this was not the former custom. A pig was all that was killed if the sha-ai or chang-ai had not been performed by deceased. This killing of a pig or mithun is called *khosa.*

If persons die accidentally or of cholera, yaws, leprosy, small-pox, or in battle or child-birth, the above is not performed and the body is buried outside the perimeter of the village.[1] In these cases no *Lŏngmăn*[2] ("corpse-price") is claimable. Nor, if a woman should die without any male issue, is it claimable for her.

---

[1] Not in all these cases. There is an intermediate death between a good death, when the ancestral songs are sung, and a bad death (*thishe*), when the deceased is buried outside the village, as in the case of a death in battle. In case of the intermediate death, which is death as the result of diseases entailing corruption of the living body, the body is buried inside the village, outside the house, but the vault is made along one side of the excavation instead of leading northwards from it, and no songs are sung. In all such cases no *lŏngmăn* is claimable, as in the case of death in child-birth, when the deceased is usually buried behind the house. In the case of full *thishe*, when the interment is outside the village, no vault is made at all.—(Ed.)

[2] *Lŏngmăn* is a payment made to the nearest male kin of a deceased person on the mother's side if deceased is a male, on the father's side if the deceased is a female. Thus in the following table :—

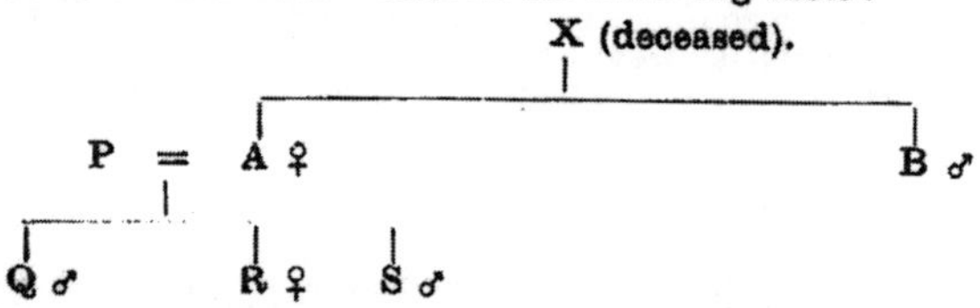

On A's death *longman* is paid by P to B ; if either or both be dead, it is paid or received by the nearest patrilineal heir.

If R die after bearing a legitimate son, *who survives her*, her husband will pay *longman* to P.

If Q die, *longman* is paid by P or by S to B, unless it should happen that Q should have been married and die without having had any children at all, surviving or otherwise.

The principle of paying for the children a woman bears as well as for the woman herself appears in Guiana, where the Caribs recognize it (Brett, *Indian Tribes of Guiana,* 354) and doubtless elsewhere, but the real significance of *longman* is indicated by its name. Rai Bahadur S. C. Roy tells me that among the Ho of Chota Nagpur, a tribe of Mon affinities, parents marrying off their daughter always stipulate that after her death her bones shall be returned to her family; this condition is accepted, but is never carried out in practice, nor is it really expected to be. Now among the Thado a woman the lobe of whose ear is split cannot join her relatives in the next world, is buried therefore as an intermediate (bad) death, and no *longman* can be claimed for her. Obviously the inference is that *longman* (=" bone-price ") is the price that is paid for retaining the bones of the mother or of her child as the case may

Before *longman* can be claimed the claimant has to kill a pig[1] for the person from whom he claims a mithun as *longman* and this is known as *longman bepna*. otherwise the claim is not admissible according to custom.

Marriage.

There are four kinds of marriage among the Thadous viz :—*chongmu*, *sahapsat*, *jol-lha'* and *kijam mang*. In the first two a proper ceremony is gone through while the latter two amount to elopement.

Chongmu.

In this form of marriage the bridegroom's parents send go-betweens to the parents of the bride to find out if they are willing to allow a union. At the time the parents of the bride if they are agreeable, kill a pig for the representatives of the bridegroom's people and they all eat it and much ju is drunk.[2] This is called *sumtansha*. At this time a settlement is made as to the amount of marriage price to be paid and how much of it should be brought on the wedding day. If afterwards the question of return of the *mān* (marriage price) should arise for some reason leading to divorce then this *sumtansha* expenditure is returnable. The date for taking away the bride is fixed on at the time of this feast and the representatives of the bridegroom's people return and inform him and his parents of the results. There may be some haggling over the marriage price but the full amount to be paid is finally settled before the bride is taken away. When everything is fixed up the bridegroom will send strong young

---

be in the husband's or father's family. Presumably were the bones returned the soul would in the life to come foregather with the mother's relatives, and it seems likely that bone-price is a survival from a custom like that of the Khasis (*v.* Gurdon, *The Khasis*, p. 140) at which the bones of the whole matrilineal clan were from time to time collected at a religious ceremony of great importance. A change to the patrilineal system would obviously entail the abandonment of this practice and ceremony, and the right to claim the bones would then become merely formal, as with the Ho, or would be commuted for a money payment as with the Thado. In this connection it is significant that the Ho have much in common with the Khasi (Dalton, *Ethnography of Bengal*, p. 55. sq.; Gurdon, *The Khasis*, p. 11), and that Mr. S. J. Duncan, who has followed Mr. Shaw at Tamenlong, is himself of partly Khasia extraction, and is familiar with Khasi custom, tells me that he finds very great similiarity between the religious customs of the Thado Kuki and the Khasi. It may be further noted that the Lhota payment called *echhiman* (i.e. "death-price") corresponding to the Thado *longman* or *dumditman*, is accompained as a rule by a nominal payment called *ming-eshi*, = 'name buying,' which entitles the family of the payer to use the dead woman's name for children born in subsequent generations.—(Ed.)

[1] In the presence of the man from whom he claims.—(Ed.)

[2] A marriage is broken off or postponed on account of the occurrence of a death in either family during the preliminaries. In case of postponement the parties are careful to note, during the time agreed upon, whether or not further calamities occur, in which case the marriage is usually broken off.—(Ed.)

men with his representatives to take away the bride on the day fixed, sending that part of the marriage price agreed on to be paid at the time, but leaving the greater part as a balance to be paid later. These representatives are feasted at the expense of the bride's people and both parties wrestle and much dung and filth is thrown at the bridegroom's party.[1] Drums and gongs are played and songs sung in the evening by all together while feasting. The next day the bridegroom's party departs triumphant with the bride and the marriage is complete except for the wrench of paying up the balance of the price by degrees.[2]

Sahapsat.

In this form of marriage the wrestling and other festivities are not indulged in and generally the bride is taken away the same day or early the next morning.

Jol-lha'.

In this no arrangement regarding marriage price is made. It is a case of pregnancy resulting from an intrigue between a young man and a girl. The man takes her to wife in consequence when her state is known. No previous arrangement exists between the parties and there are no marriage ceremonies. A *mān* however is settled upon as a rule.

Kijam Mang.

This is when a young man and girl elope and live together without or against the wishes of the parents of either or both parties. No ceremonies are performed and the *mān* is settled on in due course. In the last two forms of marriage there is no *sumtansha* and so none can be claimed hereafter in case of divorce. In these two forms of marriage a ceremony called *in lut* is usually performed by the husband after a time; it merely means going to the parents of the woman and making his peace with them. It is usually at this time that the marriage price is fixed on. *In lut* means "house-entering," the eloping pair being thus recognised as daughter and son-in-law.

The question of the amount of marriage prices among the Thadous is not definite. Chiefs and wealthy persons usually

---

[1] This throwing of mud, dung and rotten eggs at the bridegroom's party takes place at three occasions, first on its arrival at the bride's house; next when the pig is killed for the feast on the following day, and finally when the bridegroom's party departs, which must be before dawn on the day after that. The wrestling likewise takes on these three occasions, and the young men who wrestle must be perfect, none of them must lack a limb or an organ or even a little finger joint. This condition also applies rigidly to the *thempu* who officiates at the wedding.—(Ed.)

[2] After the bridegroom has taken his bride to his house, marriage is not consummated till she has revisited her father's house on a subsequent date previously agreed on, when a further instalment of the *mānpi* (bride-price) is paid. This date may be a few days, a month, or even three months later.

Soppitt (*Short Account of the Kuki-Lushai Tribes*) gives an interesting account of Changsen marriages, but the customs recorded by him cannot safely be regarded as *bona fide* Thado.—(Ed.)

claim and pay the equivalent of 10 mithun, Rs. 200 in cash, 2 *Dapi* (large gong), 2 *Dapu* (set of trio gongs), 2 *Khichang* (ear beads); 2 *Khichong* (necklaces). The ordinary person often actually pays a couple of mithun, khichang and a khichong and Rs. 25 or so in cash. In most cases the *mān* is commuted. For example a pig in some cases may be taken as one mithun.[1] I have actually come across cases where Rs. 40 has stood for 4 mithun and a jar of *ju* for a khichang or khichong. Thus the parent of the bride hardly ever receives the marriage price in full, but in the form of more or less fictitious substitutes. They love to name large amounts as the *mān* not with any idea of getting it, but to be able to boast that their daughter was married for so much; when questioned as to what precisely they received, it will be found that actually a much smaller amount has been accepted in full satisfaction by a system of fictitious values. Besides very few, if any, ever intend paying the *mān* of their wives in full themselves, as it is a recognised thing that their sons or next-of-kin male heirs should pay some if not the greater part. Thus often claims are admitted as outstanding for more than 5 generations for balance of *mān* still unpaid. Consequently the present generation is inevitably burdened by debts due for great-great-grandmothers and aunts and other relatives whose descendants they are or represent. So the Thadou tribe is full of litigation on this score and the Christian movement may do good in this direction. But if so I think the Thadou will have to have an outlet for his litigious and quarrelsome tendencies in some other form.[2]

Mankang.

This is a mithun which may be claimed by the bride's father's brother or by the best friend of her father, but in return he must give the bride a dowry in the form of necklaces, etc. To claim his mithun, however, he must at different times, kill three pigs or their theoretical equivalents, for the husband or for his male next-of-kin if the husband be dead, but it is considered a breach of etiquette for the claim to be made against any other than the husband. If the donor die before one pig is killed no claim lies against the bridegroom.

Sumkhao Sat Tan Man.

After a girl has been betrothed by the performance of *sumtansha*, if she marries some one else, then one mithun has to be paid to the bridegroom first elected for breach of pro-

---

[1] The first and the last of the number of mithun arranged must be paid in genuine beasts—cow mithun, but for the rest of the mithun substitutes of any kind will serve if the parties are in agreement.—(Ed.)

[2] As stated in the introduction, I think that the litigiousness referred to by Mr. Shaw is the result of a passing phase of social disturbance. In my experience the Thado is not particularly litigious, though the disputes which he has are apt to be of an unsatisfactory nature to the authority that has to deal with them.—(Ed.)

mise. The same applies should the man fail to carry out his contract, and a mithun is payable to the girl's parents.[1]

Chalam.

The first child that dies in a family is known by this name and no *longman* is claimable for it in consequence.[2]

Jalkhunchonman.

This is a mithun paid in lieu of a second *mān* to the parent or nearest male relative of a woman by a second husband should he be the brother[3] or direct relation of her first husband. It is customary for a brother to take to wife a deceased brother's widow although he be already married. I feel that some ages ago the Thadou must have had the system of wives being common property between relations of the husband, as no shame seems to exist when a brother or his near relation is found cohabiting with his wife and nothing is said.[4] It does not seem to lead to unpleasantness or ill feeling.

Noituichonman.

When a man dies leaving a wife who does not return to her parents again but lives on in her husband's house or in the village and some other person marries her then one mithun is paid[5] to the

---

[1] But in this case it is called *jouman*, and I think the penalty of a mithun is less straitly exacted.—(Ed.)

[2] For the purposes of *chalam* the unit taken is a father, mother and children. For the first of this group that dies no *longman* is payable. As soon as one of these children marries and has children he or she is regarded as having left the family for the purposes of *chalam*, and the newly married couple and their children form a fresh unit.—(Ed.)

[3] This custom, as stated, certainly, does not hold good of all the Thado. Many of them declare emphatically that *jalkhun chonman* is not payable when a widow is taken by her deceased husband's brother, but only if the man who takes her is a cousin or some other more distant relative of the deceased. The probability seems to me that the discrepancy arises from attempts to state in definite terms what is really a custom of some flexibility and adaptable to circumstances. Many of the Thado live in joint families, two or three brothers in a house. In the case of a man of such a family dying and his widow being taken by a brother living already under the same roof, I am doubtful if *jalkhun chonman* would be paid by any Thado. On the other hand if a widow were taken by a brother living in a distant village it is possible that a demand for it would be regarded as not unreasonable.—(Ed.)

[4] On the other hand in the only such case that I can think of, a great deal was said, and very bitter too. One point seems worth noting and that is that there is no distinction apparently between the elder and the younger brother in this respect. Whereas in some tribes, *e.g.*, the Rengma Nagas, a younger brother has, or used to have access to his elder brother's wife without a reciprocal right on the part of the elder brother, the Thado seem to have no relic of such a social condition even in sentiment, and the elder brother takes the widow of the younger just as freely as the younger takes the elder's.—(Ed.)

[5] *Jonman* is the name by which I know this payment. I am very doubtful about the correctness of the statement that under such circumstances the second husband pays *man* to his wife's parents. In my experience if a man marries a widow who has not returned to the house of her father or his representative after her husband's death, the first hus-

late husband's next-of-kin male by the new husband in addition to any *mān* which may be agreed on between him (new husband) and her parents to be paid to the latter. On second marriage full *mān* is never taken for a divorced, widowed or run-away wife. It must be at least one mithun less according to custom. This second marriage price is spoken of as *nungkitman, lamlhang chotlha' man* or *lamlhang lho'lha' man* and not as *mān* or *manpi*.

Dumdi'man.

This is of the value of one mithun.[1] Should a married woman die without having given birth to any children this amount is paid in full satisfaction of all dues to her father or next-of-kin male. No *longman* is due either. *Dumdi'man* is only paid when none of her *man* or *nungkitman* has been paid up. If any part has already been paid of the *mān* or *nungkitman* then the death of the woman merely cancels the balance. *Dumdi'manna* can be claimed if she has only given birth to girls and no boys, but now-a-days there is a new school which advocates that if girls are born then the full *mān* should be paid since the girls *mān* will be enjoyed by the husband or next-of-kin male. I am told that in such cases one mithun of the marriage price of each girl is paid to the next-of-kin male of the mother at the time of the marriage in compensation for the loss of the *mān* the mother's people suffered. If a boy has been born then full *mān* has to be paid although much of it is usually compounded for a smaller sum unless the parties happen to be at enmity, when they fly to the court in hopes of pulling a larger tooth.

Inbo' man

This is an amount equivalent to one mithun which is paid to the person in whose house a stranger has died by the male heir of the deceased person and is for cleansing the house of the evil spirit which has entered it and thus caused the death.[2]

---

band's heir male is still responsible for the full amount of the origina *manpi*, and receives the second *mān* from the second husband. Ordinarily, however (unless she marries a brother or cousin of her deceased husband) the widow returns to her father's house and the unpaid portion of the *manpi* due from her first husband lapses, and a *nungkitman* is arranged by her father with her second husband. Where the widow marries the heir or near relative of her late husband, the original *manpi* alone stands, augmented or not as the case may be, by *jalkhun chon man*.—(Ed.)

1. If a son dies unmarried before his mother, *dumditman* can be claimed as if no son had been born. *Dumditman* means "the price of a (woman's) tobacco pouch," apparently a metonym for an unfruitful wife, it may be noted that the Kayan of Borneo who is looking out for a sweetheart is said to be "seeking tobacco" (Hose, *Natural Man*, page 66).—(Ed.)

2. I fancy that former custom prescribed not a mithun but a pig and a jar of *ju*. This is still accepted as adequate provided the payer does not contest the claim.—(Ed.)

Jol-lei.

This is an amount of one mithun to be paid by the paramour of a pregnant girl to her father or male next-of-kin, if he does not marry her. If he intends to take the child when weanable, then he has to pay yet another mithun for maintenance to the father or next-of-kin at time of taking over the child. This is called *Chavaman.* If he refuses to take the child when weanable then it is treated as a member of its mother's family. However, at time when the question of *Jol-lei* is settled the paramour must then say whether he intends taking the child or not and must adhere to that.[1] The child should strictly speaking be born in the paramour's house thus according it a formal recognition of parentage.

Sukai.

Sukai is an amount of Rs. 4 paid by the bridegroom to the Chief or the village to which the bride belongs when he takes her to wife.

It is of interest to give the story of how this came about.

In the time of the chief Munthom one of his villagers took to wife one Kilnem and fled away to Khodai village. Munthom went to Khodai village to call them back but was killed by the villagers of that village. Mangjel, brother of Munthom, was too much of a coward to avenge his brother's death but when Thomhil, son of Munthom, grew up he attacked Khodai village and killed many taking a war drum and mithun horn. He then said he would take *sukai* from all who married girls of his village hence forth as the *longman* of Munthon and so the custom became established.[2]

Jachatman.

Jachatman is an amount of one mithun paid by the man who entices away or makes pregnant another man's wife. It is paid by the adulterer to the husband. In addition he has to recoup to the husband all *mān* or *nungkitman* yet paid. The woman's father or male heir will then sue the adulterer for the balance still due.

Divorce.

If a man drive away his wife without cause then he forfeits all paid *mān* or *nungkitman* and in addition has to pay one mithun as

---

[1] Should he ultimately refuse to take the child having originally said that he would do so, *chavaman* will, I think, still be claimed from him by the woman. The death of the child within three years, or the failure of the mother to maintain it for that period nullifies the claim to *chavaman*, unless, in the latter case, the failure be due to the death of the mother.

A son born in this way is among the Haokip Thado given such precedence over legitimate children as the date of his birth warrants. With the Shitlho clan, however, he ranks after legitimate sons, or at any rate after the eldest legitimate son.—(Ed.)

[2] *Sukai* (=*cunni rapina*) is a Shitlho custom, but apparently chiefs of other clans can acquire the right to claim, as if Shitlho, by performing a ceremony to this end, involving a pig and a jar of *ju*, in the house of a Shitlho.—(Ed.)

Daman. If the woman run away from her husband for no cause then the paid *mān* or *nungkitman* is returnable to the husband. It is customary for the man to attempt to call back his wife if she should go away from him. If he does not do so then it is obviously a case for *daman* and forfeiture of such *mān* or *nungkitman* as has been paid. If she refuses to return in spite of the request to do so, then *mān* is returnable. The causes of divorce are often very trivial and mostly the man is to blame in some way or other. Thadous are extremely subtle and sly in the way they work divorces so as to avoid the customary financial consequences.

Sumken.

Sumken is the dowry given to the bride by the brother or best friend of the father. The original name was *Thilken* which means "Property gift" which has been modernised to "Money gift."

Lutom.

Lutom is the gift of a black cloth (that called *pondum*) to the bride's mother by the husband for having given birth to the girl he has chosen.

Laisui.[1]

Laisui is the gift of a pugaree to the father of the bride by the husband for being the begetter of the girl he has selected.

Villeinage.

There are two kinds of service among Thadous *viz* that of *Shó* and that of *Chengcha*.

In the first case a *shó* is really a servant of the person under whose protection he is and lives in the same house with him.

In the second case the *chengcha* lives elsewhere whether in the same village or in a distant one.[2]

In neither case is it slavery in our sense of the word and merely entails menial work. In the second case it does not even amount to the position of a servant.

---

[1] Mr. Shaw has got them the wrong way round, I think. *Laisui* means a woman's waist-band, while *lutom* is a man's loincloth. They were cloths for the bride's parents, now-a-days usually commuted to a money payment of Re. 1 and Rs. 2 respectively. A woman can claim *laisui* in person—perhaps the only claim for property that a Thado woman can make on her own account.—(Ed.)

[2] I am inclined to think that the real test of the difference between *Sho* and *Chengcha* is that in the former case his lord pays the price of his villein's wife, and in return receives the *manpi* of his daughters, whereas in the case of the *Chengcha* the lord is entitled to such services as he can get from the *Chengcha* and also to *shating* (*vide infra*). If that be so the distinction corresponds precisely to that among the Sema Nagas between *akaākhemi*, who are provided with wives by their chief, and *anukeshimi* who merely cultivate his land and pay him service (including the precise equivalent of *shating*) in return for his protection, which is very often sought to obtain payment of a debt.—(Ed.)

A man becomes a *shó* usually to obtain protection under some circumstances or other in which the *shó* is uncertain of his life. There are also many *shó* among Thadous who are the descendants of captives taken in early raids or obtained by purchase from others. One of the principal dealers in *shó* was Zhuimang of Kandung village[1] in the Naga Hills who used to get his supply from Khonoma and neighbouring Naga villages. Kabuis and Kacha Nagas when in extreme poverty resort to selling their children to Kukis as *shó*. I have actually known more than one example of this in my experience.

Chengcha are usually those who have had their debts paid for them by some wealthy or influential person originally in return for service but who have drifted away.

For the release of a *shó* from his obligations one mithun is usually paid among Thadous. This clears the *shó* and his entire family. Many try to claim one mithun per head for the latter but this is not admitted by existing courts. The same applies in the case of a *chengcha* who wishes to clear himself of the tie.[2] It often happens that the *shó* or *chengcha* gets married and the person whose *shó* or *chengcha* he is pays the *mān*. In such cases if there are children (females) of the *shó* or *chengcha* who marry, their *mān* is taken by the master and not by the *shó* or *chengcha* himself. In consequence it often arises that a *shó* or *chengcha* wishes to clear himself of the bondage by paying a mithun before he has had any daughters. Such cases are now-a-days decided on their merits so that the master may not lose in the transaction in the second case and the *shó* or *chengcha* in the first. But I need hardly add that the *shó* or *chengcha* usually comes off worse in the former case but finds it best not to make a fuss about it so long as he can clear himself and his entire family of the obligations involved.

Sometimes claims are made for one mithun per head per year against the *shó* or *chengcha* but this is not according to custom and is not allowed by the Thadou among themselves.

Changseo. This is one *dan* or measure of paddy to the chief of the village. Each household pays this to its chief for the right of cultivation annually.[3] Among the Haokips only a jar of *ju* is paid ; it is called *belpeng*.

---

[1] He was really a Kachha Naga (Nzemi) originally of Mpaimi village.—(Ed.)

[2] The obligation of a *sho* whose status is acquired by what is called *bangmaisap* (='homicide fence') is regarded as very much more binding and sacred than when the status is otherwise acquired, although it is acquired by the payment by the *sho* himself of a substantial sum to the chief whom he chooses as a protector. For release from this particular bond a very heavy penalty would almost certainly be claimed, but I do not remember hearing of one's ever having arisen.—(Ed.)

[3] The theory is that the land cultivated by any Thado village belongs to the chief. *Changseo* must be paid after the crop is reaped.—(Ed.)

Khotha is the name given to the free labour supplied by one person from each household in the village, who must work one day for the chief of the village in his fields in every year.[1]

Khotha.

This is an amount of Re. 1 per head paid by the seller of mithun, buffalo or cattle to the chief of his village. It is by way of quittance to the chief for the past grazing on his lands.

Shel Kotkai.

When a man migrates from a village the chief has the right to attach all his standing crops and any stored grain. This is only if the villager migrates without the chief's permission ; if the chief has caused the man to move out, the chief has no right to confiscate his property, although chiefs are not beyond doing so in all cases. Villagers get over the difficulty by selling off their stock after harvesting and having no standing crops when they actually migrate.

Migration Due.

Rupee 1 is paid by the purchaser for every head of mithun, buffalo or cattle to the chief of the village, from which the purchase is made, as a sort of export fee.

Lamkai.

I am of opinion that this due and *Shel kotkai* is paid to recompense the chief for the loss of animals from his village, animals of which he would certainly get a portion if killed there ; also villages are spoken of as possessing so many mithuns, etc., and by reduction of their number the chief's prestige is somewhat reduced, since he takes the credit for any wealth of this kind in his village. In the old days it was a large jar of *ju* and the chief's permission had to be taken before any animals were allowed to be purchased by outsiders.

Thil Kotkai is an export fee of Re. 1/- paid for a single barrelled gun, Rs 2/- for a double barrelled gun and Re. 1/- for a *Dapi* (large gong). The idea is again that the chief's prestige is reduced, and in the case of guns it is obvious that in the old days considerable persuasion would have to be brought to bear on the chief before he would dream of allowing one to leave his village.

Thil Kotkai.

The right hind leg of all game killed by whatsoever means on the land of a chief goes to the chief of that village.[2]

Shamal.

This is the flesh between the upper side of the ribs and the hide of all animals killed. It is paid by the killer to his senior male next-of-kin. The head of any family pays in turn to the head of the

Shating.

---

[1] The *thempu* and the official blacksmith have a similar right to a certain amount of free labour, but the amounts are variable.—(Ed.)

[2] The Semas have exactly the same custom. In the Sema case, as also I think in that of the Thados, the right does not stop at game but

branch from which his family is sprung and so forth until the head or "Pipa" of the Thadous is reached where such payments end.

Shangong.

This is the neck of an animal killed. It is paid by the killer to the male next-of-kin of his mother.

N.B.—Any default in paying these customary claims would mean a fine of a mithun. The Thadous are very strict on these dues.

Gu'man.=Theft price. In cases of theft it is customary for the thief to return the articles stolen and to pay one mithun as compensation.[1]

Tolthe.'

Tolthe,' is a pig and a jar of *ju* due to the chief from the person who sheds any human blood in a village affray.[2]

Method of trial by chiefs.

Both parties bring a jar of *ju* each to the chief's house where the matter in dispute is tried. The old men of the village are usually present also and generally the influence of the *ju* makes a compromise by the chief easy as most are well under the influence of it before leaving and are so genially inclined that they will agree to a great deal.

Thadou law of inheritance.

This goes by the male line only and no female has any right to claim as heir of a person, whether male or female.

For example :—

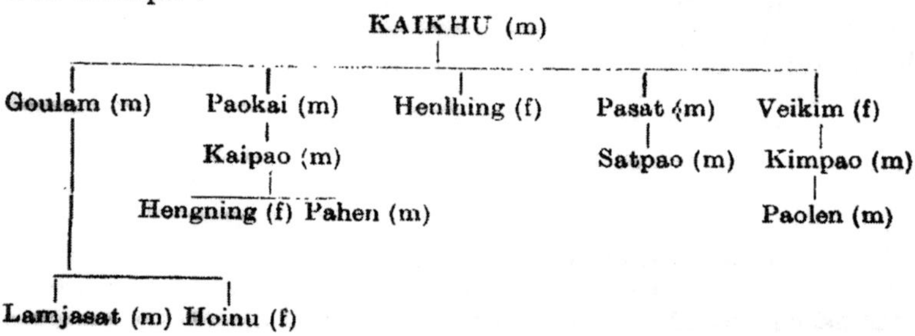

extends to a leg of all animals killed ceremonially, a right of much value.—(Ed.)

[1] The penalty of a mithun is, of course, theoretical, and would not be exacted except in serious cases or where the thief proved indecently contentious. It has been stated or implied (Crawford, *Handbook of Kuki Custom,* page 22) that a mithun is the penalty for certain kinds of thefts only that are more serious than others, namely, theft of a hornbill's nest, of an animal or bird in another man's trap, of a bees' nest or from a basket inside a house. I think, however, that a mithun is a penalty which can be enforced by custom for any theft but which hardly ever is enforced.—(Ed.)

[2] It would also be payable for rape or other serious crime, and is independent, of course, of claims lodged by an injured party. Should a

Kaikhu has three sons and two daughters, and their children are given as above. Males are shown by (m) and females as (f).

The youngest daughter, Veikim having married has a son called Kimpao who has in turn a son called Paolen. If Paolen dies then Kimpao is his heir. Kimpao's heir is his father and therefore none of Kaikhu's family can claim for Kimpao or Paolen. Veikim has married out of the family and her marriage price, etc., due for her will go to Kaikhu, if alive. If Kaikhu is dead then Goulam is the heir. If Goulam dies then Lamjasat who in turn also eats any dues of his sister Hoinu. When Lamjasat dies then Paokai is next in order and so Kaipao and then Pahen, not Hengning his sister. When their line becomes extinct for want of a male heir (called *ingam* in Thadou) then Pasat and his son Satpao inherit and so on. Henthing, being a female, has no say in any claims. If the entire family of Kaikhu becomes "Ingam," then the male representative of the eldest of his brothers inherits. A younger branch cannot do so until all the senior branches are extinct in the male line.

Adoption.

This is very seldom resorted to and even when it does take place is usually only recognized during the lifetime of the adopter on whose death his next-of-kin male takes no further notice of the fact.

Oaths.

It can be safely said that oaths have fallen sadly in value from what they used to be, but even now oaths between relatives are usually avoided if possible. A list of oaths in their order of gravity [1] is of interest.

(*a*) *Aitui don.* Drinking of the juice of the Ai plant.[2] It is prepared by the Thempu (Medicine man) who

---

man be accidentally killed, the killer has to provide *khosa*, *i.e.* a mithun and black cloth for the funeral. *Tolthe*="ground cleaning."—(Ed.)

[1] I am doubtful if this order would be found to obtain throughout all the Thado. I have generally found that (d) is regarded as preferable to (b) and I have rarely had (a) or (c) asked for in my court.—(Ed.)

[2] This oath appears to be a very near relative of the Sema oath on the *aye-shu*, where the name seems to retain a trace of the common origin though the plants used are different. A former practice of drinking the juice is possibly to be traced in the second part of the Sema word, for *shu*='drink,' though the existing Sema custom is to bite a piece of the plant. As in the case of the Thado plant the posionous property of the plant is magical not chemical. The Thado eat their plant on certain ceremonial occasions, and with the Semas the destructive principle is apparently sympathetic, for the plant dies down and disappears in the winter (v. *The Sema Nagas*, p. 165). It has however, a pungent juice and is used as a remedy for snake bite. The ordeal by drinking *bona-fide* poison is, of course, a widespread custom particularly in Africa (v. Frazer, *Folk-lore in the Old Testament*, III, ch. V.), but this Thado custom of drinking a magical potion is on rather a different footing, though, as a Thado admitted to me, their practice no doubt affords the *thempu*, who incidentally gets Re. 1/- from each party as his fee, an excellent opportunity of

utters all kinds of things to suit the occasion, and there is no definite formula since it is impromptu, while

Formula.

extracting the juice. Then the person willing to take the oath repeats his contention in the matter and then drinks down the concoction. This is done in the presence of both parties and the chief. This form of oath is considered the most grave since love charms and other magical potions are said to be made from this plant. Those possessing the evil-eye and having magic powers of turning into animals at wish and killing people are said to use this juice. Such people are called Kaoshe by Thadous.[1]

(*b*) Eating the earth of a newly made grave[2] is next in importance to which the *thempu* may add other odds and ends to suit the occasion. This addition, however, varies in different villages and in the hands of different *thempus*, and may be a little salt, ashes, a few grains of rice, a bit of ginger, or any such like matter. Here again the person taking the oath must first repeat his contention before all concerned and then eat the mixture.

(*c*) Drinking water from the barrel of gun.[3] The water is poured into it and the swearer drains the amount after stating his version of the dispute. His own gun is used by preference; any other if he has not one.

(*d*) Diving.[4] In this the *thempu* first kills a fowl at the pool where the diving is to take place. He calls on

---

mixing some chemically dangerous ingredient into the potion, and though this would be contrary to the principle of the oath it would be rash to say it had never been done. Both the ordeal by real poison (probably aconite) and by a magical poison (water with which an idol had been washed) were used by the Hindus (*Asiatick Researches*, I, 404).—(Ed.)

[1] See Appendix G—Vampires.—(Ed.)

[2] So too Semas (v. *The Sema Nagas, loc. cit.*).—(Ed.)

[3] The Lhotas and Rengmas sometimes bite the barrel of a gun, a dao or a spear in taking oath; the biting of a tiger's tooth is the normal form of Sema oath but as with the Thado it is of little or no weight, man-eating tigers being rare in the now thickly populated hills. By Nagas some hair is plucked from the head and bitten along with the tooth or gun-barrel, etc., as the case may be.—(Ed.)

[4] Unlike the ordeal by poison, this ordeal by diving appears to be limited to south east Asia, and to have a distribution roughly conterminous with that of elements of the Mon race. Thus we find the same ordeal as that of the Thado among the Moï of Annam (Baudesson, *Indo-China and its Primitive People*); in Siam, where poles were used as by Tangkhul Nagas (La Loubère, *Royaume de Siam*, I, 334; Turpin, *Histoire etc. de Siam*, ch. iv); in Burma (Scott and Hardiman, *op. cit.*, I, ii, 485), where this form of ordeal was applied to women as well as to men (Sangermano, *Burmese Empire*, pp. 72, 190 [1885], Symes, *Embassy to*

the spirit of the water to do justice in the case as the blood of the fowl trickles into to it while its throat is being cut. Then the two parties stand breast deep in the pool and repeat their respective versions. They must stand with the water touching the nipples of their breasts otherwise when sitting in the water it would not cover them. On a given signal they dive, or rather sit down, under water. The first person who breaks the surface with any part of his person, be it his hair or clothes or part of his body, loses. Both are then dragged out by their supporters. If a man, after standing breast high, cannot get under at all he likewise loses.

(*e*) Official Diving Oaths. In this no *thempu's* preparations are made. On the signal from the officer the parties dive for it after standing breast high as before. The conditions otherwise being the same.

(*f*) Biting a spear or a dao. The man taking the oath bites the spear-head or dao after giving his version of the case and thus wins.

(*g*) Biting a tiger's tooth. The same as (*f*) but a tiger's tooth replaces the weapon.

In these days the last oath given is practically valueless as Thadous themselves admit. It is only resorted to in trivial matters if a compromise is impossible because of deep-rooted enmity between the parties. After this form of oath a smile is usually noticeable among the crowd of onlookers.

Ava, ch. xviii); in Pegu (*Voyage of Ralph Fitch, 1583–1591*, Hakluyt; Hamilton, *Account of the E. Indies*, II. 58), and in Assam, where it is practised not only by the Thado but by the Tangkhul Naga, by the Memi apparently (Hodson, *Naga Tribes of Manipur*, 110), by the Khasis (Hooker, *Himalayan Journals*, II, ch. xxviii; Dalton, *Ethnography of Bengal*, 57; Gurdon, *The Khasis*, 94) and in Manipur. Hodson (*The Meitheis*, 92, sq.) seems to imply that its use in Manipur was restricted to cases between hillmen, but Gurdon (*loc. cit.*) quotes Col. Maxwell as describing such an oath between two Manipuris who held on to stones at the bottom of a river. A very similar form of ordeal indeed but applied to a single accused person is described from Bengal by Warren Hastings in his paper 'On the Trial by Ordeal among the Hindus' *Asiatick Researches*, I, xxiii. The accused person in this case has to remain under water holding the feet or the staff of a Brahman during the time occupied by certain prescribed actions. An ordeal by water used to obtain in Europe in which the accused was thrown into the water with a rope round his waist. If he sank he was innocent and was hauled out. If he swam he was guilty. (Verstegan, *Restitution of Decayed Intelligence*, 1655, p. 52). It survived ultimately as a test for witches, and curiously enough precisely the same test for witchcraft was used in Burma (Sangermano. *Burmese Empire*. 121). Among the Thado of the Naga Hills there is a variant of the form described by Mr. Shaw, in which the contestants have to pick up stones from the bottom.—(Ed.)

There are no such things among Thadous. If any money has to be raised it is usually done by the chief himself unless the villagers offer to help, which they very often do in cases of administrative fines imposed on the chief for any reason.

Civic Funds.

Among some of the Naga Tribes there is a recognised house where the young men sleep at night and where they keep their guns, spears daos, shields and other weapons of attack and defence. Among the Thadous this does not exist these days but they have a word for it, *shom*, which, in my opinion, shows that it used to be a recognised establishment.[1] Just after dark is spoken of as "*shom leng phat*" which is an additional reason to presume that such an organisation did exist. It means "Going-to-the-Young-men's-house-time." After eating their evening meal they used to move off there for the night. I am told that it was not very long ago that there was a young women's house[2] where the unmarried girls all slept but as this led to too much trouble among them it was abolished. This house was also known as "*shom*."

Young men's House.

---

[1] The Lushei still retain this institution under the name of *Zawlbuk*, but I am doubtful whether it can be regarded as a genuine Kuki institution. It is, however, typically Naga, and in the Sema Naga tribe, where it has disappeared except for certain ceremonial purposes when an imitation is built (*vide*, *The Sema Nagas*, p. 37), I am inclined to regard this disappearance as the result of an overlay of Kuki culture. My own view is that it is an Indonesian or Austroasiatic institution, rather than a Tibeto-Burmese one, and that the traces of it perceptible in Kuki tribes are due to survivals from other elements absorbed by the invading Kuki. See Note 2 on p. 73 of *The Ao Nagas*. The Thado have certainly, however, possessed the institution for a time. and still speak of shooting stars as stars "going to their *shom*."—(Ed.)

[2] I have never heard of this, and such Thado as I have asked have denied that they ever heard of it either, but of course if, as I suggest, the whole institution is Naga rather than Kuki in origin, it may well be that tradition should in some case remember the previous existence of girls' 'morungs,' which some Naga tribes possess.—(Ed.)

CHAPTER V.

RITES AND BELIEFS.

Rites and Beliefs. Pathen.

The Thadous believe that life is given to everything by Pathen who rules the universe. He has the power to subdue the evil influences of the Thilhas and it is to Him that they do their sacrifices in order to regain health or escape any adversity they may happen to have fallen into. He is supposed to have made the heavens and earth and is all-powerful.

World.

To the Thadou the world is the land they live in and the surrounding country, for the peoples of which they have names, and there it ends. This may be an additional reason for their self-importance. The sun and the moon [1] go round the earth and they cannot believe that the earth revolves. The idea of its being a sphere is not comprehensible since, to their minds, the people on the sides and underneath would surely fall off. They give no reason for gravity and merely state that as a thing is heavy it must come to earth again. Only very light things which are carried away by the wind fly about for a time and these must eventually fall to earth too, as the wind does not always blow and there is some weight in any object whatsoever it may be. No explanation of rain exists beyond stating that it rains just when the Pathen pleases. The stars also go round the earth but certain stars are usually seen in one direction which is owing to their great distance from the earth.[2] They have a tradition of a flood which took place when they were at the upper end of the Gun river but this was before they became ordinary beings and in the time of their mythical ancestors.

Thunder and Lightning.

These [3] they explain as an exhibition of the powers and anger of Pathen, who visits those with whom he is displeased by striking

---

[1] The markings on the moon's face are said to be a tree, as by the Angami, Ao and Rangpang Nagas and in Polynesia (Ellis, *Polynesian Researches*, III, p. 171.)—(Ed.)

[2] They seem to have certain definite beliefs about stars, which are associated, as so often, with the dead. In the folk-tale of Ashijoul the heroine ascends into heaven as a star, at least that is what I infer from her name and fate, (v. Appendix A), and at any rate the morning and evening star, called Valpa, is identified with a man named Thăngbāpū, who was a great warrior, while the Pleiades are seven brothers trying to cover themselves simultaneously with the only cloth they have between them. Shooting stars are said to be stars retiring to the Stars' Morung for the night. Orion on the other hand, or rather his Belt and Sword, are described as the hole of a species of rat which digs down very straight and deep at first (the Belt), and then turns off at right angles (the Sword).—(Ed.)

[3] The rainbow is described as the spirit rope (probably for the ascent of spirits to the sky. See *The Ao Nagas*, p. 304 n[2] 305 n[1]).—(Ed.)

them with lightning. Thunder is to remind them that Pathen is still very much alive as the Thadous admit they are very careless and forgetful.

Earthquakes.

There are two versions about this. The first is that a large serpent encircles the earth (perhaps something to do with the serpent which disputed the passage at the *khul* when Chongthu came out upon the earth. He cut it into seven pieces) and goes round and round. This serpent overtakes his tail sometimes and nips it which causes him pain and the earth shakes in consequence.

The other version is that Chongja shakes the earth from his underworld home just to see if Chongthu's party are still alive. For this reason the Thadous always shout out "We are here, we are alive" while an earthquake is on.

I prefer to accept the latter as the version generally accepted as correct.[1] I understand the former as being the story given to children.

Khichang.

This is the red cornelian bead worn by the men in their ears. One in each ear hangs horizontally on a piece of string from a hole pierced in the lobe.

The story of how they became known to the Thadous is that in the days of Galngam; when they all lived at Lhanpelkot and Thijongbung, the man Galngam went into the jungle one day and met Hangshai of the Lionmen. They made friends and the latter invited the former to his village. Galngam went and saw much hard red fruit on trees which Hangshai told him was the fruit of the Lionmen and offered as many

---

[1] One cannot, I think, justly distinguish between a correct and an incorrect version. Both explanations occur elsewhere in Assam (*v. Folk-Lore*, XXXVI, pp. 113 sqq), the second version, or something very similar, being held by the Kabui of the Manipur State, with whom very many of the Thado are in touch, by the Akas of the lower Himalayan slopes north of the Brahmaputra and by the Kachins. Traditions on the same lines are widespread outside Assam, being found among the Karens of Burma (Marshall, *Karen People of Burma*, pp. 230, 289) the people of Bali, Sunda, Timor and other islands of the Indian Archipelago, the Tami of New Guinea, the Conibos of Peru and even in Africa (*vide* Frazer, *Golden Bough*, V, viii § 5). The first version given by Mr. Shaw agrees closely with that of the Abor, again on the north bank of the Brahmaputra, and that of the Lushei, while the Shans combine the two versions attributing great earthquakes to this serpent in words almost identical with the Thado account and slight earthquakes to the other cause (Milne, *Shans at Home*, 54), while the Fijians seem to combine them in the same individual (Brewster, *Hill Tribes of Fiji*, 80, 81, 85, 255, 269). This story of the serpent coiled round the world biting his tail is strongly reminiscent of the *midgards ormr*, the serpent that encircles the world, of the Edda of Norse mythology. This serpent is regarded as personifying the ocean (Stallybrass, *Grimm's Teutonic Mythology*, II, 794) and it is significant that Frazer (*loc. cit.*) points out the natural association between earthquakes and the sea.—(Ed.)

as Galngam could take away with him. Galngam did so and these he distributed to the Thadous on his return to their village. They could not eat them so they wore them in their ears as they do to this day. There are said to be very few of the real old ones and they are so well treasured that their possessors are most secretive about them. A good old bead may easily be valued at 5 to 10 mithuns even in these days, but transfers at such prices are rare as the possessors do not now-a-days part with them.

Mithuns.

The first mithun known to the Thadous was to their mythical ancestors, when they were in the underworld. They used to have 4 horns. Chongthu when he came up to the earth brought a two-horned one with him and the keeper was called Lepokpa. One day this mithun was killed for a feast and the skin was placed in a neighbouring stream to soften. It disappeared and shortly afterwards one Lendou saw another mithun of the same markings as the previous one so they presumed the skin had come to life again. This all occurred at Sisep and the mithun was known as *Noimang shel*.

Later Sat-song, the son of Chongthu, found a mithun grazing in his millet fields and caught it. This mithun is spoken of as the *Van shel* (Sky Mithun).

In Doi.

This is the house-god. It is not taken away by the next-of-kin male on the death of the house-holder. Each house-holder has his own *in-doi*. It serves the whole family so long as the members all live in one house, but on separation new *in-doi* may be made. There is no fixed time for this and it is usually done when a separate household feels that it is suffering from a lack of health or of wealth and that the want of the *in-doi* may be the cause.

In making a new *in-doi* the *thempu* plays an important part

The following things are to be collected :—

A piece each of the *shething* and *thinghi* tree. Small bits of *gopi* (a garden bamboo), *vomgui* (a creeper), goat, pig, fowl and egg. Also small portions of a gourd, *khaopi* (a tree the bark of which makes excellent rope), and *hailhi* (a particular species of gourd) A sword and spear and a woman's brass wristlet called *chao* have to be produced.[1]

Then the *thempu* taking a very small bit of each of the above with the spear, dao and wristlet in his hand says :—

" Pathen bless so and so (The person whose *in-doi* is being made.).

---

[1] The *in-doi* (= " house magic " or " house charm " has a very close parallel in the *siap aioh* of the Kenyahs in Borneo (Hose and McDougall, *Pagan Tribes of Borneo*, II 124). So far as I know it is typical of the Kuki culture as distinct from the Naga. See also Appendix G.—(Ed.)

Bless him as you blessed the *Sheloinampha, i.e.*, the best of the *shething* trees (to be the *in-doi* of man).

Bless him as you blessed the *Thinghitoinampha* (=the best of the *thinghi* trees).

Bless him as you blessed the *Gopichengnampha* (the bamboo), *Vomguipha* (the creeper), *Vohpimaikem* (the pig), *Kelchalkihe'* (the goat), *Pengjompa* (the round gourd), *Ḥailhipha* (the long gourd), *Chemkolpha* (the old dao), *Tengmunpha* (the spear), *Chaoveipha* (the wristlet), *Khaopithosom* (the tree whose bark makes rope), *A'tolngo* (the white fowl) and the *Katuilungtheng Katui lungva'* (the clean and clear egg).

The *thempu* then carries on the blessing praying that the householder may have many sons and daughters, riches and power and a long life. After this the genealogical tree of the household from Chongthu has to be repeated in full and the *thempu* asks Pathen to exempt the present maker of an *in-doi* from the consequences of the sins of his forefathers. So saying the bits of articles enumerated are put into a small gourd and hung up on the outside of the front wall of the house near the top usually above the door out of the way of children and fowls searching for something to play with or for food. So the ceremony ends and there is much *ju* drinking and eating. There are no special animals to be killed; that merely depends on the circumstances of the person performing the ceremony. The *in-doi* thus made is carried with him by the maker where-ever he goes until his death, when his son or sons have to repeat the ceremony if they intend having an *in-doi* also. The house-god therefore is apparently only for the protection of the person for whom it is made, which is also evident from the ceremony given above.

Chang Ai.

This is a feast to the entire village and is the only known ceremony in which a Thadou woman plays the leading part. In the old days when Thadou villages consisted of houses in their hundreds it meant a very expensive affair which could usually only be done by the wives of chiefs' or of very wealthy men. In these days as households in the majority of Kuki villages reach double figures only, it is not such a great affair. The woman performing it has to feed the whole village for one day and she puts up a platform of earth about 6 inches above ground level which is held in position by a border of small stones placed upright. Within this border small upright stones are placed and represent the number of *bings* (woman's baskets) of paddy which is being consumed on that day. In the centre are two stones also upright with one larger than the other known as *Shong mol* (spirit stones). They say these do not represent the spirit of the woman and her husband but are the sign for Pathen to know where Chang-Ai has been performed before he selects a good place at " Mithikho " for that person.[1] This feast can only be done three times. Much singing eating and drinking goes on the whole day and night in the house of the person performing it. The *Sheltoldel, Boncho* and *Lholhil* dances are performed on the third occasion, when the person is said to have assured herself a safe entrance and specially selected place at " Mithikho."

Women who have performed this feast are permitted to wear the dark blue cloth with the embroidery at the two ends in red and white cotton of a special design. The name of the cloth is *thangnang*.

Sha Ai.

This is performed by men and implies a feast to the entire village for a day. Some have been known to have done so for more days. In the old days only those who have killed all the different kinds of dangerous animals were allowed to perform this ceremony but now-a-days it is mostly a question of wealth and all want to make out that they have done so. However one animal at least must be killed even these days to justify the ceremony although trapping an animal is sufficient for this purpose.

On the day of the ceremony the *thempu* appears and with *ju* in his hand calls upon the Pathen to permit the " Y-shaped post " to be erected. The Pathen is supposed to tell the *thempu* that He has left the charge of the earth to Noimangpa so in turn the *thempu* asks the latter where the post may be erected. Noimangpa is supposed to give his authority by saying that wherever the *thempu* spills some of the *ju* on the earth there it is to be erected so the *thempu* does so and then digs a small piece of the earth out, and the actual erection is done by the young men of the village. After this the mithun to be slaughtered is to be tied to this post which must be of the *shething* tree and no other. It is then killed by piercing it with a spear or sharp bamboo. Generally the *thempu* does the killing after blessing the man who is performing the Sha-Ai after the gene-

---

[1] Nevertheless, I strongly suspect these two stones of being a degenerate form of the two stones set up by so many Nagas as representing the husband and wife, and as phallic vehicles for the fertilization of the land and its produce, from human to vegetable by the soul matter of those who have demonstrated by their prosperity that they are fit persons to do so (*v. Carved Monoliths, etc., J.R.A.I.*, LIII). The connection with the dead still obtains in the association with *Mithikho*, and the fact that the stones are erected by a woman rather suggests that the ceremony dates to a matrilineal period before the intrusion of the patrilineal Kuki, which would perhaps, not inappropriately, associate the custom of erecting stones with the Mon-Khmer element which seems once to have dominated these hills and which still survives in the stone-erecting matrilineal Khasis and Syntengs. This feast is called also, I think, *Buh ai* (v. Shakespear, *Lushei-Kuki Clans*, page 205 sq., illustrated at p. 207).—(Ed.)

alogical tree from Thadou has been repeated down to this person. Then there is the usual orgy during which *Saipi Khupsu'*, *Sagol Pheikhai* and *Theiphit* are danced three times each, while the feast is being prepared but *ju* is going round all the time. Generally the entire village is unfit to be seen the next day.

Chon.

This is considered the most highly prized feast of the lot and can only be performed by those who have done the Sha-Ai three times.[1] In this everything has to be done seven times. Seven mithuns are to be killed and everything else must be in multiples of seven. This has not been done for a very long time and so the exact rites are not clearly known. It was originally done by Thadou himself and only three or four persons are supposed to have ever done it since, but even then it was not done properly as the *Chontul* which was the only weapon by which the mithuns or other animals could be killed on such occasions, was buried and lost owing to a quarrel between the Dongngel and Thadou families at a very early date. Even the songs and genealogical trees had to be repeated seven times. The whole ceremony taking days to complete and the expense incurred being fabulous. Even after the death of such persons the corpse had to be carried round seven times and everything pertaining to burial rites had to be done seven times so that they resorted to smoking the bodies of such persons to avoid decomposition before the entire rites were completed.

The performance of the *Chon* gave the soul of that person a paramount seat in Mithikho and ensured eternal happiness.

Village ceremonies.

These are performed by the *thempu* for the village when any rumour or news comes through of Cholera or any such like fatal epidemic. One is called *Aikam*. The most serious form is with a *nguldu* (Hoolook ape), the *ai* root, a piece of *thingsaphulip* and of the *thingthu* tree. The gibbon is cut in two and the blood mixed with the other things. All the people of the village then come and anoint themselves with a little of the mixture and also taste a little. The anointing is generally on the forehead. After this the *thempu* takes the remainder of the mixture and the two halves of the gibbon and places them on the frame work of the arch made a short way out of the village on the main path. Half of the hoolook being on either side of the path. At the time of preparing the mixture and killing the hoolook the *thempu* calls on Pathen to protect the village from the epidemic and the entire village is "taboo" for 15 days. No one is allowed to enter or

---

[1] I find in my notes that the Thado have a series of three "feasts of merit," to use Mr. Mills' apt term. For the first a three-pronged post is set up, for the second a forked post surrounded by bamboo poles (cf. the Sema *aghuza*, *The Sema Nagas*, p. 227), and for the third a stone. The three-pronged post is a familiar sight in Thado villages.—(Ed.)

to go out of the village, and on the day the ceremony is performed no cocks must crow in the village, so they are all taken into the jungle out of hearing for one day and kept there in baskets. It is said that one gibbon dies each moon and so they are not heard making a noise between the old and the new moon. The death is the toll taken by Pathen from them in order that they may be quiet then. In consequence a gibbon is thought the best animal to sacrifice in case of approaching fatal epidemics.

Another village ceremony entails the killing of a dog to keep away evil spirits, as *thilha* detest dogs, as already mentioned apropos of the killing by Chongthu of his favourite dog. In this case the taboo is for 5 days only but the rites otherwise are the same.

The third is a village taboo accompanied by the other ceremonials, but without any sacrifice. This entails a 3 day taboo.

A fourth is the one day taboo for crops or feasts or the like. In this the *ai*, etc., play no part unless the particular reason for the taboo requires it for some further cause than for merely closing the village to all strangers.

After a field has been cut and burnt, *Daiphu* is performed.

Field Pujahs.

For this the *thempu* has to make small earthen images of the following :—

Saipiha (Elephant's tooth).
So'long nupa (Slaves).
Vengke (Partridge).
Thoche (Squirrel).
Shel (Mithun)
Khichang (Ear bead).
Langbel (Mica).

With these he takes an egg and some cotton and goes to the field and asks Pathen to excuse the cultivator of that field for all the damage he has done by cutting and burning the land. All the objects are then placed on the bole of a tree and the *thempu* then returns to the village The day following nothing is done but the day after that the *thempu* goes to the field to see whether the objects which he placed there are still where he left them. If any of the images are missing or broken it means that someone of that household will either die or suffer illness as Pathen has considered the damage done excessive. Consequently *kilhalho* will be performed in the village to ward off any ill effects which may be expected from the *thempu*'s interpretation of the *Daiphu*.

The *Changlhakou* follows the reaping and storing of the paddy crop. It consists in the killing of a fowl for the spirits of the paddy for their kindness in yielding so much. The story is that once upon a time a terrible famine was rampant all over the earth. No one had anything to eat. Then a woman staggering with weakness came to the village of the Thadous and asked to be maintained, but no one would feed her at first because they had not even enough for themselves. Eventually she was taken in by an old lonely widow and in return for the kindness the strange woman gave the widow some paddy, which she (the strange woman) stated would never die, so that she (the widow) would never want for rice. This came true and the widow became very rich and paddy seemed to come to her even if she did no cultivation.[1] So the Thadous do this to the spirits of the paddy in return for the kindness once shown to one of them who was an old useless widow, and ever since the Thadous have thrived on rice.

Unwanted Children.

These were either allowed to die after birth by not feeding them or handed over to the old women of the village to dispose of in some way or other. It is said that the old women used to put thorns into the soles of the feet of such children before burying them so that their souls should not be able to chase them in the after-world where they may meet.[2]

Head-hunting

The Thadous consider themselves great head-hunters[3] and have not given up the practice as was seen so recently as the Kuki Rebellion

[1] In the Golden Age that preceded the *Thimzin*, rice, firewood, and everythingelse that has to be carried in this weary world moved of itself to the desired place when ordered, but as a woman who was with child died on every day that this power was used the practice of calling in the paddy and the firewood was abandoned. The Ao likewise believe in this Golden Age (Mills, *The Ao Nagas*, 108), while the Angami look for its return. The beliefs of the Karen of Burma in *Apu Lagan* and the Kayan of Borneo in *Apu Leggan* and that of the Fijian in *Tavuki* are pobably all connected (*vide* my note on Mills, *loc. cit.*). The Angami call it *Tikidzü-rüke ketsonhye*, 'topsy-turvy of the Universe.'—(Ed.)

[2] Infanticide of bastards is also followed by pricking with thorns the soles of the child's feet among Angamis, at any rate in the Khizami group, and the reason given is virtually the same, to prevent the return of the ghost.—(Ed.)

[3] It would be an error to regard the Thado as a typical or even a *bona fide* head-hunter. True head-hunting in Assam, at any rate, and probably over a much wider area (*vide* 'Head-hunting' in the new (1929) edition of the *Encyclopaedia Britannica*), is a conscious attempt to convey the soul of the individual beheaded into the victor's possession as a source of life and fertility, the head being regarded as the location *par excellence* of the soul. The Kuki is really a slave-hunter, who also takes heads having probably acquired the practice by contact with genuine head-hunters, and having fused it with his slave-hunting propensities and beliefs, so that he now takes heads in order that the soul, conceived of as a person and quite different from the true head-hunter's conception of it as a sort of life essence (*cf.* Marshall, *The Karen People of Burma*, p. 221 sq.), may serve his dead in Mithikho. The practice of the Kachins, who seem merely to produce the head as evidence of prowess (Scott and Hardiman, *op. cit.*, I, i, 430), is probably another instance of the effect of the contact with a head-hunting tribe of non-head-hunters who have copied

in 1918-19. They place great value on a head because each head means an additional slave for the soul at Mithikho; also that unless a man take a head he is not keeping up the traditions of his ancestors who were all famous head-hunters.

Before a party leaves on a raid the *thempu* makes a mixture from the *ai* plant and then annointing each warrior on the forehead says "May your enemies become stupified so that you may kill them easily and may Pathen bring you safely back with many heads to your count." This is called *Gal-him*.

The Thadou places most value on a child's head, male or female, as it means that to obtain it he must practically enter the enemies' village. Next in value is that of a woman since this would mean going very near to the village. After that comes the head of a known warrior of the enemy since it would require much prowess to kill him and then last of all the ordinary man or youth.[1]

---

the practice without sharing the beliefs from which it arose. It may be noted that the Assam tribes north of the Brahmaputra are not head-hunters. The Thado practice seems to have a close parallel in that of the Kayans, Kenyahs and Klemantans of Borneo, the Iban perhaps, corresponding to the Naga in the *rôle* of genuine head-hunter. The Kayan like the Kuki regards it as necessary to put a head on the grave that its soul may serve the deceased in the next world (*vide* Hose and McDougall, *op. cit.*, I, 190; II, 105). On the other hand the Sebop Klemantans have a story of the origin of head-hunting which is entirely Naga in spirit (*ibid.*, II, 138 sq.). My conclusion is that Borneo has been subject to the same head-hunting culture as Assam and to the same intrusion of a subsequent slave-hunting culture, which I associate in Assam with the Kuki and Kachin races and which I am tempted to associate with the Kayans in Borneo. Col. Shakespear (*op. cit.*, p. 60) denies that the Lushei was ever a head-hunter, but also that he ever sacrificed slaves at the graves of chiefs, but the evidence of Woodthorpe (*Lushai Expedition*, pp. 181, 282, 293) is conclusive against him in the latter respect, and both the Thado (Soppitt, *op. cit.*, p. 14) and the Chins had the same custom (Carey and Tuck, *op. cit.*, I. 196); the Ao Nagas believe that the souls of slain foes serve the taker of the head in the next world, which I ascribe to the intrusion of Kuki into Naga culture (Mills, *The Ao Nagas*, p. 200).—(Ed.)

[1] Frankly I regard this list of valuations as suspect. It is too logical and suggests the attempts which have been made to rationalize the preference felt by most Nagas for a female head over a male one, *vide* Johnstone, *Experiences in Manipur and the Naga Hills*, p. 30, and Hodson, *Naga Tribes of Manipur*, p. 114. In these cases the statement may, as Shakespear in his note on the latter passage suggests, be an attempt to excuse a practice known to be regarded with disapproval, though there is some evidence to the contrary, *vide*, *The Angami Nagas*, p. 163 sq.; the reason given by Hutchinson (*Account of the Chittagong Hill tracts*, p. 146) is obviously an aetiological effort of the Kukis who recount it, and my own opinion is that the value of female heads is higher than that of male primarily on account of a higher fertility rating (*v. The Sema Nagas*, p. 178.) When Johnstone says that to kill a baby in arms is a greater feat to an Angami than to kill a man, he is drawing on his imagination entirely, and he should have made it clear that to an Angami unless it has cut its teeth an infant's head does not count at all, though I believe the Kukis have been known to take the infant from the mother's womb and decapitate it, and this is specifically stated by Rawlins (*Cucis or Mountaineers of Tipra*, 'Asia-

After returning from a raid with heads the village turns out in full strength with drums and horns and the raiders will then sing the song called *Hanla* in which the number of heads is to be sung. They then enter the village in procession. For three days they are fed on food separately cooked and eaten off banana leaves. This food is called *Gal an.*[1] Immediately on their arrival *Minlo* is done which is merely the reciting of the genealogical tree of those who have taken heads. The *Gal an* is supposed to be the enemies' food and no one else must

---

tic Researches,' II, 188). This latter practice is also reported of the Kagoro of W. Africa (Tremearne, *Tailed Head-hunters of Nigeria*, 180). —(Ed.)

[1] The first food eaten by a warrior who has taken life must be eaten with the unwashed hand which has been deliberately imbrued with the victim's blood. This custom is obviously intimately connected with the practice observed by the Lushei of licking from the spear-head the blood of the first man killed (Lewin, *Wild Races of South East India*, page 269). The custom is obviously a form of that in which the enemy's blood is drunk, probably in order to imbibe his soul or his vital principle, which is a very widely spread custom, to be traced no doubt in a final degenerate form in the Sema custom, pointed out to me by Mr. Mills, of compelling every warrior who has shed blood, or assisted thereat, to take a ceremonial meal before entering the village. This 'meal' is purely formal and consists of a mere mouthful of cooked rice, but the fact that the warrior must take it before entering his village suggests very strongly that the real point is that he eats it with bloody hands. The Sema insistence is now on the eating, but the Thado insistence is on the blood on the hands, affording a connecting link between the modern Sema custom of a mere ceremonial meal before entering the village and the original custom of quaffing an enemy's blood.

The Melanesians of Florida and the Ibo of Nigeria do just what the Lushei does, lick the dead man's blood from the blade that killed him (Codrington, *The Melanesians*, p. 305; Leonard, *The Lower Niger, etc.*, p. 180). Actual drinking of the blood is reported of the Kafirs of the Pamirs (Leitner, *Dardistan*, 53, 61,), of the Maoris (Lang, *Polynesian Nation*, 72, where a parallel from Nubia is cited) and of the Scythians (Herodotus, IV, 64). A degree further is the tasting of the liver, heart or brain of the dead enemy. The liver is tasted by the Lushei (Lewin, *loc. cit.*), and by the Tinguian, Bagobo and Mandayan of the Philippines (Cole, *The Tinguian*, 374, *Wild Tribes of Davao*, 94, 203), and the heart or brain or both is eaten or tasted by the same three tribes of the Philippines as well as by the Italones (Sawyer, *Inhabitants of the Philippines*, p. 268), as probably by some of the Bornean tribes; also by the Kafirs (Leitner, *loc. cit.*) and by the Maori (Donne, *The Maori*, page 281), who refer to their victim as "the first fish," and is reported also of the Chinese (Sawyer, *loc. cit.*).

Although the general intention is probably the absorption of the vital essence of the slain, other possible reasons must not be overlooked, such as the desire to acquire the qualities of the deceased, or the desire to insult and to degrade the deceased; the Ibo explains the practice as intended to slake the desire for bloodshed and thus prevent the slayer's running amok among his own tribe; and that the idea of preventing the slain from avenging his death on the slayer by establishing a physical community with him may give rise to the practice, is suggested by the fact that cases have been reported in Europe of murderers eating parts of their victims flesh with this idea, shared also by the natives of Queensland (Tremearne, *Tailed Head-hunters*, 183).—(Ed.)

partake of it. The village is taboo for those three days and the women folk must make *Thu'po* for each of the successful raiders from cotton which is worn in the knot of hair behind as a sign of their great deed.[1] After the three days the village re-enters its normal routine.[2]

In the old days when a chief died it necessitated a raid as the more slaves the chief had for his soul at Mithikho the better.

Petty Pujahs.

These are many and mostly for curing different kinds of illness or for warding off the same. Or they may be for some reason such as poverty or loss of property.

I merely give the names of some since they are all really household pujahs and do not concern the village. They are:—

Uitheng, Neovei, Doivei, A'them, Veishe,' Koldoi, Gamla kithoi, Tuigaldou, Tombil, Sahapban, Bo'them, Loulam, Tuilam, Thingvei, A 'themkoldoi, Janchan, etc.

Some of these are for the waterspring, path, tree or stone which they think has caused the trouble, be it illness or a wound or a sore. All these merely entail killing a fowl by the *thempu* or by the sick man himself.

Shalhakou.

This is a pujah performed for a person who returns successful after a hunt.

First the wife of the hunter puts some *ju* into the mouth of the killed game and then the *thempu* does likewise saying "All you beasts of the world and flying game taste this *ju*, it is much better than any *ju* you all will ever have, so come here for it when you are thirsty." By this it is meant that they will be enticed to come to that village and the hunter will kill them all.[3] The *thempu* will call on Kholkipkholjang site, where the

---

[1] See Plate 3 fig. 3.—(Ed.)

[2] The Thado takes the head only as a rule, not other limbs also, as a Naga does so often, though among the Lushei Woodthorpe records an arm on Volonel's grave (*Lushei Expedition*, page 282). When a Thado takes the head he takes the whole head unless he has felt particularly bitter against the dead man, in which case he takes the head above the jaw, leaving the rest. This is done when the life taken is an act of revenge, and apprises the victim's relatives of the state of mind of the slayer. When not affixed to a grave the head is impaled outside the village on a pointed branch or on a stake the top of which has been cut away to leave a vertical point projecting upwards from the centre of the stake which is cut off level round the base of the point. This point apparently transfixes the skull projecting through a hole in the cranium, though the only specimens actually seen by me consisted of crania only (some with the hair still attached), the skulls having been reported to have been divided between Chengjapao and the Haokip chief Tongkhupao. What is probably the last specimen of a Thado's human trophy is now in the Oxford University Museum. I collected it in 1922. —(Ed.)

[3] *Cf. The Angami Nagas*, pp. 239, 240.—(Ed.)

Thadous saw gathered all the animals of the world, before he pours the *ju* into the mouth of the killed game.

There is always much drinking and singing, when any game is killed and brought into the village, at the expense of the hunter.

When a Thadou dies a bamboo is erected over his grave which gives in niches on it the tally of the game which he has killed in his lifetime.

CHAPTER VI.

VILLAGE AND OCCUPATIONS.

Village.

The Thadou usually selects the dense jungle for his village site, either on the top of a ridge or on the slope just below. There is no special orientation of the houses that are promiscuously scattered about the place. Being migratory he attaches little sentimental value to an old site which has been occupied for any length of time. When the mood takes him he leaves his house and goes elsewhere. He has no village perimeter like the Nagas and takes no pride in the village either. The chief's house is generally the largest while the majority have houses about 20ft. by 14ft. on an average. Before the Chief's house, and those of some of the wealthier villagers, is usually found a platform made of wood and bamboos upon which men congregate of an evening or at any time to discuss any village politics or disputes. Those that are able, either from wealth or the number of inmates, make a palisading around the house—forming an enclosure to keep out the mithuns and probably protect a small kitchen garden. This palisade is made of logs split into planks roughly and then tied together with cane or bamboo binding to keep them in position, with posts at intervals to hold them upright, and cross strands of wood or bamboos to keep them in line. It is all a very crude and apparently carelessly-put-together construction. A few banana trees are some times found, otherwise, fruit trees are conspicuous by their absence Pigs, fowls, dogs and children play about anywhere they please and in the rains all the ground is a quagmire with a few logs thrown down here and there to avoid sinking shin-deep into the filth. The sanitary installation is the pig for the grownups while the dog is specially kept to assist the mother of a child who has not learnt yet to do for itself. Very little care is taken of the water supply where people may be seen drawing water while others are either bathing themselves or washing their clothes or hair. However, as the bathing propensities of the Thadou are practically zero the contamination is slight.

To form a new village omens are consulted and also dreams, the interpretations of which are strictly followed. There are two kinds of omens consulted. One is with an egg. A small bit of the shell is removed at one end and the egg is then placed on three sticks under which a small fire is lighted. If the egg bursts or overflows then it is bad, but if the liquid comes out and congeals on top like a cap and none of it trickles down to the sticks holding up the egg or to the ground then it is a good omen and a village is established. The other omen is with water. A small hole about the size of a dinner plate and about 6 inches deep is dug. This is lined with any kind of leaves and then water poured in quickly to fill the hole. After the pouring if the water goes round clockwise it is bad but if counter-clockwise it is good. These omens are consulted on the proposed site by the *thempu* or village soothsayer of the village to be.

Houses are made of wood posts with wooden rafters. Thatching grass is used for the roof which is held in place by split bamboos and bamboo or cane lashings. The walls are bamboo matting. The whole structure is raised about 4 to 6 ft. at the back according to the nature of the ground surface, while the front rests on the ground.[1] The house contains one large room and a verandah in the front. In the verandah the mortar for pounding paddy is placed, on one side. About the middle of the room a hearth is made where all the cooking is done. Some times this is on one side of the room. It is made of mud about 6 to 9 inches deep which is placed on the split bamboos which are laid flat on the trusses which support floor. It is usually about 3 ft. square. In the centre are three stones of conical shape placed slanting inwards so as to hold the utensil for cooking and the fire is placed between the stones. Over this cooking place there are two or more platforms hanging from the roof upon which things are dried. The sleeping bed is either of planks or split bamboos laid flat at the back end of the house. Sometimes it is to be found on one side. Shelves, brackets and hooks are on all sides made of bamboo or wood tied and held in place by bamboo or cane lashings. A length of bamboo is usually found placed across one corner of the room upon which clothes are hung. A few cooking pots, some gourds and a basket or two make the total of the property.

Some pieces of flesh either drying or dried and a few bamboo tubes for drawing water will also be found about in the room. Before building a house no regular consultation of omens is indulged in but a few rather like having their dreams interpreted on the eve of the erection, probably by way of curiosity rather than of custom.

The fact that the Thadou does not erect his house entirely on a "machan" or platform, but with the front always resting on the ground leads me to believe that they must have originally been ocean-shore, river, lake or creek-bank dwellers rather than mid stream.[2] I do not consider that the idea is a

---

[1] The reason given for putting part of the house on the ground level is the weight of the wooden mortar in which paddy is husked. Field houses where no mortar is kept, are raised entirely from the ground and approached by a ladder.—(Ed.)

[2] I think Mr. Shaw has overlooked the fact that the habit of building a house partly on piles is just as likely to originate in the use of a steep

remnant of building in trees or the like to be safe from wild animals, because then they would have no portion of the house resting on the ground which is the general practice and which the very old men do not remember to be in any other form.

The average size of a Thadou house is about 20 ft. long by 14 ft. broad. The chief and the wealthy villagers indulge in much larger ones. These larger ones only consist of one large room, as the smaller ones, but inside cubicles are some times found for the slaves or servants to sleep in. I wonder if the cubicle arrangement is a remnant of some form of captivity which the slaves were subjected to in the old days? No one has been able to enlighten me on this among the Thadous.[1]

The paddy is left in the fields and carried up in such quantities as is required from time to time. Gongs are concealed in the jungles mostly, although some place them inside the *lel*, a conical shaped basket, with other treasures such as new clothes, beads, etc.

On the whole the Thadou house is a miserable construction and the average man takes very little interest in his house except to keep the rain out. Very likely the migratory feeling dissuades him from wasting his energies on a house he may vacate at any time that the whim takes him. When asking the reason why I have often been told "We are like birds and are lazy," which describes the Thadou very accurately.

Domesticated animals are mithuns, buffalos, pigs, goats, dogs and fowls.

The mithun are left to roam about the jungles on their own and are really only half tame. The same applies to the buffaloes. Sometimes they are persuaded to collect near the village for salt, but this is only done to keep them from wandering too far and thus calling for the use of tremendous amount of energy when the time comes to kill them.

---

slope as a village site, as in the use of a river or lake-shore. If the principal purpose of lake dwellings may be taken to have been defensive, and as this purpose would not be served by houses half on land, perhaps the former alternative is the more likely.—(Ed.)

[1] It may perhaps be taken that the original house was similar to the Bornean "long house" and accommodated the whole community, which from building cubicles inside came to building semi-detached and finally detached apartments outside, *vide* Peal, *Eastern Nagas of the Tirap and Namtsik*, J.A.S.B., i, of 1896; *On the Morung, etc.*, J.R.A.I., XXII, iii. The preferred plan of a Thado village is still a double row of houses facing each other across a street orientated according to the slope of the ground; houses must not face down the slope, but across it. A house that looked up or down the street would be liable to catch all the spirits going about "as a basket fish-trap in a weir collects the fish moving up or down stream." Presumably spirits about in the street are less dangerous than in the house. That, at least, is Korean view for "Korean devils are........far more powerful indoors than out, and so the Koreans are at special pains to exclude their devilships from..........interiors" (Miln, *Quaint Korea* p. 236).—(Ed.)

Pigs are fed regularly and come to the call of "*Lui*" from their owners while "*Chi*" is the word used for dogs. The voice is the only distinction recognised by the pigs and dogs as to whether their master is calling one or the other. Pigs play a very important part in the sanitation of a village which does not debar them from being a delicacy on the breakfast table. Male pigs are castrated after they are 3 to 6 months old and are never allowed to grow up to full size naturally. This does not seem to reduce the reproductive properties of the stock, but the standard in size is low.[1]

Dogs are kept for two purposes mainly. One is for the chase.[2] The other has already been referred to earlier in this chapter. No special breed of dog is kept. The dog is not always fed and hence the poor condition in which they are often seen. Nagas are very fond of dog's flesh[3] and so a good trade exists in this line between the Kukis and Nagas. Thadous are not averse to dog flesh but do not place it in the front rank. Male dogs are not castrated.

Goats are kept for trade and food, and are not fed but allowed to graze in the jungle. Sometimes miniature houses are built for the goats to sleep in at nights. The same for the fowls. Fowls are also scavengers of the village and are not fed.

I have very seldom come across cats in Thadou villages. Apparently they have very little use for them otherwise they would not be omitted from their stock of domesticated animals.[4]

---

[1] This method of dealing with pig is universal in these hills, and it appears again in the Philippines, where the Tinguian castrates them, as do all Nagas, at two to three months old. In the case of the Tinguian the stock is apparently propagated by breeding with the wild species (Cole, *The Tinguian*, p. 412), but that is not the case in the Naga Hills, where I have only once heard of the domestic pig breeding with the wild one. In that case the young were brindled like the wild young as in the Philippines, but this is not the case with the ordinary litter. Probably this practice of castrating all the males when still very young obtains widely in south east Asia, but I cannot find that is reported except by Methold who in his *Indian Observations* reports the "strange increase of the Swine of that Country (Siam) amongst which there are found no Boares, yet have they Pigs according to the custome of other Swine" (Purchas, *His Pilgrimage*, 1626, p. 1007).—(Ed.)

[2] As by Nagas, hunting-dogs are treated by the Thado with due respect. When hunting-dogs die they are buried with four corner-posts (*vakot*) to their grave. Other dogs are eaten before they reach old age or else sold.—(Ed.)

[3] They regard it as having medicinal properties v. *The Ao Nagas*, p. 17 n2. With the Thado, however, its curative properties seem rather magical than material; an account of how Chongthu discovered them is given by McCulloch (*Valley of Munnipore*, p. 56).—(Ed.)

[4] Cats are rare in most parts of the hills, and I think the rarity is primarily due to the fact that the cats find life in the jungle easier than in the village and stray away and turn wild, where they readily mate with the small leopard-cat, or so it appears. In most Naga tribes cats are the subject of many superstitions. *The Angami Nagas*, pp. 82, 242, 340, *The Sema Nagas*, pp. 65, 59). The Lhotas (Mills, *The Lhota Nagas*,

One hardly ever sees the Thadou on affectionate terms with his dog or any other animal. One often doubts whether such a thing as affection is included in his composition at any time.[1] He exhibits all the traits of a bully, very clearly, in his daily life. He kicks his dog, beats his wife, speaks roughly with everyone just because he is annoyed over something which is not connected with his dog or wife, etc. He suffers permanently from an enlarged liver, which, after all, is to be expected from the capacity for "*jù*" that he possesses at all and any time of the day and night taken in conjunction with the climate. He is also very fond of eating rats of all kinds and this may be a reason why he does not like keeping cats which would reduce his supply of this delicacy. Practically all animals and birds are eaten by the Thadou and fish are a particularly appreciated diet.

Cultivation.

The Thadou's staple diet is rice but the Lhouvum and Lhoujem are said to be particularly fond of *bal* (taro) and rely on it a good deal.[2]

There are many kinds of rice but all are grown on the hill-sides and are not irrigated. They have to depend on the season entirely. Other crops are beans, millet, Job's Tears, sesamum, maize, chillies, mustard leaf, cotton, ginger, turmeric, onions, pumkins, cucumbers and gourds.

The Thadou does not sow his seed broad-cast like some Nagas [3] but with a small hoe called *tucha* digs a small hole and puts in a few seeds and then covers them up. The Nagas who live among the Kukis sow broadcast and then lightly hoe over with some earth by merely scratching the ground with their small hoes. This may be one of the causes that the Kuki generally gets a better yield than the Naga. Tree jungle is best liked by the Thadou,[4] and they hardly ever cultivate more than two

---

p. 63) are reputed never to keep cats, though they sometimes purchase them for food, and Mills remarks that the Aos do not care about cats as they soon run wild and supplement their meals with the domestic fowl (*The Ao Nagas*, p. 135). The hill man here is always in the dilemma between feeding his cat, when, he says, it will not trouble to catch rats, and not feeding it, when it goes off to the wild on its own account.—(Ed.)

1 I can by no means subscribe to this estimate of the Thado; on the contrary his family affections are strong enough to make it frequent for several brothers with their families to share a common house, which to Nagas would be utterly unworkable, and his domestic behaviour is just as good as other people's. He is about the only tribe in these hills which ever takes the trouble to rear and tame wild animals as pets.—(Ed.)

2 It is said that it is only of comparatively recent years that rice has supplanted taro as the staple crop of the Thado, and taro (*colocasia*) is still largely cultivated.—(Ed.)

3 Similarly the Sema Naga dibble in the seed, whereas the Ao sow it broadcast.—(Ed.)

4 The Thado's ideal of really satisfactory cultivation is to fell virgin

years on one field. They show a tendency now-a-days to take up irrigated rice cultivation, and the heavy initial outlay of energy required in the preparation of this type of field may eventually lead to the Thadous' dropping their migratory inclinations when this form of cultivation gets a greater hold on them.

In *jhuming*, which is the name given in Assam to the dry cultivation, the jungle is cut in January or February annually. It is then allowed to dry thoroughly and is burnt. After that the field is cleared of debris and the sowing begins. Three to four times is the usual number of weedings when the crops are growing. In the one field nearly all the crops mentioned are often seen planted promiscuously. The crops are cut with a sickle which has a sawlike edge. The heads are collected on the field and there thrashed and winnowed, and the paddy is stored in the field house called *lou bu'*. It is carried up to the village as required and pounded into rice for daily consumption. The harvest starts in October and ends about the early part of December according to whether the crop is of the early or late ripening type. The Thadou, however, prefers the late ripening kind of rice which he says has a better flavour and is more sustaining.

Hunting.

In hunting the Thadou is particularly expert. Nothing pleases him so much as to be out after game with his muzzle-loading gun or arranging and setting up traps to snare wild animals. He is a good tracker and has an uncanny knack of knowing where the game is likely to be. For large game such as elephant he puts a spear into his gun and wounds his victim in such a place that the beast finds it very painful to move, then he kills it while it is thus anchored. Another form is to dig large pits with sharp pointed bamboos placed firmly upright in them, so that when the animal falls it is literally pinned. This form of pitfall is also used when driving any kind of game. Next we have the *pel*, a large falling trap made of logs of wood which fall on and crush the animal, used for tigers, bears and the like. A smelly piece of decomposing flesh is placed inside to attract the animal. When the beast touches it, it releases a trigger and thus causes the heavy platform of logs to fall and crush it. For smaller game there is the *pelkop* which is a smaller fall trap of a different pattern. Logs of wood are placed upright in the ground parallel to each other thus making a passage. Over the space between these walls a large log weighted with stones is hung so that when the animal passes through the passage it is crushed. Another

---

forest and grow a single crop of rice among the fallen logs and then repeat on fresh forest for the next year. This method gives the highest possible return for the lowest expenditure of labour, but is so extravagant in land that it can rarely if ever be indulged in now-a-days.—(Ed.)

trap for squirrels and such small animals is made with a stick planted in the ground and pulled down with a piece of string, at the end of which is a noose. When the game passes over the noose it releases the spring and the animal is held strangled in the air by the noose, which is whipped up by the string on the peg which kept it down.[1] This is called *thangte.* Small deer and wild pigs are sometimes caught in it. In addition spring-gun traps are also made. The height at which this is to be is ascertained by doubling the circumference of the animal's footprint. There are innumerable other forms of traps for birds and game all based on the spring-release system.

For fish they make a bamboo weir across a river and then poison the stream with various kinds of seed, leaf, root and bark poisons which are to be found in these hills. The weir holds up the stupefied fish which are then collected.[2] Another form is to make a weir with a platform run at one end, and the fish, in their frantic efforts to go down stream, jump into this run which is high and dry and there die or are caught. This method is used about October, just at the end of the rains, as the Thadou says the fish then begin going down stream. I have seen some very large catches made in this way. Yet another form is to make a weir as above but with an attached platform on the downstream side at the top upon which the fish jump and are caught. For the smaller fish bottle-shaped traps are affixed to the base of these weirs in which small apertures are made and the fish swarm through them to be held in the bamboo traps until removed.[3] In the smaller streams just a weir across below a pool is made early at the end of the rains and then when this pool is seen to be full of fish which have come down owing to the want of water higher up the Thadou jumps in and puddles it. This chokes the fish and they are easily caught as they come up to the surface. In addition to all these traps[4] and poisons there are the ordinary night

---

1 V. *The Sema Nagas*, p. 79.—(Ed.)

2 This method seems to be in use throughout the Indian archipelago; at any rate it is practised in Borneo, in the Philippine Islands and in the Torres Straits. It is also used widely in South America.—(Ed.)

3 The basket fish-trap, to be effective, should be set with the opening facing down stream in the spring and up-stream in the autumn. The mahseer come up (? to spawn) in the rains and go down again for the cold weather.—(Ed.)

4 One form of Thado fish trap which Mr. Shaw has not mentioned is interesting on account of its distribution. It consists of a piece of bamboo split into half a dozen slats joined by the node and kept splayed out by a bamboo ring at the end and a smaller one in the middle, making a skeleton cone, the longditudinal ribs of which are lined with rachides of the cane plant so tied that the points of their formidable hooked thorns are directed towards the node of bamboo. From this node a spike projects inside the cone on which a white bean is impaled to act as a bait. The fish enters the cone without difficulty, but the thorny hooks make it impossible for it to back out. The trap is opened at the node,

lines which are fastened to a rod consisting of a length of bamboo well planted in the ground and bent over. Projecting horizontally on the water and just above it is a smaller piece of bamboo with a "V" shaped cut at its extremity. Through this the line from the bent bamboo is brought with a cross piece of stick tied to the line and placed under the V-shaped cut thus holding the rod bent. An ordinary bazaar hook is used with a small crab, frog, snail, fowls' entrails or a minnow attached. This is hanging in the water about a foot or so below the surface. When the fish takes it the cross-piece of stick is pulled out beyond the end of the V, and the bamboo straightens, retaining the fish with its head well out of the water suspended on a stout line.[1]

Many kinds of tree-gum are used also for birdlime when trapping the smaller sorts of birds.

The Thadou has no compunction in killing a male or female of any kind of game. They are all edible flesh to him which is the only thing that really matters to his mind.

Game laws have been brought in by the State and some attempt is being made to restrict his unsatiable desire for game. The Thadou interpretation of this law is that the Sahebs want to shikar game and catch fish and so this preservation has been brought in to avoid having too many blank days while so doing.

Manufactures.

It is said that the following things were originally made at Thijonbung and Lhanpelkot by one Tamlopa Thadou :—

Da'pi .. Large Kuki gongs.
Da'thilu .. A set of of three gongs.
Tuidol[2] .. Large basin.

---

which is divided in half to facilitate the extraction of the fish by the node end when the node is untied. A stone is tied to the node as a sinker and anchor when the trap is set. Balfour (*Thorn-lined Traps, etc.*, 'Man' 1925, 21) shows that the use of such traps extends from the Naga Hills to the Solomon Islands and Santa Cruz. The Chins use them, as do the Lhota and Konyak Nagas, but though the Thado uses them, the Kachha Nagas (Nzemi), among whom the Thado live, apparently do not. The trap is a cruel one, fish taken in it being literally covered with gashes inflicted by the hooked thorns in the attempts of the victim to escape, but it is simple to construct and exceedingly effective..—(Ed.)

[1] I have seen this spring fishing rod among the Thado, but never among Nagas. A virtually identical method of taking fish, minutely described, is reported by "Fins" in *Country Life* (October 27th, 1923), as used by the Arawak Indians of South America. Cole, (*The Tinguian*, p. 385) mentions baited lines on sticks stuck into the ground, but does not state that they are arranged like the Thado and Arawak lines to strike the fish automatically when the bait is taken.—(Ed.)

[2] The Tuidol (Page 146 (a). fig. 1) is particularly associated with the killing of elephants. It has elephants cast in relief round its frieze and is filled with *ju*, and the killer of a wild elephant must quaff the whole—a sort of sconce, in fact. Mr. Duncan is my informant.—(Ed.)

Lumdal	.. Brass plates placed on shields.
Chaldep	.. Brass dao-shaped plate worn upright on head in full dress.
Chinking	.. An iron rack [1] with flat serpent-shaped ends to the arms projecting from a central stem.
Chemkol	.. An old type of genuine Thadou knife.

Now a-days none of these things are made and the art has been lost,[2] Burmese or other foreign made gongs and utensils and knives having now taken their place.

Cloths are made in the same way as the Nagas from cotton grown by them but the pattern is different: They are:—

Thangnangpon	.. Very dark blue cloth with embroidered ends in red, white and yellow cotton.
Saipikhup	.. Same as *Thangnang pon* but with different pattern for the border.[3]
Pondum	.. Plain dark blue with no border.
Ponmongvom	.. White cloth with one black stripe at each border.
Ponlhe'	.. A plain white cloth with no borderings.
Del	. A white cloth used either as a "pugri". or a "dhuti."
Phoi	. A thick white cotton cloth made with coarse thread. In between the warp and woof wads of cotton with the seed extracted are worked in at the time of weaving and fastened at the middle of each wad. The ends stand out and thus make a pile surface on one side of the cloth.
Ponpho'	.. This is the same as *Phoi* but without the wads of cotton worked in.
Ni ..	.. A petticoat worn by women. It is of red and black alternate stripes.
Ponve	.. A plain back cloth worn round the torso by women. There is a plain white one also by the same name.

---

1 It is a sort of collection of hooks branching from a central stem on the lines of a candelabrum. We may compare, perhaps, the decorated brass hooks of Borneo (Hose and McDougall, *op cit.*, II, 220). See Page 146 (b), fig. 2.—(Ed.)

2 Beautiful brass and bronze tobacco pipes, dao-handles, flint and steel boxes, *ju* syphons, vases, and gauntlets for women used to be made by the *cire perdue* process. This art, though rarely practised now, is not extinct, *vide* Appendix C.—(Ed.)

3 The cloth takes its name from the resemblance of the pattern to the leg of an elephant (*saipi*).—(Ed.)

The first two, *Thangnangpon* and *Saipikhup*, were only worn by chiefs and those who had done the *Chang-ai* and *Sha-ai* pujahs and by no one else. It was necessary to perform a pujah called "*Kithenthou*"[1] by killing a pig on the completion of those cloths as the borders were supposed to represent the images of "*Thilha.*"

Now this is not observed and anyone able to have them made may wear them, while the patterns of the border are varied according to taste.

The ordinary hand loom is used in making all these clothes and one or more lease-rods are used when weaving in patterns according to the complications of the design, with one or more heddles.[2] The work from the reaping of the cotton to the weaving is all done by the women. To extract the seed from the cotton a machine consisting of two wooden rollers closely fitting is used through which the cotton wads are passed.[3] This is called *patlhe*. Then it is ginned with a bow which is called *patsai*. Next it is rolled into lengths of raw cotton, like elongated wads, on a stick which is withdrawn when its wads are completed. These wads are then spun into cotton on a machine called *mui* which is a revolving piece of thin iron worked by hand on a frame.

Their cups are lengths of bamboo planed with a dao while their plates are made out of wood. The cooking utensils are mostly earthenware bought from Manipur but many are now going in for iron and aluminium.

Their daos and spearheads are made by the *thishu'* of the village out of scraps of iron got from bazaars or stolen. The bellows used consist of two adjacent large sized bamboo tubes with a piston to each padded with fowls' feathers and worked

---

1 *Kithenthou* is performed by the *maker* of the cloth, a woman, of course, who kills a chicken and puts one of the feathers in her hair and a string round her neck.—(Ed.)

2 The loom is a simple tension loom exactly like that used by Nagas (*e.g. The Sema Nagas*, p. 50) and elsewhere in the Indonesian area. The Thado, however, in addition to the single laze-rod used by Nagas, employs a large number of pattern laze-rods such as those used by the Iban and Dusun of Borneo on their precisely similar looms. The Thado is ahead of the Naga, too, as also of the Iban, in the shuttle he employs, for whereas the Naga and the Iban use a simple spool, the Thado puts his spool into a bamboo shuttle with a smooth nose and a hole at the side through which the weft is released. The apparent difficulty of threading the weft through the small hole in the side of the bamboo shuttle from the inside is ingeniously got over by blowing into the shuttle, which immediately causes the loose end of the weft to protrude through the aperture.—(Ed.)

3 These rollers have rough spiral cogs in reverse directions cut at the end of each roller so as to draw the cotton through as a mangle takes clothes to be wrung. Both this ginning machine and the spinning wheel are of the pattern used in the Manipur valley and in the plains of Burma.—(Ed.)

alternately.[1] They are connected with the fire by smaller bamboo tubes well below the fire level with earth forming the actual connection. To temper the iron a hole in the ground is made and water placed in it with which some clay is stirred up.[2] A hard stone or piece of hard wood is used for an anvil. Now even this art is slowly fading away as they are buying ready-made daos and spearheads from Manipuris and from Cachar markets. In fact the same may be said of clothes as there seems to be a preference for foreign made stuff which appeals greatly to the Thadou generally with his excessively lazy and careless disposition. He never intends doing more than he can possibly help he would do less than that if he could conceivably manage it—so gradually foreign goods are getting a hold on him and the habit is not a little promoted by the advent of missionary work in Thadou villages.

The Thadou is naturally handy with his *chem* (dao) and *rheicha* (axe) and takes great interest in all constructional work. Perhaps there is to be found here the makings of first class carpenters and blacksmiths with training—and perhaps in time excellent contractors. But this all means work—a very detestable thing to the Thadou.

He is a great drinker of rice beer called *ju*. There are three kinds namely *jukha, vaiju*[3] and *anthom*. The first is distilled while the last two are made by fermentation caused by adding yeast. He prides himself on the amount he can consume and competitions take place to see how much a man can drink in one breath without discomfort to himself and the party.[4]

The bulk of the work falls on the women-folk who in addition have to bring up their children without the help of ayahs and nurses no matter how things go. This accounts to a great extent for the fact that the women age very rapidly, while the men seem to keep remarkably youthful till much later in life.

---

[1] The familiar Indonesian type used from Assam to the Philippines and from Siam to Madagascar.—(Ed.)

[2] If mud is not used the surface of the steel has a cracked appearance and the weapon is brittle. Salt is added to the tempering mixture.—(Ed.)

[3] *Vaiju* is readily distinguished from other varieties of rice wine, as the husks of the paddy are also used in making it and give it a distinctive flavour. An identical liquor is brewed in the distant Konyak Naga village of Ukha, far to the north-east.—(Ed.)

[4] When guests are entertained great care is taken to see that each man gets the same measure of liquor, and if a man cannot finish this he usually gets a friend to do it for him, for when they have all finished another round is measured out. When drinking through siphons from jars the measure is indicated by a length of cane or stick standing in the lees at the bottom. When the top of the stick appears the drinker stops and the jar is filled up again to make a fresh infusion.—(Ed.)

CHAPTER VII.

LANGUAGE.

Language.

The Thadou language is spoken by all the descendants of Thadou and by the Non-Thadou clans absorbed by them. Most of the Old Kukis can speak Thadou fluently although they have languages and dialects of their own such as Kom, Khotlhang, Waiphei, etc. The fact that the Old Kukis [1] use Thadou as a *lingua franca* is possibly an indication of the manner in which the earlier Kuki immigrants were overrun by the later.

Sir George Grierson classifies Thadou in the Northern Chin sub-group of the Kuki-Chin group of the Tibeto-Burman Family (*Linguistic Survey*, III, iii), and an account of the language has been given by Mr. T. C. Hodson in his *Thado Grammar*.

The language has undoubted affinities with Metei (Manipuri), Kachin, Garo Lushei and the various dialects spoken by the Old Kukis. I agree with Mr. Hodson when he contradicts Lieut. Stewart who affirmed that most of the Thadous knew Manipuri. Lieut. Stewart was correct if he meant only to speak of those on the ranges of hills bordering the valley of Manipur, but, further in, where the Thadou is really to be found in his true state, the knowledge of Manipuri is conspicuous by its absence.

It is not a written language and so this perhaps accounts for the variations of pronunciation and phraseology which differ, although very slightly in some cases, from village to village. There is a story among the Thadous that very long ago Pathen (the Creator) gave the Thadou, Naga and Manipuri a separate language each, written on skin. The Thadou owing to his admitted habitual laziness and casualness lost his script which was probably eaten by rats, dogs or pigs.[2] The Naga, because of his almost insatiable hunger ate his. The Manipuri, who is not a flesh eater, and who is also provident and thrifty, carefully kept his and eventually studied it. So neither the Thadou nor the Naga has a written language while

---

[1] The Thado are sometimes spoken of as New Kukis in contra-distinction to the Old Kukis, consisting of the Hrangkol, Chiru, Biete and other tribes who preceded the Thado migration from the south (*vide* Shakespear, *Lushei Kuki clans*.—(Ed.)

[2] The Angami Nagas, the Sema Nagas, the Padam Abors (D. S. Dunbar, *Abors and Galongs*, p. 51, *M.A.S.B.*, V), the Kachins (Hanson *The Kachins*, p. 117) and the Karens (McMahon, *Karens of the Golden Chersonese*, p. 143; Marshall, *Karen People of Burma*, p. 280) all have this story in slightly varying versions.—(Ed.)

the Manipuri has. This applies to the old Manipuri script which is now-a-days obsolete owing to the use of Bengali characters throughout Manipur.

The fluidity of the language makes it far from simple to form grammatical rules as Mr. Hodson also found, but for the purpose of this book it is not proposed to go into details though a revision and expansion of Mr Hodson's "Thado Grammar" is needed by officers who have to work among Kukis and who desire to learn the language.

The purpose of this chapter is merely to give a general outline of the language and to supplement the information given by Mr. Hodson. It is to be hoped that some one will publish an exhaustive work on the language before it changes, as it seems likely to do, under the influence of semi-educated Thadous, whose tendency is to twist it to what they suppose to be English forms and thereby to outrage both languages at once.

Alphabet.	*Vowels.*
A ..	.. as "a" in "father."
A ..	.. as "aw" in "awe," or the "a" in "ball."
A ..	.. as "a" in "company."
E ..	.. as "a" in "may."
E ..	.. as "e" in "then."
I ..	.. as "ee" in "keen."
I ..	.. as "i" in "in."
O ..	.. as "o" in "bone."
O ..	.. as "o" in "dot."
U ..	.. as "oo" in "fool."
U ..	.. as "u" in "pull."

All the above have a glottal stop shortening them in certain words which some contend represents a silent consonant which is either "k" or "h."[1]

	Consonants.
B ..	.. as in English.
C ..	.. used only in combination with "h."
D ..	.. dental.
F ..	.. Not used.
G ..	.. as in English.
H ..	.. as in "hen" and also aspirates the consonant which it is combined with. There are two schools of thought as to whether the "H" as an aspirate should be

[1] The silent consonant if not 'K,' must be 'T.'—(Ed.)

		placed after or before the consonant it is combined with. I belong to the first school and so place it after the consonant it is to aspirate in all Thadou words.[1]
J, Y and Z	..	These are all interchangeable and the only possible method is to use one of them which should be the "J" for preference since it is most generally in use.
K ..	..	All as in English.
L ..	..	
M ..	..	
N ..	..	
Ng ..	..	as "ng" in "bringing" and not as in "finger."
P ..	..	as in English.
Q ..	..	Not used.
R ..	..	as "r" in "rank."
S ..	..	as "s" in "this."
[2]T & V	..	as in English.
W & X	..	not used.

Tone.

It is a tonal language and so can only be properly learnt from among the people themselves. I give one example :—

Kol .. Precipice or cliff.
Kol .. Burma or Burmese.
Kol .. Foreigner.

Which meaning is intended can only be ascertained from the text and intonation, whether high, medium or low.[3]

---

[1] In my opinion the aspirate should sometimes precede and sometimes follow the consonant qualified. It seems reasonable enough to write H before R. e.g. *Hrangkol ;* on the other hand to write it before K as is done in Burma is merely perverse. No one can pronounce Khamti as "Hkamti." In the case of L & H there is in Thado a distinct variation of use.

Thus

lhun=to reach, arrive

hlün or *hlon*=to accompany.—(Ed.)

[2] T is generally at any rate dental not palatal.—(Ed.)

[3] There is a clear tonal distinction between *Kől*=cliff (high register) and *Kŏl*=Burman (low register), but *Kŏl*=foreigner (mid register) has also, a shorter vowel in the ŏ, at least that is how I hear it. I suspect that in Thado, as in Sema and probably other Naga languages, the tone is deliberately used as a method of distinguishing different words, *vide* J.R.A.S., Jan. 1927, Bor and Hutton, *Use of Tones in Sema Naga.*

Grierson, *On the Representation of Tones in Oriental Languages*, distinguishes nine tones which he represents by a mark before the syllable in which the tone occurs, thus :—

Euphony.

There are many changes in form of the word for which they can give no other reason than "It is the custom" or "It sounds better that way." For examples :—

1. **Kicha** .. To be afraid,
   becomes
   Kichatsha .. To frighten.
2. **Man** .. To catch,
   becomes
   Matsha .. To cause to be caught,
   and
   Matding .. In order to catch.
3. **Lho** .. To weed,
   becomes
   Lha .. (the "aw" sound) weeded.
4. **Len** .. To be big,
   becomes
   Letsha .. To make big,
   and
   Letding .. In order to be big.

	Level	Rising	Falling
High Register	¯ka	ˊka	ˋka
Mid Register ..	—ka	⁄ka	⁻ka
Low Register ..	_ka	ˏka	ˎka

These indication marks can be combined when necessary to signify compound tones. Eg. ¬ ^ ⌣

The mark for the level mid register will normally be omitted, as if used it is liable to be mistaken for a hyphen, but as the tone it indicates is the ordinary one the sign can be taken for granted. It is not very likely that all these tones are found in Thado, but Mr. Bor and I have identified four or five, e.g.

fire	=	*—mei*	sit	=	*ˋthou*	opposite	= ki *ˋdong*
clouds	=	*ˎmei*	rise	=	*ˏthou*	tender	= a *_dong*

But probably for practical purposes the use of four tonal marks would be enough for the Thado language, that is, omitting the mid register ¯ka, _ka, ˋka, and ˊka.

I give below a few similar words differentiated by marks as they might be in a dictionary. I do not think it will entirely eliminate the difficulty of identical spellings, but it should help. In texts I imagine the difficulties will have to be borne.

The following may be taken as examples :—

fire	*mei*	drink	*ˋdon*
tail	*mei*	tube	*_don*
cloud	*ˎmei*	nurse	*nau-don'*

[The sign ' is used to indicate a glottal stop]

beginning of house-building	*gêl*	rain	*gū*
plan, think	*gêl*	poison	*gū*
thin	*agĕl*	bone	*_gū*
kind of tree	*—gĕl*	bamboo	*_gu, —go* (which ?)
hail	*giel*	kindle fire	*gou*

I think the first two *gels* and the first two *gus* are the same, in which case I defeated by them, but they are no worse than *bat* and *bat* in English.—(Ed.)

5. **Dong** .. To ask,
becomes
Do'ding .. In order to ask.

Yet it cannot be stated as a general rule that words ending in **a, n, o** and **ng** all follow these peculiarities, because many do not change their root form.

Noun.

An agglutinative language such as Thadou can hardly be said to possess any true case endings, but the Agentive, only used when an action takes place, acts as the subject of a transitive verb and is indicated by the suffix *in* or *n*, but the suffix is dropped sometimes when it is not required and the sense is shown from the context. The Ablative and Dative cases are formed by adding *Koma*, or *Henga*.

The Possessive Case is indicated by placing the possessing before the possessed word thus *Chem kung*="dao' shandle;" where the possessed word is omitted, *a* is suffixed to form a possessive—e.g., *hiche Lengjang a hilo Doujon a ahi*=this is Doujon's not Lengjang's. The Instrumental Case is formed by adding *in* or *n*.

Adjective.

This follows the noun it qualifies. *A* is prefixed to the root word and the negative form is made by adding "*lo*" or "*hi*" to the root. Thus *Chem ahemlo khat ume*, means "There is a blunt dao." The word for word translation would be "Dao sharp-not one is."

Comparisons are effected in three ways :—

1. By use of "Sangin":—

Hiche sangin hichekhu alene
This than that larger.

2. By use of adversative sentences :—

Hiche aneo, hichekhu alene.
This small, that large.

3. By using "**Sangin..........jo**":—

Hiche sangin hichekhu aphajoe.
This than that is better.

4. By use of "**Sangin..........pen**":—

Hiche sangin hichekhu alenpene.
This than that is bigger.

Superlative degrees are formed as follows :—

1. By use of "**la-a............pen**":—

Hiche la-a hichekhu alenpene.
This among those is the biggest.

2. By using "**pen**" only :—
   Hiche alenpene.
   This is the biggest.
3. By adding "**penpen**" or "**chacha**" when speaking of one out of many big or small things respectively:—
   Hiche alenpenpen.
   This biggest.
   Hichekhu aneochacha.
   That smallest.

Pronouns.

Demonstrative pronouns are formed as follows :—

(1)	**Hiche pasal hi** ..	This man (here).
(2)	**Hiche numei khu** ..	That woman (there).
(3)	**Hiche**	This (near).
(4)	**Khuche**	That (At a distance).
(5)	**Hikoma**	Here (close).
(6)	**Khukoma** ..	There (Some distance away).

Interrogative pronouns are :—

(*a*).	"**I**" or "**Ipi**" ..	What?
(*b*)	**Ida**	Why?
(*c*)	**Itile**	When?
(*d*)	**Itina**	How?
(*e*)	**Ijat**	How many? (Articles).
(*f*)	**Ichan**	How much? (Length, size, etc.)
(*g*)	**Ijatve**	How many times?
(*h*)	**Hoja** ..	Where?
(*i*)	**Hoikoma** ..	Where to or from?
(*j*)	**Hoilanga** ..	Where? Which direction?
(*k*)	**Koi**	Who?

Personal pronouns are :—

(1)	**Kei**	I.
(2)	**Keho**	We (all of us).
(3)	**Nang**	Thou.
(4)	**Nangho, Naho** ..	You
(5)	**Ama**	He, she or it.
(6)	**Amaho**	They.
(7)	**Eini**	We two (Speaker and spoken to).
(8)	**Keini**	We two (Speaker and another).
(9)	**Nangni**	You two (Spoken to and another).

(10) **Nang le nang** .. You and you (Pointed out).
(11) **Ama le kei** .. He and I.
(12) **Ama le nang to** .. He and you.

Possessive pronouns are:—

(*a*) **Ka** .. .. My
(*b*) **Na** .. .. Thine.
(*c*) **A** .. .. His, her or its.
(*d*) **Keho** .. .. Our.[1]
(*e*) **Naho** .. .. Your.
(*f*) **Amaho** .. .. Their.

To express "own" the Thadou uses **mongmong** but the ordinary possessive pronoun conveys the same idea yet not so emphatically, thus :—

1. **Ka in mongmong** .. 'My own house.'
2. **Keho bong mongmong** 'Our own cattle.'

Relative pronoun. Where this is used in English with a subordinate verb, the Thadou uses a qualifying adjective composed of a noun or verb root with **chu** suffixed.

1. The man who came yesterday,
   Janha ahungpa-chu.
2. The child who died,
   Naoshen athi-chu.
3. The horse which I sold,
   Shakol kajot-chu.

Reciprocal pronouns are formed as in the following instances :—

(*a*) We beat each other,
   Keini akidentoutoulhone. [2]
(*b*) They two steal each other's property,
   Amateni thilkeo akigutoutoulhone.

Reflexive pronouns are formed as in the cases given below:—

1. I broke it myself,
   Hiche keima mongin kachu' shet ahi.
2. I ate it myself,
   Kei mong kane ' ahi.

Cardinal Numerals are shown clearly in Mr. Hodson's "Thado Grammar" so I shall not deal with them here. However there are some points worth elucidating.

---

[1] There is also a dual possessive *i-* ='belonging to the two of us.'—(Ed.)

[2] The infix—*ki*—almost always, if not always, gives a reciprocal sense to a verb, *vide* note [8] on the story of Khutshibi (*infra*, p. 117).—(Ed.)

There are no **ordinal** numbers as in **English** but only the following :—

First	..	**Amasa.**
Second	..	**Khat bana** (This means the one after the first).
Third	..	**Ni bana** (One after the second and so on for the rest).
Last	..	**Anu nungpen.**

Ordinal Adverbs are formed by adding " **VE** " thus :—

Once	..	**Khatve.**
Ten times	..	**Shomve.**

Multiplicatives thus :—

Singly	..	**Khat khat nin** (By one and one).
By fours	..	**Li li-n.**
By 20,000s	..	**Taima taima-n** or **Taima ma-n.**[1]

Fractions :—

One half	..	**A ke.**
One quarter	..	**Ake ke.**
Two-fifths	..	**Chan nga-a chan ni** (Share five-in share two) and so on.

Verb.

It is doubtful whether a verb in an agglutinative language can properly be said to have moods at all therefore I merely give a list of illustrative sentences to convey a general idea of the verb and its habits.

I nabol em ?	What art thou doing ?
I nabol um ?	What are you doing ? (Plural)
I nabol ta vem ?	What didst thou do ?
I nabol ta vum ?	What did you do ? (Plu:)
I nabol ding ham ?	What wilt thou do ?
I nabol diu ham ?	What will you do ? (Plu:)
Iti nabol lo vem ?	Why dost thou not do ?
Iti nabol lo vum ?	Why do you not do ? (Plu:)
I nabol hi ' am ?	What didst thou not do ?
I nabol hu ' um ?	What did you not do ? (P)
I nabol lo ding ham ?	What wilt thou not do ?
I nabol lo diu ham ?	What will you not do ?
Bolin ..	Do. (S)
Bolun ..	Do. (P)
Bolhi ' in ..	Don't do. (S)

[1] *Taima*, I am told, means 10,000 not 20,000. However, it is only a purely theoretical term, and never used in practice, and as the score is the unit for calculation in some Naga tribes, it is possible that *taima* is used by some Thado for a score of thousands (*shang*) instead of for a decade of them.—(Ed.)

Bol hu ' un ..	Don't do. (P)
Boldingin ..	Will have to do. (S)
Boldiuvin ..	Will have to do. (P)
Bolloding ahi ..	Will not be done. (S)
Bollodiu ahi ..	Will not be done. (P)
Ka bol e ..	I do.
Na bol e ..	Thou dost.
A bol e ..	He, she or it does.
Ka bol lo or Ka bol lo ve.	I do not do.
Na bol lo	Thou dost not do.
Ka bol tai ..	I did.
A bol tai ..	He, she or it did.
Ka bol nange ..	I will do.
Na bol inte ..	Thou wilt do.
A bol inte ..	He will do.
Keho bolunge ..	We will do
Naho bolunte ..	You will do.
Amaho bolunte	They will do.
Kei cheponge ..	I will not go.
Nang che ponte	You will not go.
Che taite ..	Let us go (Two persons).
Che taute ..	Let us go (More than two).
Che taihen ..	Let them go (Two persons).
Che tauhen ..	Let them go (More than two).
Che po hi ' te ..	Let us not go (Two persons).
Che po hu ' te	Let us not go (More than two).
Bolinlang ..	Having done. (S)
Bolunlang ..	Having done. (P)
Boldanlang ..	Not having done. (S)
Boldavinlang ..	Not having done. (P)
Bol-na-ding ..	In order to do.
Bol-lo-ding ..	In order not to do.
Bol-intin ..	If (it) had been done.
Bol-hi '-intin ..	If (it) had not been done.
Hiche na bolle ..	If you do this.
Hiche na bol lo le	If you do not do this.
Na bol phat-a ..	While you do.
Na bol tengle ..	When you do. (S)
Amaho bol tengule	When they do. (P)
Ama bol jongle ..	Even if he does.
Nang bol hi ' jongle	Even if you do not do.
Ka bol jo le ..	When I finish doing.
Na bol jo lo ..	When or if you do not finish.
Ka bol che po ve	I have not done all.
Ka bol jing e ..	I am doing.
Ka bol nang e ..	I will do (Not definite when).

Ka she nom e	..	I wish to say.
Ka she da e	..	I do not wish to say.
Na bol jo lo joug le.		Even if you do not finish doing.

These illustrative sentences will suffice to give some idea of the peculiarities of the Thadou language with its niceties of phraseology and meanings.

APPENDIX A.

SEVEN THADO FOLK-TALES

THADO FOLK-LORE.

The seven folk-tales which follow have been recorded by me from the same narrator—Lenjang of Taning, in the original Thado and then translated. Where the Thado itself is given the literal translation will be found underneath each word, and a freer translation of the whole at the end. Where the Thado is not given, as in No. vii, I have been very careful to keep as close to the meaning of the Thado as linguistically possible (any interpolations required by the English being shown in brackets) except in the matter of participles, which I have freely translated as finite verbs in order to obtain sentences that end, instead of carrying on interminably from participle to participle as in the original story. Indeed the same liberty has been taken to a lesser extent in recording the original Thado of the first six stories, as I found it otherwise extremely difficult to keep the thread of the original. The references at the end of the English versions of stories iv. and v. are to the notes on the Thado which immediately precede them. The titles are given by the narrator in response to a request for a title. I gathered that they were not themselves traditional.

The tales given here are scanty specimens of a very voluminous folk-lore, but fairly typical. Many themes familiar in English folk-lore are found. Thus in one tale a girl is carried off by a demon. Her six elder brothers perish in the attempt to rescue her, but the seventh and youngest succeeds in reaching her. By simulated affection she coaxes from her demon lover the whereabouts of his external soul. The hero succeeds in ascending to the house of God (Pathen) in the sky and obtaining possession of the pigeon in which it is kept. The girl flees with him, they are pursued and raise obstacles behind them, a cliff, a swamp, etc., in the pursuer's path by means of magical objects purloined from the demon himself.[1] In the final struggle between the demon and the hero, the former is disabled by the latter's breaking the pigeon's leg. Again in the story of Ashijoul we find the spiteful bully wearing a full blown flower in his hair, contrasted with the modest and kindly lad who prefers to wear a bud only. The two go out to woo Ashijoul, and the former maltreats those he meets by the way, the other is kind to them. The former is sent about his business with contumely while the latter finds favour with the lady and with the help of the animals he has befriended performs the impossible tasks required by her parents of a suitor for their daughter's hand. On their way home a wer-lioness treacherously devours the bride and takes her place, but a fruit-tree springs from the bride's blood, the bride-groom plucks and puts by the fine fruit from the tree top, from which emerges the true bride who cleans up the house while the couple are in the fields. She is one day caught by her husband, who kills the wer-lioness, from whose corpse springs a plantain tree, and whose severed head becomes a stone. In spite of warnings Ashijoul tries to pick a plantain leaf from the tree, which devours her, and her husband rescues her by cutting down the tree and finding her reduced to miniature inside the tree (cf. the somewhat similar episode in story vii, The Magic Fiddle). She recovers, and again disobeys him by spreading a cloth to dry on the stone that had been her rival's head and is devoured by the head. The husband fails to break it and the story ends by his pulling down the whole village fence and burning it upon the stone which splits with a loud report and discharges its contents to heaven. The fact that *Ashi* means a star may be connected with this but I can find no meaning to attach to *joul*. One rather curious episode is the somewhat fanciful inclusion of a cloud among the "animals" scornfully treated by the villain and helped by the hero. It amazingly rewards him by bringing the other clouds to carry for him up to the house of his prospective father-in law an enormous stone which he has been told to fetch. The clouds carry the stone and the hero walks in the midst of them singing "Ho, ho" as if he were doing the work himself. Most of these stories are extremely discursive and contain many repetitions of approved formulae. They contain much in common with Naga folk-lore (*e.g.* compare the story of Ashijoul with that of Muchupile or Hunchibili, *The Sema Nagas* p. 357, *The Angami Nagas*, p. 280, and Mills, *The Lhota Nagas*, p. 188), but much that is distinctively Kuki and in contrast to Naga Folk-lore in general, in particular the introduction of

---

[1] So too in the *Story of Kungori* (Lewin, *Exercises in the Lushai Dialect*, p. 84) not only do we find these magical objects, in this case the "seeds" of fire, thorn and water, but two episodes from Jack and the Beanstalk, the *Fee fi fo fum* episode, and the Beanstalk itself.—(Ed.)

magical paraphernalia in a material form. The heroine of Hunchibili no less than Ashijoul is able to re-incarnate herself in the fruit of a tree, but the Naga stories seem to lack entirely such Aladdin-recalling treasures as Khutshibi and the Magic Fiddle, or the *lohaldang*, which is no less than our old friend "Stick-out-of-bag" scarcely disguised at all, The stories of *Khutshibi* and of the Magic Fiddle contain a number of incidents closely paralleled in the folk-lore of the Lepchas (*vide Lepcha Folk-lore*," J.A.S.B., xxi.)—(Ed.)

i. Man and Spirit.

Masangin mi le thilha takhat ahin ; min thilha athat-
Formerly man and spirit alike being man spirit kept
thatnin ahile thilha achen Pathenpa-koma " Min ei-that-
beating and so spirit going to God (said) Man me keep
thatne ei-thatgamding ahithai." Pathenpan thilha-koma
beating me to kill outright is. God to spirit
" Chol-lai-vum na-bolinlang tuikhu-a na-koile-
Yeast-centre-black you having made in water hole you
chun, amit-lai vum-intin, chutheing mutheitapon-
place his-eye-centre black-will-be and thence will be unable
atin." Hiche-kal min thilha amutheilo ahithai.
to see. Since then man spirit unable to see has been.

Free translation of the above :—

In the beginning man and the spirit were alike, but man kept beating the spirit, so it went to God and said " Man keeps beating me the way he will be killing me entirely." God said to the spirit "If you make some yeast cakes with black centres and put them into his well, the centres of his eyes will become black and then he will be unable to see you." From that time man has been unable to see spirits.

ii. The Change of Skin.

Masangin ganhing miong akilipmin, ahitile
Formerly animals mankind changing (their skins) thus
aphapui atiin, uphoh le tang akihousain, ashei-
not good saying toad and lizard causing to contest the one
masa-sa changhin. Tangin "Gul kilip, tang kilip"
to say first will get. Lizard Snake change lizard change
atile, uphoh-in " Mi kilip, phoh kilip " atile, anu-
saying toad Man change toad change saying hav-
nungtan hiche-je-in gul le tang akilipmin,
ing been behind for this cause snake and lizard changing (skin)
mi akilip-theipui. Mi kiliple teshi aumtheipui,
man change could not. Man if changing old could not be

atething akiliple gullhang ahikitne.
when aged changing (skin) young man would have become again.

Once upon a time animals and men used to change their skins. As it was not regarded as fair[1] a contract was arranged between the toad and the lizard, the first of which to say the word was to have the privilege of changing skins. The lizard said "Snake change, lizard change" and meanwhile the toad said "Man change, toad change" but he was slower. For this reason snakes and lizards change their skin, but man cannot. If he could he would never become old, for when ageing he would change his skin and become young again.

---

[1] That is to the reptiles, who did not change their skins then. The toad is apparently not classed with the reptiles, so perhaps the Thado has not observed that he also changes his skin. Legends of this sort about death are, of course, widespread (*vide* Frazer, *Folk-lore in the Old Testament*, Vol. I, ch. ii), but the Kenharingan version (Evans, *Among Primitive Peoples in Borneo*, 176) may be compared with this one.

iii. The Dao-Sharpening.

Chim-that-the.

Chimthatpan[1] chim athatle kaikongin atôh ahŏlle.
Dao-sharpener dao sharpening craw-fish fundament prodding
Chimthatpan gova ji aban. Gova ji
Dao-sharpener bamboo tip-end sliced. Bamboo tip-end
apa ngei akhoe Apa akithaile chenai
jungle fowl's cheek pricked jungle fowl scuttling red ant
athaidoh-in chenai avāle ngălchăngpa[1]
having scratched up red ant running along wild Boar's
tīl apetle ngalchangpa akitŏmle ba chen-na
testicle biting wild Boar rushing about bat's abiding place
shaishophung ashulhun; ba alengle saipipa kul-a
wild banana tree overturned bat flying Elephant's ear in
alenglutne saipipa[2] akitomle meithainu in ashulhue
flying into Elephant rushing off widow house knocked down.
Meithainun "Saipipa, ida ka-in na-shulhu-
widow Mr. elephant why my house have you knocked
ham?" Saipipan "Ba ka-kul-a alenglutnin." "Ba,
down? Elephant Bat my ear in having flown into. Bat,
ida saipipa kul-a na-lenglutham?" Ngalchangpan
why Elephant's ear-in you fly into? Mr. wild boar
ka-chenna shaishophung ashulhue." "Ngalchangpa,
my living place wild banana tree overturned. Mr. wild boar,

---

[1] *Pa* suffixed to the names of animals or persons is a sort of honorific = Mr. or the "Brer" of Brer Rabbit, etc., in Uncle Remus.

ida ba chenna shaishophung na-shuhlhuham ?"
why bat's living place wild banana tree you overturn ?
Chenaiyin ka-til apetnin." "Chenai, ida ngal-
Red ant my testicle having bitten. Red ant, why Mr. wild
changpa til na-petham ?" "Apan ei-thaidoh-e."
boar's testicle you bite ? Jungle fowl me scratched up.
Apa, ida chenai na-thaidohham ?" "Gova ji-
Jungle fowl, why red ant you scratch up ? Bamboo tip-
in ka-ngei akhôe." "Gova ji, ida apa ngei
end my cheek pricked. Bamboo tip, why jungle fowl's cheek
na-khôham ?" "Chimthatpan ei-bane." "Chimthatpa,
you prick ? Dao-sharpener me sliced. Dao-sharpener,
ida gova-ji na-banham?" "Kaikongin ka-tôh
why bamboo-tip you slice ? Craw-fish my fundament
ahŏle." "Kaikong, ida Chimthatpa tôh na-
prodded. Craw-fish, why Dao sharpener's fundament you
hŏlham ?" Kaikongin asheiding ahetapui. Kaikongin
prod ? Craw-fish to say did not know. Crawfish
"Mei-a nei-golechun moltheipthumintin lilai-a nei-
In fire me if toasting will be fruitless in deep pool me
koilechun sanpiintin chapang deidei-
if placing will become very red boy will be delighted
umine" atiin, lilai-a alelutle "Ka-chenna lil
to watch said pool in jumping in my abiding place pool
thujinjen" atiin lilai-a achengthai.
very deep said pool in remained.

The Dao Sharpener was sharpening his dao when the Crawfish came and prodded his anus. Mr. Dao-sharpener sliced off the tip of a bamboo end. The tip of bamboo pricked the cheek of a jungle-fowl. The jungle-fowl, scuttling off, scratched out a red ant, which ran and bit Mr. Wild Boar in the testicles. The Wild Boar dashing about kicked down the wild plantain tree which was the bat's home. The bat flew out and fluttered into Mr. Elephant's ear. The elephant dashed off and knocked over the widow's house. "Mr. Elephant" said she, "why have you knocked down my house ?" Said the Elephant "The bat flew into my ear." "Bat, why did you fly into Mr. Elephant's ear ?" "Mr. Wild Boar threw down the wild plantain tree I live in." "Mr. Boar, why did you do that ? "The red ant bit my testicles." "Red ant, why did you bite the Boar's testicles ?" "The jungle fowl scratched me up." "Jungle Fowl, why did you scratch up the ant ?" "The bamboo tip pricked my cheek." "Bamboo tip, why did you prick the jungle-fowl's cheek." "Mr. Dao-sharpener sliced me off." "Mr. Dao-sharpener, why did you slice off the bamboo tip ?" "The Crawfish prodded my posterior." "Crawfish, why did you prod the

Dao-sharpener?" The Crawfish did not know what to answer. He said, "You can do nothing by toasting me at a fire. If you put me in a deep pool I shall turn very red,[1] and the boy will be charmed to see it." He jumped into the pool. "The pool I live in is very deep," said he, and in the pool he stayed.

[1] One cannot help suspecting condensation here and the loss of some such incident as that of Brer Fox and Brer Rabbit and the briar patch.

iv. The Elephant-apple Carrying.

Ailhanglhum 'puthe.

Nupani acha apu-y-in gamla ha lai-y-a
Wife-husband-pair child carrying in jungle yams to dig
achele, mun khat-na ailhanglum-thei,[1] amĭnin
going place at one elephant apple fruit having ripened
anehlŭnle chuin athei akishiemhlŭnin apuhlŭnle
eating then fruit having made up loads carrying
apujouhlŭntha-hih-in, ajipan "Athei keikhat dalha-
having been unable to carry husband fruit, part leave
hite" atile, ajinun "Ahipui, thei hibang thei-tui dalha-
saying wife no fruit very fruit-sweet will not
puihite. Icha[2] thai-jol-a[3] pengna atha peng-
leave our child womb-threshold-in birthplace new will be
nante, icha dalhahiting thei puhite" atiin. Acha ha
born our child for leaving fruit will carry said child yam
khu-shunga akoi-y-in athei apun ahunghlŭn-
hole-within having placed fruit having carried come to-
thai.[4] Chuin acha chu nishihle akăpkăpjin, nikhat
gether. Then child indeed all day having cried one day
hlominu amuthai. "Vahleningthing nenange" atiin,
wer-lioness found having brought up will eat having said
apuyin avahle alenphatnin nunga-ni-to
having brought having reared when grown big two girls with
akilômin, lo-a akunle[5] shunin lo
having accompanied to field in field going in the day field
ahloule anumeitenin asheipihlŭnin "nanu le
weeding the two girls having explained your mother and
napan naneolaiyin ha chovin napuihlŭnin
your father when you were small yam digging having taken
mun khat-na ailhanglhum thei aminin
you place one-at elephant apple fruit having ripened
ailhanglhum apulhonin nang na-dalhahlŭnin hlominun
elephant apple having taken you having left you wer-lioness
na-puyin 'kavahletthing nenange' atiin,
having taken you when I have reared big will eat said
navah ahi. Tunjong vai nalhunphateing kitomin-
is rearing you. Even now when you get back home having
lang in-shung na-lutlole phapunte.

become terrific into house you not entering will not be well.

Hlominu kot-sa kot-lhanga[6] apangin
Wer-lioness on one side and the other of the door waiting

nathatding nague." Chuin amajong inshung
to kill you wishes you Then he too into the house

alutdingteing akitomin alutle hlominu akichan
when entering becoming terrific entering wer-lioness being

athat-ngamthapui. Chujovin amipan hlominu
frightened kill was not brave. Then the man wer-lion-

athatthai. Chuin amajong anu le apa-koma achein-
ess killed. Then he too mother and father-near went

"Thushim sheijinge" atiin, masanga akhanchanu asheile,
Story will tell said first beginning having

anu le apa akăpthai. Chuin anu acheïn
said mother and father wept. Then mother having gone

athei agasatkeïn anăp anit-khumin sampôn
fruit having cut in half blew her nose[7] hair-combings

ahinkoiyin "Nangjea kacha kahiti-bol" atiin
having placed on account of you my child thus did said

ahungin achapa-to mun-khat achengtave. Hiche-
having come son together with dwelt. Thence-

kalchun ailhanglhum thei-shunga apon-khu sampôn
forward elephant apple fruit within filaments hair-combings

ahiin amugil aum-khu anap ahiin.
are kernel that is phlegm of the nose is.

A married couple carrying their child went into the jungle to dig for yams. At one place they found some ripe elephant-apples[1] and ate the fruit and made up loads of what remained but found them too heavy to carry. The husband said "Leave some of the fruit," but the wife said "No, the fruit is very sweet, we won't leave it. More children will be born to us from the womb that bore this. Let us leave the child and take the fruit." So they put the child in a yam-hole and carried the fruit home. The child cried all day long, and one day a wer-lioness found it and said " I will bring this up, and eat it." So she took it and reared it. When the child had grown big he went to the fields with two girls and while weeding the field during the day the girls told him how his parents had taken him a-yam-digging when an infant and had left him behind to take ripe elephant-apples, and how the wer-lioness had found him and was rearing him to eat him. " Even now," said they, " when you get back home you had better go into the house looking very ferocious, for the wer-lioness is waiting inside the door on this side or on that wishful to kill you." So when he went into the house he was very ferocious, and the wer-lioness was scared and dared not attack him. Then he himself killed the wer-lioness, and he went to his parents, and he said "I will tell you a tale." And when he told them the beginning of it, they wept. Then his mother left them and cut in half an elephant apple and blew her nose and put the phlegm and the combings of her hair into it, and said "For your sake, my child, I do this." And she came back and they all dwelt together, and from that time forward the hair-combings are to be found as the fibres of the elephant-apple and the rheum of the nose is its kernel.

---

1 **Ailhanglhum** is the tree *Dillenia indica*, the "**o-thenga**" of the Assamese, having a big heavy green fruit, with a very fibrous flesh and a slimy kernel.

2 **I-cha—i** is the dual form of the possessive pronoun of the first person.

3 **Thai** is all the abdomen below the naval; **jol** is usually a horizontal stick laid on two uprights as in the doorway made for ceremonial purposes outside a village, but it may be also used for a horizontal stick similarly placed on the ground.

4 **Hlün** here is the root implying accompaniment, and in this as in several preceding verbs gives a dual sense.

5 **Kun** is the root which implies leaving the house, to go to work or to hunt, trade, etc., the departure from the house being the essential sense conveyed.

6 **Kotsa kotlhanga,** i.e., on each side of the door inside the house, not outside and inside the door. Kotsa is the right hand side of the door when facing it from the inside and **Kotlhang** is the left hand side. The **hlominu** is, I think, imagined as moving restlessly backwards and forwards inside the door of the house (? lashing her tail).

7 **Anăp**=mucous from the nose, **anit** is the act of blowing one's nose by wringing it with the finger and thumb and snorting, **khum** is the act of putting inside a receptacle.

V. Khutshibi.

Meitai khat achah pashal khat aumthai. Avaichan
widow one child male one remained. Being poor

achahpan acha khat apuun, aju-a achele vadung khatna
child fowl one brought to sell going river one (at)

Milonghon gulpi khat ngoi-a aputave. Gulpi
Nagas[1] big-snake one in fish-trap had brought. Snake

chu Milonghon akihomtave. Chuin pashalpa
indeed Nagas had (agreed to) divide. Then boy

chu achen, "Thathiu'n! Ke acha lavin, gulpi
went do not kill my[2] fowl take snake

lhatavin!" ashei. Chuin amahon alhatave, aacha
release said. Then they released his fowl

alatave. Achuin Milonghon achethai. Ama pashalpa
took. Then Nagas went. He boy

alungdongin vadung-a achelele chuin vadung-a mi
grieving river-in going along then river-in man

khat-to akishutoin. Mipan "Hungin!" atie. Anung-a
one met. Man Come said after him

achele " Gulpa, nang umhihlechun ke Milonghon
going Friend you if not remaining me Nagas
eithatding ahitan. Nang-in nihin sātthai.[3] **Hungin**
me-about to kill were you my life saved. Come
Ka-in-a cheite." Achehlunle lampa agulpan asheiin
my-house-in will go. Going together on path friend said
" Gulpa, ka-nu le ka-pan thilkeo aphapha
Friend my mother and my father property very good
pejonglechun kilahih-in. Ka-nu mecha khutjem
if giving do not take my mother little finger ring[4]
'eipen' tithang" atie. Chuin achelhunle a-in-kom
give me say said. Then going together his house near
aphalhunin amipa alut ngămtapui Chuin agulpan
having reached the man enter was not brave. Then friend
" Ven, gulpa, chung-a vakol lengpikhu" atile chuin
look friend above stork[5] fly big there said then
agulpan avetle avetka-in akengnin amanin lilaia
friend looking while looking legs both seizing in pool
alutpithai. Chuin alutle anoi ahule chuin agulpan
made enter. then entering below being dry then friend
akhănna anu-apa -koma asheile, anu-apan
experiences mother-father with speaking mother-father
atile " Ka-nao, na-gulpao nahinsat. Tun ka-in-a
saying my son, your friend life-saved. Now my house in
thilkeo nadeidei kiputhang" Chuin aman
property you wish-wish take away[6] Then he
" Hepi-hepu, ke mi vaicha ka-i-to
Grandmother and father I man poor me[7]
kilommopunthe nakhut mecha nakipu khutjem chu
cannot but befit[8] your hand little finger wear ring that
ei-pethang !" atile ; anomtapui. Chuin agulpan
me-give said (she) was not willing. Then friend
Henu, napelole chekiningthing .
Mother, you not giving having gone back
kaŏhna-a ohkithangi kei-shanga
my-be-trapped-place-in will be trapped again me-above
nakhutjem na-itjohle." Chuin anu " Ahile, Icha
your ring you choosing. Then his mother it being so my child
iitjohhidam" atiin, akhutjem apethai. Chuin mipan
will rather choose said ring gave then the man
ahinpuin ahungthai.
having taken came.

Ahunglhunphatnin anukoma " Henu, kōng
at the time of arriving back his mother-with Mother, dish
hinlān" atile anun " Ima-beh-in kong
bring saying his mother " There being nothing dish
kalāīn ipiding ham ?" Chuin anu kong
I having brought what for eh ? Then mother dish

alan apele, akōng-gei chu akhutjemin
having brought giving dish-rim ring-by
akīvin, bu le me akong-a ahungdimin
having struck rice and curry in dish having appeared
anehlunthai. Chujuvin ajiding adonghlunthai
they two ate. Thereafter for wife they two asked
Anumeithen shūmtam shieltam dapi
Relations-in-law many rupees many mithun big gong
dabu kichăng kichung angeole anu
little gongs[9] single bead string of beads asking mother
alung adongin,[10] "Hijat thilkeo jānkhăt-kaä
heart having searched This much property within one night
nahinkoile kăchā kipuithang." Ama-nu
you depositing my daughter take-in-exchange. His mother
alung adong akăpthai. "I-in-a bu-bel bon
heart Search wept. In my house rice-plate even
umloa, mān ijad huiya kilādeham?" atiin
is-not price so much whence am to bring having said
achethai. Alhunphatnin achapan anu adongthai
went. At time of arriving boy mother asked
"Nape naüm?" ati. "Epenai ahivangin shum-le
Did you give said to give though be rupees and
shiel tampi angeove," atile, achapan "Ipipiham
mithun much demanded saying boy how
sheithang," asheithai. Chuin akhutjemin akovin
say said. Then ring (by) called
jankhat-kāïn ange ejadjed akoithai. Chuin anumeinu
one night-within ask as much as placed then girl
akipuithai. Chuin ashu-akol tampi ahithai. Chuin
brought back then retinue much was then
haosha[11] ahithai.
chief was.

Nikhat ashuhon loulhoh vetdinga achele, akhutjem
One day servants field-clean to look at going ring
in-a kongvo-shunga akoiin ahaithai. Ahungkaïn
in house bag inside[12] having placed lost Before came
mikhat akhutjem aguthai. Ahunglhunphatnin
a man ring stole. At time of coming and arriving
Khutshibi[4] aholmothai Chuin alung adongin
Khutshibi searched in vain then heart having searched
awicha le amengcha angoe, "Naholdohlole nangni
dog and cat put to You not search find if you two
kathatding." Chuin awicha-le amengcha aholin
I will kill Then dog and cat searching
achehlunthai. Wichan "Kanao mengcha,
went together. Dog (by) My younger brother cat
itidinghitam?" Mengchan "Hëu, pal-kom
how is this going to be? Cat (by) Elder brother fence-near

chăn!" hiti. Achanhlunle yucha khat
wait so said. Having lain in wait together rat one
amanthai. Mengchan "Hëu, nang alulang
caught Cat (by) Elder brother you head side
chăngin kei atholang chăngding netahite"
taking I fundament side will take we (two) will eat
atile, yuchan "Ei-nehlunhih-in na-titi
saying rat (by) Me-you two don't eat if your whatever
hol-pe-in" atile, "Kapu Khutshibi min
will search give saying My grand-father Khutshibi man (by)
agun, hi-chu galan." Yuchan le noi-a ku ashin
stole this bring rat earth under hole burrowing
a-in noia achedoh-in alel atuvangin
house under having emerged "jappa"[13] having pierced
aholle; amupui; chuin amipa-chung aholle;
searched did not find then man-over searched
akhutna akibun; ahinlan; mengcha-le wicha apethai.
on hand remaining having taken eat and dog gave
Chuin mengchan "Ken ka-mei-a pung" atile. Wichan
Then cat (by) I my-tail-on will carry said dog (by)
"Ken ka-kam-a möm-nang"[14] atile. Wichan amömin
I my-jaws-in will hold saying dog (by) having held
ahunghlunle vadung khatna lilai-a nga amu; ahăple
going together river one pool-in fish saw barking
Khutshibi ahlalutnin; nga-meibong khatnin avălthai.
Khutshibi fell in broken-tailed-fish[15] one (by) swallowed
Chuin wichan "Kanao, i-itiding-hitam?" atile.
then dog (by) My yr. brother what about it saying
Mengchan "Hëu, vadung chan" hiti.
cat (by) Elder brother river Lie in wait thus
Achanhlunle satuilu te-nupa
Having lain in wait together other male and female
amanhluthai. Mengchan "Hëu, nangin achal
they two caught cat (by) Elder brother you (by) male
nenlang, ken anu nenge" atile. Satuilu tenupa
if eat I (by) female will eat saying otter pair
"Ei nehlunhih-in natiti bolpiinge" atile.
me do not having eaten you whatever will carry out saying
"Hea ngameibong khun kapu Khutshibi
there broken-tailed-fish that my grand-father Khutshibi
avălle, galan!" Satuilunin agamanin athătnin
swallowing bring otter (by) having caught having killed
agil ashouvin akhutjem aladohthai.
stomach having disembowelled ring brought out
Shoung-chunga aphoule mu-vanlai-in ahunghlohthai.
stone-on drying kite (by) came-snatched.
Chuin wichan "Kanao, itiding hitam? atiin, meng-
Then dog My younger brother what about it? said Cat

chan "Hëu! **Lhangdung changhiti," atile. Achang-**
Elder brother hill Let us go up said. On re-
lhunle khuili tenupa amanlhunthai.
aching the top marten male and female succeeded in catching.
Chuin mengchan "Hëu! nangin achal nenlang
Then cat Elder brother you male eating
ken anu nenge", atile. Khuili tenupa "Ei nehlun-
I female will eat said. Marten pair Us do not
hi-in! natiti bolpiding" atile. Khua mu-
eat whatever you say will do said. There kite
vanlai khun kăpu khutshibi ahlohin, galan!" atile
that father Khutshibi has seized, catch said
Chuin khuili anchălpa thinga akalin anupan
Then marten male on a tree having climbed female
toula mu lie atōpan, doi-y-in abolhlunin
on ground kite shadow sat on with magic having done
amanlhunthai. Amu athătnin akhutjem ala-
succeeded in catching. Kite having killed ring took
dohthai. Chuin mengcha apethai. Menncha le
out. Then cat gave. Cat and
wichan ahinpun ahunghlunle lămpa mengchan
dog carrying while coming on path cat
wicha-hienga "Ilhunthing ipun 'Meh tuwi
to the dog When we have arrived grandfather viands nice
bu tuwi hung nehlunin' tiintin, itivekuyongle
rice nice come you two eat will say although calling very persistently
ganepu-hi-ti" atiin. Achelhunle alhunlhunin
don't go eat up said. When they arrived as soon as arrived
apun bu nedinga akule. Iiti akuvangin mengcha
master rice to eat called. Thus on calling cat
anompui: wicha achein aganethai. Chuin
did not obey dog having gone ate up. Then
wicha ahungdohle kimpuma mengcha-to
dog when coming out in the porch with the cat
akidilthai. Hichekalchung wicha le mengcha akitomôthai
fought. Thenceforward dog and cat have not agreed.

---

1 **Milong** is used more particularly for Kabuis and Kachha Nagas, but is also used generally for any Naga as distinct from a Kuki or a Manipuri.

2 **Ke**—an alternative form for **Ka**, probably used here to avoid the awkwardness of identical vowels in juxta position.

3 **Nihinsatthai**=(You) have saved my life.
Nahinsatthai=You have saved (his) life.
Kahinsatthai=I have saved (your) life.

4 **Khutjem**=literally "hand-ornament"—**Khut**='hand,' **jem**='gem.' The exact meaning of **Khutshibi** I have been unable to

ascertain. It is the name given to the ring or to the genius of the ring.

5 **Vakol**—a bird not certainly identified; said to be seen flying over head in line and wedge formations at a very great height indeed, to be long-legged and of large size, though not like the **Mulaopi** (?=the roc) which can carry off men.

6 This **ki**-always conveys a reciprocal sense and here implies "in exchange for what you have done"

7 **Ka-ito**—the *i* gives a sort of deprecatory emphasis and the sense conveyed here is "as it is only me, a very humble individual".

8 **Kilom**='becoming' (precisely).

mo=not

Punthe=cannot be.

The idea conveyed is that the meanest ornament will fitly become so humble an individual. Thado women commonly wear on their fingers brass wire rings of no value at all.

9 **Dabu** is a set of three small gongs which should be in tune at a semitone apart.

10 **Adong** by itself='ask,' only with **alung** ('heart') does it mean 'be troubled.'

11 **Hao**='rich'

sha= (1) 'thick', (2) 'animals'. Probably the first meaning is the one in this compound which implies a man of substance

12 **Kongvo**=a small flat bag-like basket of woven cane used, in particular, by women when sowing grain.

13 **Alel**=the tall covered basket used for carrying and storing property. It is made of cane and bamboo in two thicknesses with bamboo leaves in between to keep it water-proof. For illustration *vide* Shakespear *Lushei Kuki Clans*, page 10.

14 **Mŏm**=to carry in the mouth without biting; **pit**=to carry in the closed teeth.

15 Apparently a particular individual, not a species.

There was a widow with an only son. As they were in need, the boy took a fowl to sell, and coming to a river found some Nagas who had got a big snake in a trap, and had agreed to divide it. So the boy went up to them and said "Don't kill it, take my fowl and let the snake go," so they let it go and accepted the fowl, and went away. While the boy was walking sorrowfully along the bed of the river, a man met him. "Come", said the man, and, as the boy followed him, "my friend, only for you the Nagas would have killed me. You have saved my life. Come! let us go to my house." As they went along together the stranger said to his companion, "Friend, whatever valuables my parents offer you, don't take them. Ask for the ring on my mother's little finger." But when they got near the stranger's house the boy was afraid to enter, so the companion said "Look, friend, at that great stork[1] flying up there," and as he was looking he caught both legs and pulled him into the pool. Down below it was dry and when the stranger had told his parents his

---

1 See above note 5.

adventure they said "My son, you saved your friend's life. In return take anything in this house that you fancy." So he replied "Grand-parents, I am a poor man; the ring on your little finger is fitting enough for such as I.[1] Give that to me" said he, but she was reluctant to comply. Then his friend said "Mother, if you don't give it I will go back and get caught again in the trap as before, for you will be valuing your ring above me." On that his mother said "Very well, my child, I would rather have you," and gave the boy the ring, and he took it and went home.

As soon as he got home he said to his mother "Mother, bring a dish," she answered "and when I have brought it, what use?—and we with nothing to put in it." But when his mother had brought the dish he tapped with the ring on the brim of the dish, and rice and curry appeared in the dish and the two of them ate it. By and by the two of them asked for a girl as a wife for the boy, but as the girl's relatives asked much cash and many mithun, big gongs, little gongs in sets,[2] single beads, and bead necklaces the heart of the mother was troubled. "This property you must hand over to us by to-morrow morning" said they "if you want our daughter in exchange." So the boy's mother's heart was troubled, and she wept. "And me without one rice-dish in my house" said she "where will I get so great a price?" and with that she went home. When she arrived the boy asked his mother, "Did you give the price?" Said he, "Even if I would be giving it" said she "they asked very many rupees and mithun." "Tell me how much," said the boy, and with the help of the ring he produced all that was asked within one night, so the bride was brought back, and the boy became a chief with many retainers.

One day when going to see his servants weeding his field he missed his ring, which he had put in a bag[3] in his house. A man stole the ring during his absence. As soon as he got home he searched for Khutshibi, but in vain. Then in his trouble he put it to his dog and his cat "If you two do not search for and find (Khutshibi), I will kill you" said he, so the dog and the cat went a-searching together. Said the dog "Young cat, my lad, what about it?" "Sir," said the cat, "let us hide by the fence," so they lay in wait together and caught a rat. "Sir", said the cat, "let you start at the head and I will start at the tail, and between us we will eat him up." Said the rat "Please don't eat me, you two, and I will find and give you whatever you want." "A man has stolen grand-father Khutshibi", was the answer, "fetch it!" The rat burrowed underground and came up inside the man's house, and gnawed a hole into and searched

---

1 See above note 8.
2 ,, ,, ,, 9.
3 ,, ,, ,, 12.

his clothes-basket,[1] but did not find the ring, so then he searched the man's person and found that he was wearing the ring, so he took it and gave it to the cat and the dog and the cat said "I will carry it on my tail" but the dog said "I will carry it in my mouth," and as he was carrying it they saw a fish in a pool in a river and he barked at it and Khutshibi fell into the river and a broken-tailed fish[2] swallowed it. Then the dog said "My boy, what about it?" "Hide by the river, Sir", said the cat. They did so and caught a pair of otters. "If you will eat the dog otter, sir, I will eat the bitch" said the cat. "Don't eat us," said the otters, "and we will do whatever you tell us." "Bring us that there broken-tailed fish that has swallowed our grandfather Khutshibi." The otters caught the fish, killed it, disembowelled it and got out the ring. As it was drying on a stone a kite swooped down and took it. "What about it, young man?" said the dog. "Let us climb that hill, sir" said the cat, and on reaching the top they managed to catch a pair of martens. Said the cat "Let you eat the jack, sir, and I will eat the jill," but the martens said "Don't eat us, and we will do whatever you wish." "That kite there has seized Father Khutshibi; catch him" said they. Then the male marten climbed a tree and the female sat on the shadow of the kite on the ground, and by using magic they succeeded between them in catching the kite. So they killed the kite and extracted the ring and gave it to the cat. While the cat and the dog were carrying it along the homeward path, the cat said to the dog "When we get home our master will call us both to come and have a really good meal. However much he keeps on calling don't you go and eat it up." The moment they got in their master called them to come and eat, and although he called them thus the cat did not obey, but the dog went and ate it up. Then as the dog was coming out he fought with the cat in the porch. Since that time the dog and the cat have not agreed together.

N.B.—An elaborate version of this theme appears in Bompas' *Folklore of the Santal Parganas*, XXII— 'Sita and his Animals', as well as an impoverished one in XXXIII, 'Ramai and the Animals'.

vi. The Vine-cutters.

Lengbanthe.

Pasal khat acha pasal sagi ahi. Ni khat
Male one children male seven were. Day one
lo avatnule alo laia lengpe[1] alen khat
field when cutting field in midst vine great one

[1] See above note 13.
[2] ,, ,, ,, 15.

aume. Apavin "Chathe, hiche lengpe ki-bănthetnu-
was. Father children this vine let us cut for
hite! Abăn-than-lolo Hlo-kotna [2] kithunghinte."
a wager! The one who does not cut right through lion's door way shall sit.

Ni khat anu chimpong nolin apangin
Day one mother dao to sharpen set to
achathe-a heimthetnin anolin apava akalelangin [3]
children's extremely sharp having sharpened father's wrong side
anolin achevin akibanthetnule achathen abanthanin
having sharpened having gone cutting for a wager children having cut through
apavin abanthanjoupui. Chuin achathen "Hepa,
father did not cut through. Then children Father
chedathan." Apan "Ithisha ida jou kishei-
do not go. Father My spoken pledge why false say
dam?" atiin. Achein Hlokotna akithungthai.
again said. Going Lion's doorway sat in.
Sanga [4] ahungin "Koi nahim ka-kotna kithung?
Wild cat coming Who you? my doorway sit
nengkhate" atiin, aman "Ei-nethang! Ka-pulading
will eat said He Eat me Will come to fetch me
chunga āshijad noia telnajad ka-chimthatna
above stars how many below leaves how many my dao sharpener
Aichi-shoung [5] ka-thal shuina vŏ-buh [6] tei"
Aichi stone my arrow shavings boar's lair so many
atile, sangain akichan ajamthai. Humpi ahungkithai.
saying wild cat afraid ran. Tiger came along
"Koi nahim ka-kotna kithung? nengkhate" atiin,
who you my doorway sit will eat having said
aman "Ei-nethang! Ka-pulading chunga
he Eat me Will come to fetch me above
ashi-jad noia telna-jad, ka-chimthatna
stars how many below leaves how many my dao sharpener
Aichi-shoung, ka-thal shuina vo-buh tei"
Aichi-stone my arrow shavings boar's lair so many
atile, humpin akichan ajamthai. Chujovin hlo
saying tiger afraid ran. After that lion
ahungin, "Koi na-him ka-kotna kithung?
having come who you my doorway sit
nengkhate" atiin, aman "Ei-nethang! Ka-pulading
will eat having said he eat me. Will come to fetch me
chunga ashi-jad noia telna-jad, ka
above stars how many below leaves how many my

chim thatna Aichi-shoung, ka-thal shuina vo-buh
dao sharpener aichi-stone my arrow shavings boar's lair

tei" atile, hlo ahungin anethai. Chujovin
so many, said lion having come ate. After that

achathe pasal sagi apula achele, lampa
children male seven to fetch going path

ani-koma, ageipan, anin bu
father's sister with spent the night father's sister rice

le sa ju ashimpein akipuin achele,
and flesh liquor having prepared having taken going

ahlo in alhunlin janin hlopan
lion house having arrived in the night lion

naichim-hinga "Pachin, phel[7] gil" atiin,
to mouse Mr. mouse bow cut saying

naichim achein guphel agilin, ayingin pasal sagi
mouse going bow cutting in morning male seven

păl-lēa apangin hlopa-koma "Kă-pa na-ne
wall-on waiting lion-to My father you eaten

hungthohteimin" atile, hlopa ahung-dohle
shew how saying lion coming out

aguphel-a akāple, aguphel abonggămthai
with their bow shot (at) their bow broke utterly.

Chujovin hlopan athatgamthai. Chujovin anu
After that lion killed entirely. Then mother

alungdongmanin in-chunga[8]
having grieved at heart on the top of her the house

alumin akāle, Pathenpan guphel-a ape'le
lying down weeping God with bow shooting

agayin, chujovin ashophatnin acha pasal
impregnated then at the time of birth child male

ahin thi-kang[9] le thi-guphel-to asho'thai.
getting iron bean and iron bow-with was born.

Ahunglenphatnin agulhoñ-to kang-a
At time of becoming big with companions with bean

akikaple agulhon kang akapkein
making reciprocal shots companions' bean having struck

agulhon "Hiti hatnan na-pa le na-ute
companions thus strong if your father and your elder brethren

phu-latang!" Amayong anu-koma achein "Henu,
retaliate-bring So he to his mother going Mother,

Ka-pa le ka-ute ipin athatham?"
my father and my elder brothers what killed?

asheiyin Anun "Gaplēng-chan na-phatnin
having said his mother paddy drying platform like when you are

sheinange" atiin, achapa akite' loiloiloile
will say said her child quickly-measuring

gapleng-chan aphatthai. "Henu, tūn
rice drying platform like attained. Mother to-day
sheithang, gapleng-chan kaphatthai atile.
say rice-drying platform like I have attained saying
anun "Na-gullhanting sheinange." Chujovin
mother When you are adult will say. Then
agullhanphatnin anun "Na-pa le
at the time of becoming adult mother Your father and
na-ute thatna hlo ahi" atile,
your elder brothers killer lion is saying
"Aphulanching" atiin, athi-guphel akipu'in
Will revenge him saying iron-bow having taken
achele, lampa-a ani-koma ageipan
going path-on with father's sister having spent night
anin "Ka-nao, hoiya na-chedeham?" atile,
father's sister My child whither are you going saying
aman "Ka-pa le ka-ute phulading kahi,"
he My father and my brothers to revenge I am
anin "Ka-nao, Che-hih-in! Na-ute hijad-bon
aunt My child, do not go Your brothers as many as all
thigamthai. Na-changin thatjoupōnăthe" atiin,
are dead entirely. You alone will not be able to kill having said
aman "Ahivangin, chetheiyinge." Chuin anin
he nevertheless shall be able to go. Then aunt
"Na-ute le na-pa phu na-lajoudingle
your elder brothers and your father revenge if you will take in
shoung thătle-inlang ahunghla-ka-in
full stone throwing up before it has fallen back
ju-leng[10] khat chiep lhanlang chule ka-vocha thu
liquor mark one suck completing then my pig fist
shom[11] maninlang in-dung in-vai
ten seizing house length house breadth
ship-khup-minlang hiching chu na-boljoule,
pitching over this indeed if you do completely
na-ute le na-pa phu-lānăté." Aman ani
your brother and your father revenge shall bring. He aunt
shei-shei aboljouvin, chuin anin a-vocha
say-say having done completely then aunt her pig
athatpiin aposhain, ju alhohpiin satao
having killed made to carry liquor having siphoned animal's fat
um khat ashiempi "Hlopa in na-lhunteingle
gourd one prepared lion's house when you reach
ju pēnătin lhoung ong-ka-a[12] bulhanlung; nang
liquor will give machan hole-between pour completely your
ju doninlang. Sa penatin lhoung ong-ka-a
liquor drink. Flesh will give platform hole between
paimanginlang, nang sa nen Ju na-pe
having thrown away your flesh eat liquor you given

na-ute thi ahin, sa na-pe na-ute sa ahi."
your brothers' blood is flesh you given your flesh is
Chuin ama achele hlopa in alhunphatnin hlopan ju
then he going lion's house when reaching lion liquor
apein, aju abulhan ama ju
giving his liquor having poured away his liquor
adonin; sa ape'le, apaimangin ama
having drunken flesh when gave having thrown away his own
sa ane. Jahnin hlopan "Pachin, phel gil" atile,
flesh ate. At night lion Mr. mouse bow notch saying
pachinin "Hepu, ha bei-in." Janin hlopa acha
Mr. mouse Grand father tooth are not. At night lion fowl
ahungkhunle "Ki-ki-i-i, Chongpu ti-ni, jinpa
crowed out Cock-a-doodle-do Chongpu death-day stranger
hăt-ni" atile, hlopan aacha lol ame-e. Chuin
strength-day saying lion his fowl gullet squeezed. Then
acha akhunkitle "Ki-ki-i-i, Chongpu hat-ni,
fowl crowing again Cock-a-doodle-do Chongpu strength-day
jinpa ti-ni," atile, hlopan a-acha bu ape-e.
stranger death-day saying lion his fowl cooked rice gave
Ayingin amipan thing khat ahoh akho-in
Next morning the man tree a bark having stripped
akathouma satao-um athătke-in, ama apangin,
fork animal's fat gourd having broken [13] he waiting
ahlopa-koma "Ka-pa le ka-ute na-bol
to the lion My father and my elder brothers what you did
hungthohteimin!" Chuin ahlopa ahungdoh-in
come show how. Then the lion having come out
"Thohtaleng." Amei apongsāngin achople amipa
Will show. His tail having lifted jumping man
aman-diichet. Chun amipan aguphelin akam-hom
just failed to seize. Then man with bow maw-aperture
akaple alumthan, amipa akumding
shooting having lain (as though asleep) man to come down
akichan khuiva ahunlengin amipan "Pa-khui khuiva,
afraid bee coming flying man Mr. Honey Bee
kă-sā-kāp gavetteimin! Athiha ahingham
the animal I have killed please examine. Dead or alive
gavetteimin" Khuiva achein atoh vuvuatin, alu vuvuatin,
please see Bee going anus buzzing head buzzing
ashunga aluin athin hal-khat apon achethai. Chuin
inside entering liver a piece carrying went. Then
khuingal ahungkitnin amipan "Pa-khui Khuingal,
hornet coming along man Mr. Hornet Bee
ka-sa-kap gavetteimin! Athiha ahingham?"
the animal I have killed please look at Dead or alive
Khuingal achein atoh vuvu alu vuvu atiin ashunga
Hornet going anus buzz head buzz saying inside

aluin athin halkhat apon achethai. Chuin amipa
entering liver a piece carry went. Then man
ahungkumin ahlopa lu-to a-ute lu le
getting down lion head elder brothers' head head and
apa lu-to ahinpun ahungle ama khulche-ke-in
father's head bringing coming he during his peregrinations
anu min anagemjiin anun kot anakānin
mother man visiting-by-night mother door having fastened
a-in ahunglhunphatnin "Henu, kot nei-honin!"
the house when arriving at Mother, door open me
Anun, "Kacha na-hipui. Honpunge." "Henu, na-cha
mother my son you are not will not open Mother your son
ka-hinai. Nei-ta'sănlole tăpkung-a pătjăng janinlang
I am me if not believe at hearth thread having stretch-
ka-kāp-thănle na-cha hiingting, ka-kap-thanlole
ed I shoot dividing your son shall be if I do not shoot and
na-cha hipunge." Anun ajanin akaple
divide your child will not be Mother stretching shooting
akapthanin, ahivangin anu atha sang-hih-in,
shoot-dividing nevertheless mother true not believing
ahonpui. Amanjong anu-koma "Henu, yingkating
did not open. He to his mother Mother in the morning
shum-shung[14] venlang, āgil[15] venlang chule
on the paddy mortar look hen-roost look then
kolmung vetthan!" Yingka anu athouvin shum-shung
horizon look at Morning mother rising on the paddy-
avetle hlopa lu a-umin, agil avetle
mortar looking lion head being chicken-roost looking
achate le aji lu a-umin, kolmung avetle
sons and husband head being horizon looking at
achapa chimpongle aval amun, alungdonmanin, hlopa
son dao-shake flesh saw having grieved lion
muñmul ajoutnin akāle, akhutchal āttănin, athithai.[16]
whiskers stroking wept fore-finger having cut off died

---

1 **lengpe** a variety of wild grape.

2 **hlo** certainly means a lion, and it is a curious thing that several Assam hill-tribes whose habitat is far removed from that of lions should have such clear traditions of the animal. It has been suggested that the lion's range was very much further east than it now is before the intrusion of the tiger from the east, and the Indian lion, now limited to Kathiawar in the extreme west, seems to have been well known in the Central Provinces a hundred years ago. The Kuki however may have picked up his knowledge of it from the Mon or Burmese, who must have known of it through the intrusive Indian culture of the Talaings, and the Abor may have got his *via* Tibet. It is to be noted that Nagas have no word for lion and no tradition of it.

3 **akalelangin**, 'on the wrong side,' i.e., not on the back of the dao, but on the wrong side of the edge. The old type of Thado dao **(chimkol)** and the modern type of pseudo-kukri

pattern both have a plano-convex edge which must be sharpened on the convex side. Sharpening on the other side will merely blunt it. It can be used only with a downward stroke from the right or an upward one from the left unless specially made in the reverse form for a left-handed man. The long narrow curved Kuki blade derived from the Shan type (**chimjam**) has however, a normal cutting edge which is sharpened on both sides.

4 **sanga**—the leopard cat, *felis bengalensis*.

5 **Aichi-shoung**. The significance of this appears not to be known; **shoung** is a stone, but I could not get any explanation of **aichi**, except that **chi**=**hard**. **Ai**=a ceremony, but there seems to be no connection.

6 **vobuh**. The wild pig collect great piles of sticks and grass in the jungle, apparently as a protection against their natural enemies. Solitary boars sometimes sleep in them, and the sows farrow there.

7 **phel**—not the bow-string, as one might perhaps have expected, but the bow itself. The incident recalls Herodotus' account of the defeat of Senacherib King of Assyria. The old Testament merely says that the Assyrians were smitten by the Angel of the Lord (II Kings, xix, 35; II Chron, xxxii, 21; Isaiah, xxxvii, 36) so that "When they arose early in the morning behold they were all dead men," but Herodotus (II, 141) says that a number of field-mice poured in upon them and devoured their quivers and bows, and the handles of their shields, so that on the next day, when they fled bereft of arms, many were slaughtered.

8 **in-chunga**—'on the house top'—A Thado house has a slanting roof, ill fitted for reclining, nor is it usual for persons to climb them for that purpose, though not of course, impossible. The visualization like some others in this story, e.g., that of the seven sons sitting on the wall, rather suggests a more solid material culture, the flat roofs of a brick-built city, perhaps, such as the walled city of their fore-fathers of which the Chins sang to Major Fryer (*Khyeng People of the Sandoway District, Arakan*, J.A.S. 1 of 1875).

9 **kang**. This bean is a seed like a very large flat horse-chestnut, and comes from the gigantic pod of the sword-bean creeper *Entada scandens*. It is used throughout the Assam hills, at any rate south of the Brahmaputra, for games in which a competitor has to strike the beans set up by others. In Manipur an ivory disc is used. The Karens of Burma know the game with the seeds, and Cole (*The Tinguian*, p. 277) describes from the Philippine Islands a form of the same game identical with one form popular among the Angami. It extends to Oceania. In Fiji the bean is called *walai* and the game *lávo* (Deane, *Fijian Society*, p. 16), *cf.* the Sema name *alaa*. In Samoa it is played with cocoanut discs (Brown, *Melanesian and Polynesians*, p. 341). Among the Thado, as among most Assam hill tribes, the game is seasonal, and is only played between the harvest and the sowing, though McCulloch notes that in Manipur, where it is played with an ivory disc and beans and called **Kang-sânaba**, "it is played only in the spring" *Account of the Valley of Munnipore*, p. 26).

10 **ju-leng**, "peg," *v. supra*, p. 93 n. 4.

11 **thu shom**, lit.=10 fists. A pig is measured by taping its girth behind the shoulders with a sliver of bamboo, straightening out the resulting circumference and halving it by doubling the tape and measuring that half against the height of the

closed fist across the fingers. A ten fist pig therefore, is one that has a girth of twenty fists round the upper ribs.

12 **ongka,**—the cracks between the planking, or the bamboos, of the raised floor of the house.

13 **athatke**—he broke the gourd that the fat might run down the tree trunk and make it slippery so that the lion should be unable to climb.

14 **shum-shung**—paddy mortar—usually a vertical section of a tree-trunk hollowed in the middle.

15 **agil**—hen-roost—a platform usually above the door and under the eaves of the front gable of the house communicating by a small door with a loft in the roof of the house cut off from the living room by a mat partition. Almost all Thado houses have this accommodation for their fowls.

16 And on this account, it is said, a Thado killing a tiger always singes the whiskers, and makes quite sure that they shall cut off no fingers.

There was a man who had seven sons. One day when clearing a field they beheld a great vine in the midst of it. Said the father "My sons, let us make a contest of cutting this, and the one that fails to cut clean through, let him go and sit in the gateway of the lion." [1] So on a day his wife, having set herself to whet, whetted her children's daos exceeding sharp, but their father's she whetted on the wrong side.. [2] So they went to their cutting contest and the sons cut through the vine, but the father cut not through it. Said the sons, "Father, do not go," but their father said "Why belie the word I gave?" So he went to the lion's gateway and sat there. A wild cat [3] came by. "Who are you that sit in my gateway? I will eat you" it said, and the man answered "Eat me! as the stars in the heavens, as the leaves upon the earth, so is the number of those that will come to find me; my sword has been whetted on the Aichi-stone, [4] and the whittlings from my arrows equalled the lairs of wild swine [5] in volume." The wild cat was afraid and fled. A tiger came. "Who are you that sit in my gateway? I will eat you" said he. The man repeated his former saying, and the tiger was afraid and fled. Then the lion came. "Who are you that sit in my gateway? I will eat you" he said. The man said "Eat me! As the stars in the heavens, as the leaves upon earth, so is the number of those that will come to find me; my sword has been whetted on the Aichi-stone, and the whittlings from my arrows equalled the lairs of wild swine in volume." The lion came and ate him.

Thereafter the seven sons went in search of him. They slept on the way at the house of their father's sister, and she got ready rice and meat and drink, and they took it and came to the house of the lion. In the night the lion said to the mouse

---

NOTES [1] to [5]—*v. supra.*

"Mr. Mouse, gnaw bows."[9] So the mouse went and gnawed their bows. In the morning the seven young men waited on the wall, and called to the lion "Show us how you ate our father," and the lion came out and they drew their bows but the bows brake in twain. Then the lion made an end of them. Then their mother grieving in her heart lay on her house-top [10] and wept, and God loosed His bow at her, and caused her to conceive. And when her child was born he was a man-child and he had with him at birth an iron bean [11] and iron bow withal. And when he was grown and played with his fellows, he used always in his turn to strike his play-fellows' beans with his bean, till they said "If you are so strong, go and take revenge for your father and your brethren." So he went to his mother and said "Mother, what killed my father and my brothers?" "When you are as high as the platform for drying the paddy, I will tell you" said she. The boy grew up quickly to the height of the platform. "Mother" he said "tell me to-day. I have reached the platform," but she said "When you are a man I will tell you." Then when he became a man, his mother said to him "The slayer of your father and your brethren is the lion." "I will take revenge" said he, so he took his iron bow and set forth and by the way he spent the night at the house of his father's sister. "My child," she said "Whither goest thou?" He said "I go to avenge my father and my brothers." Said his aunt "My child, do not go. Your brothers, every one of them, are utterly cut off. You are alone, and alone you cannot kill him." But he answered "Nevertheless I can undertake it." Then his aunt said "If you would avenge in full your father and your brothers let you throw up a stone, and before it has fallen back to earth, drink this jar empty down to the peg,[12] then catch that pig of mine, twenty palms in girth,[13] and pitch it over the length of the house and over the breadth of the house. If you can accomplish this, then indeed shall you take revenge for your brothers and your father." And all that his aunt had said he did. So she killed her pig and gave it him to take with him, and she drew off wine * for him and made him ready a gourd full of fat (saying) "When you reach the house of the lion he will give you wine; pour it all down a gap in the platform [12]; drink your own wine. He will give you meat; cast it away through a gap in the platform [12]; eat your own meat. The wine he gives you is your brethren's blood, and the flesh the flesh of your brothers." Then he went to the house of the lion, and when he came there the lion gave him wine, and he poured it away and drank his own wine; he gave him meat, and he cast it away and ate his own meat. At night the lion said "Mr. Mouse, notch bow,"

NOTES [9] to [14]—*v. supra.*

* *i. e.*, rice wine, of course; commonly translated as "rice-beer," but it is much more wine than beer.

and master mouse came back and said "My Lord, I have no teeth left." In the night the lion's cock crew with a "Cock-a-doodle-do, Chongpu's death day, stranger's strength day," and the lion squeezed his gullet. Then the cock crew again "Cock-a-doodle-do, Chongpu's strength day, stranger's death day," and the lion fed him. On the morrow the man stripped the bark off a tree and broke the gourd of fat at the fork [13] (in which he sat) and waited. He called out to the lion "Show that which you did to my father and my brothers." Then the lion came forth with "I will show." And he lashed his tail and leaped at the man and well nigh seized him. Then the man shot with his bow into the open maw, and the lion lay still. But the man was afraid to come down, and as there came by a bee flying he called to him "Pray, Mr. Honey Bee, look at that animal I have shot, whether it be dead or alive." The bee went and buzzed at its vent, buzzed at its head, and went inside and flew off with a scrap of the liver. Then there came by a hornet; said the man, "Pray Mr. Hornet Bee, look at that animal I have shot, is it dead or alive?" The hornet went and made a buzzing at the vent and a buzzing at the head and went inside and carried off a scrap of the liver. Then the man came down and took the lion's head and took the heads of his brothers and his father and brought them home. Now while he was away a man had been visiting his mother by night and she had fastened the door and when her son arrived the house was shut and he cried "Mother, open me the door." "You are not my son," she answered, "I will not open." "Mother" said he, "I am indeed your son. If you believe me not stretch a thread across the hearth and if I shoot at * and cut the thread you will know that I am your son, and if I fail to sever it, I shall be no child of yours. She stretched the thread, he shot it in two, but nevertheless she did not believe him and opened not. So he said to his mother "Mother, when dawn comes look on the paddy mortar, [14] look on the hen-roost [15] and then look towards the horizon." Early his mother rose and looked on the paddy mortar, and the lion's head was there, and she looked on the hen-roost, and her sons' and husband's heads were there, and she looked at the horizon, and her youngest son was flashing his dao to her and she saw the gleam of it, and her heart was troubled and she wept. And as she wept she was stroking the lion's whiskers, and she cut off her fore-finger thereby and died.[16]

Notes [13] to [16]—*v. supra.*

* The arrow would be aimed through the interstices of the bamboo matting of the wall.

vii. The Magic Fiddle.[1]

There was once a king[2] who had seven wives and seven mares. The seven wives were pregnant for seven years and the seven mares were for seven years in foal. On this account he was troubled at heart and went to ask the advice of a priest[3] in the plains. The priest told him to keep his seven wives and seven mares at a place seven days' journey distant from him, on which they would all give birth within seven days, "And when you look on your son," said he, "you will go blind."

After all that he was washing his face one day, when his son came by on horseback. On looking up to see who it was, he went blind. Then he called his son and told him to bring to him his mother and the other wives.[4] He brought them. After that the son of a widow in the village had a dream. He dreamed that God[5] appeared to him and told him to go and cure the King's eyes. He said "I am a poor man, how can I go and cure them?" God said "Go to that range of hills. There there is a tree on which sits a roc[6] and a tree whereon perches a great horned owl. Cut down these two trees and make of one a fiddle and of the other a boat and a paddle."[7] Next morning he went to the king and said "Give me serving men and I will perform a ceremony that will cure you of your blindness." The king gave him serving men and he took them to the range of hills. There he felled the two trees and made the implements as God had instructed him. When they were finished there was nothing more to be done. He was warned in a dream to kill a pair of goats and a pair of pigeons

---

1 The Magic Fiddle—in Thado **Shilangda adoi**. For **Shilangda** v. Appendix vi. There seems to be a definite purpose in the selection of this instrument to carry the hero in flight, as it seems to be always represented with a bird carved at the end of the key-board, while the shape of the body of the instrument appears to imitate the wings and tail of a bird.

2 **Lengpa** is the genuine Thado word for a king or a ruling prince. Like many expressions in this tale, however, its use envisages a condition of society which is not Thado as we know the Thado to-day.

3 Priest—one version has **thempu**, the correct Thado word, another has **bamon**, *i.e.* 'Brahman,' clearly indicating foreign influence.

4 The Thado has simply **na-nute gakouvin**, 'call your mothers,' but the effect is bizarre in English.

5 God—in Thado **Pathen**, the Creator.

6 The Thado word is **mulaopi**. This word designates a mythical bird large enough to carry off men, and may be correlated to the **rukh** of the *Arabian Nights*. Yule suggests that the legend of the **rukh** contains a tradition of the *Dinornis* or the *Aepyornis*, extinct birds of enormous size, *vide* his note in *The Travels of Marco Polo*, II, pp. 415 sqq.

7 The Thado words are **kung** and **kungkhen**, and the explanation

and to anoint with their blood the things he had made, and that when he had done this the fiddle would fly with him and would alight outside the house of the King; then if he surmounted the range of hills before him he would see raindrops falling as great as a man's hand, and from there across the sea[1] he would see Doikumpu burning the corpse[2] of his sister's son, but before the rain should reach him Doikumpu would go leaving the corpse only partly burned. He should then go and burn his body with that fire and follow after Doikumpu and say to him "Uncle, feeling hurt that you did not burn me properly I have come to life again." On hearing that, he (Doikumpu) would perform ceremonies and cure the burns. So he sent to the King for a he-goat and a she-goat and a pair of doves, and killed them and mounted the fiddle and flew to the King's house. From there he flew again to the range in front of him and thence he saw the raindrops, and across the sea he saw smoke. Again he flew and tied up the fiddle on the far shore, and did as he had been instructed in the dream, and it befell that Doikumpu cured him accordingly.

Every day his aunt[3] tied up rice for him and he went out in search of game, but found none. One day she told him never to go in a certain direction, so he wondered why she so straitly forbade him, and took his food and went that way. He reached God's spring, and its water was glistening like molten silver.[4] By the side of it he undid and ate his food. Having eaten he was about to drink of the spring when he

---

given is that they mean a boat and a paddle, though the Thado do not use boats. The words might equally well mean a dish and a spoon. No boat re-appears in the story as told now, but it may have originally been needed for the crossing of the sea, or the idea of the **Shilangda** from the later part of the story may have intruded into the earlier part and usurped the boat's functions.

1 The Thado word—**tuikhanglen** (=' water-confine-big') appears definitely to mean the sea, though few Thado have ever seen it. It is described as the place where all water is collected from the rivers, and is not applied to lakes and rivers themselves.

2 The Thado do not burn their dead, though the practice exists among some of the Assam Hill tribes, who may be connected with them. Thus the Maru Kachins, the Khasis, the Chakma all cremate. The " Kookies or Lunctas " of whom Macrae wrote in 1799 (*Asiatic Researches*, VII, 194) also cremated then, as some of the Old Kukis do still, and the story may point to an extinct practice of the Thado. Equally well the incident may relate to the Hindu practice.

3 Being the mother's brother's wife of the dead boy whom the hero is impersonating he addresses her throughout as **hepi**, and the story goes on as if the relationship actually existed.

4 The Thado has **hahtui**; **hah** is the white alloy (? of lead and tin) of which the women's armlets worn above the elbow are made, and **tui** is simply ' water '—here the molten liquid.

noticed seven clothes rails,[1] and then seven of God's daughters came to wash at the spring. Each one hung her petticoat over her own rail and washed herself. When the boy saw them he fell very much in love, and he snatched the petticoat of the youngest and ran off. God's youngest daughter saw him as he ran and called out "Hi! Hi! Doikumpu's nephew! Last night I had a stomach-ache and my petticoat is soiled with my dung, are not you disgusted? Look at it!" As he stopped to examine it, he turned into an ant-hill.[2] As he did not come home, his aunt and uncle took a spud, a hoe and a fan and went to look for him. When they saw the ant-hill, they dug, and in the very midst they found the boy, tiny and tender like the hidden leaf-bud in the centre of the stem of a plantain tree. They fanned him with the fan till he came to himself; they took him home and cherished him till he recovered his former condition. Then his aunt said to him "Do not ever go there again, but if you do, and if they call to you again as before, on no account look behind you at them." Then one day he went again and as before the daughters of God[3] came back to wash again. Again he snatched the petticoat and fled homewards. God's daughter called out "my petticoat is soiled with my dung, look!" but he did not stop to look but ran back to the house.

Then the daughter of God came to ask for her petticoat. He said he would not give it back unless she agreed to marry him, and she answered "Why would not I marry you. You have touched me, laid hands on me, and my own people will not like me any more." Then the boy said "Well, take oath, then" and God's daughter said "If I do not marry you, let me become ashes," so arranging to come back in six days she went away. When she got back home she was afraid to tell her father and mother but her eldest sister said to her parents "My youngest sister has married a mortal,[4] are you pleased?" And her father answered "In a house where there are many girls, do not some get married to mortals and others to fairies like ourselves?" So his daughter went back to Manmashi six days later. Then when his wife had come to him Manmashi said to his aunt and uncle "I have delayed very long, my mother will be troubled," and they answered "If

---

1 **Talhang**—a bamboo laid horizontally on supports for hanging clothes on.

2 **Hlemlhung** is a mound of earth thrown up by termites.

3 God—in Thado **Pathen**, the Creator.

4 The Thado word is **Manmashi** which means a human as distinct from a spirit and is generally used with reference to the legendary epoch when the distinction was less marked than it is now (*v.* · *Supra*, pp. 28, 41). The word is really here used ambiguously as a proper name and continues to be so used for the rest of the story. In the next sentence I have translated

your mother is alive, what are you doing here? go home," so he took his wife to go home, and he searched by the sea-shore for the fiddle but could not find it. Then his wife said "Kill me and cut me in two and one half will go back to my home and the other half will become a fiddle. Take the fiddle with you and when you are hungry play on the fiddle and I will always bring you rice and meat. And when Manmashi said "I will not kill you," his wife said "If you do not kill me, there are so many kings and chiefs by the way that men will take me from you and we shall be separated for good." So Manmashi cut her in two pieces and one became a fiddle and the other went back to heaven. Then Manmashi took with him the fiddle and went his way, and when he was hungry he played on the fiddle, and his wife came bringing two dishes of rice and two of meat and they two ate together. So he went on and came to the village of a king. The king said he was not to stop in any house there, so he went and stopped by the spring, and played on his fiddle and his wife brought two dishes of rice and two dishes of meat. Then the king's servants, coming to fetch water, saw his wife and went and told the king, saying, "O King, you were not willing to let the man stop in a house, but he has a fiddle and when he plays on it, a beautiful girl comes, bringing two dishes of rice and two dishes of meat, and she is more beautiful than any of your seven wives," said they. Then the king summoned him. Said the king "I will exchange my *lohaldang*[1] for your fiddle." Manmashi said "Of what use is your *lohaldang*?" The king replied "It beats of itself whatsoever it is told to beat" and he told it to beat a *schimd*[2] tree that there was below his house, and the *lohaldang* went and starting at the very top beat it right away all down to the ground. Then they exchanged and Manmashi took the *lohaldang* and went, and by the way he fell hungry and found no means of eating. So he said to the *lahaldang* "Go, beat the king and bring me the fiddle and his daughter." So the *lohaldang* went and beat the king and brought his daughter and his fiddle Then Manmashi played on the fiddle and his wife came bringing three plates of rice and three of meat and they ate, and having eaten their fill they went on and came to the village of a king. The king would

---

as "fairies like ourselves" the words **ipathenchanpi**, literally meaning 'ones like us two God.' The conception of the people of the heaven is very much of that of the Good People of our own folk-lore.

1 I have been unable to get a definite meaning for **lohaldang**. The word does not appear to be Thado and **lohal** is probably the Hindustani **lohar**=iron, and one account described the implement as an iron staff. The apparatus is familiar enough and appears in our own folk-lore as a stick in a bag.

2 Thado **khengthing**, the tree known to science as *Schima Wallichii*.

not let them stop in any man's house, but made them stay in a cow-shed. So Manmashi played on his fiddle and his wife came and brought three plates of rice and three of meat. When they had eaten their fill of rice they gave the plate to the cow-herd. The cow-herd went and told the king. "You were not willing that he should stay in any man's house," said he "but this dish and whatever he has is good and his wives are fairer than yours." The king sent to fetch him and they fetched him. When he was come before the king, the king said "Let your wife wrestle with my wife and the one that wins shall possess the loser, so they wrestled to-gether and Manmashi's wife was beaten. Then the king took Manmashi's wife. Then Manmashi went on, and when he had got well on his way he sent the *lohaldang*, saying, "Beat the king and bring back his daughter and my wife." The *lohaldang* went and beat the king and brought along his wives and his daughter and Manmashi's wife. Then they went on, and when they were about to reach his house, (Manmashi said to the women) "You stay here. I will go and buy and bring tobacco,[1] but his wives did not agree, so they all went on together and arrived at the house. And when they had entered the house (they found that) it was small and there were no plenishings[2] in it at all. On that God's daughter turned the house into a mansion[3] and made the old mother young again, and after that the daughter of God went off home.

One day Manmashi went to call in at the King's house. The King said "Sit down" and he sat down, and it became time for him to play on his fiddle. But when he said "King, I am going" the King said "Do not go." Next he said "King, my bladder is full,[4] I am going to empty it," but the King said "Do not go out. Do so where you sit.[5]" Then having sat a little longer "King, my bowels are full. I go to empty them." Said the King "Do it where you sit. My servants will remove it,"

---

1 It is the almost invariable custom, when friends meet among the Thado, for one to hand the other a pinch of tobacco leaf to chew. Presumably Manmashi pretended to want it to offer to his relatives, in reality intending to try and prepare his house for the reception of his wives.

2 **Thilkeo**—the heterogeneous assertment of implements and possessions with which any Thado house is filled—baskets, dishes clothes, gourds, arms, gongs, stools, etc., etc.,

3 The Thado version told to me had **bangla** *i.e.* bungalow, obviously a modern touch, the house of an European Official being the most superior kind of house the narrator could think of.

4 The Thado even when addressing a king needs no euphemism; he says plainly **Kajun ashoe, kajun gathange,** lit. "my urine becomes, I will void my urine." The idiom of Manmashi's next sentence is exactly the same. The root **tha** appears to be used only in this connection.

5 The image in the narrator's mind is probably that of a Thado house built on a platform of bamboo with plenty of interstices.

but Manmashi said "No, I have something, I must do in my house, O King." But the King said "What must you do, speak. I will send from my house to fetch it a woman who never goes out in the sun.[1]" Manmashi said "Then go, and on my bed behind the pillow there is that which is wrapped in a white cloth. Bring it, but do not cause it to give out any sound.[2]" So the girl went, but in bringing it she made it sound. As the sound came from it her face was slapped and the fiddle disappeared. And she came and told Manmashi, and Manmashi was grieved in his heart and wept.

Then Manmashi went to his house and taking the *lohaldang* went to look for her. He went and searched at God's spring, but found no one there. A chrysalis [3] was drawing water. Manmashi asked "Why are you drawing water?" It replied "It is for the daughter of God to wash with." Manmashi said "I will come too; take me with you." Said the chrysalis "You cannot come, but if you insist on coming catch hold of my hook [3] and come." So he caught hold of the hook and ascended to heaven. When he reached there another man had arranged to marry his wife, and that night there was drinking and dancing, and in the morning an elephant came to fetch her.[4] Manmashi said to his wife "Don't go," but she answered "I must go. As you did not love me and let a servant touch me, my heart is broken,[5]" and she started to mount the elephant, on that Manmashi fell angry [6] and said to the *lohaldang* "Go and knock to pieces the howdah on that elephant," and the *lohaldang* went and knocked it to pieces. Then God said "Why are you two, husband and wife, treating one another like this?" and his daughter replied "He let a servant touch the fiddle, and I was angry and ran away home." God said "Where is the fiddle?" Then his daughter brought the fiddle and shewed it to him. He broke it. "It is over this that you two are quarrelling" said he and threw it away.

---

1 *I.e.* a dependant of such position in the household that she is never sent out to work in the fields as most women are, and is by implication a person entitled to respect and confidence.

2 Because the slightest sound produced even by giving the instrument a tap would call its familiar, who would be offended as she had specially enjoined her lover to carry the fiddle himself—**kicholvinlang.**

3 **Ol** is a chrysalis, particularly such as are found in the ground, and **olgennel**, (the chrysalis with a hook) the word used here, is a particular variety which is said to have its tail permanently curled up in the form of a hook.

4 Another exotic touch. Thado brides are not fetched on elephants, at any rate not now-a-days.

5 **Ka-lha ashie,** literally "My soul is spoilt," an expression used by persons in great grief.

6 **A-lung a-hangin,** literally "his heart was reckless," **Hang** is used of persons who display courage in the face of danger; **a-lung a-hang** is the ordinary expression for losing one's temper.

Then to Manmashi, "Take your wife and go," said he. Manmashi took his wife with him and came back and arrived at Doikumpu's. He said to Doikumpu "Uncle, give me your hoe, your spud, your fan and your knife." He answered "Nephew, if you ask for things, why would we grudge them?" and gave them. Then Manmashi's wife said "It is through your aunt and your uncle that we two were united, why do you ask your uncle for all his things?" So Doikumpu gave him the knife. They accepted the knife and came along together till they reached the outskirts of the village. There the wife scraped the dirt from her breasts with the knife and rubbed it on to a piece of cotton wool and gave it to Manmashi. "Take this," she said, and put it into the King's eyes and instruct him to take it out when you will be reaching your own house." So Manmashi went and did just as his wife told him and came, and as he reached his home the King took out the cotton wool, and both his eyes were opened.

One day after that Manmashi's wife said to him "Go and call in at the King's house" and sent him off. When Manmashi went there the King was angry. He said to Manmashi "Sit down," and when he was seated "Your mithun bull shall fight with mine. Your dog shall fight with my dog, your cock shall fight with my cock, your boar[1] shall fight with my boar. Will you come to me or shall I come to you?" Manmashi was troubled at heart and went home sobbing.[2] His wife said "What has happened that you weep?" You go to a friend's house, take drink and meat and come back sobbing." So he answered "The King is going to make all our animals[3] fight" Said his wife "Very well, arrange for the fighting on the third day from to-day. Then his wife for their mithun provided a wild mithun,[4] for their dog she provided a tiger,[5] for their

---

1 By most of the Thado all boars are castrated at two to three months old by which time they have generally reproduced themselves (*v.* note 1 on p. 86), but in the Hôlthang clan the chief usually keeps a real boar and takes a pig from every litter in the village as his fee, the boar being kept loose, of course, to roam as he will.

2 The Thado word **kăp** is the same as that used above and below for 'weep;' it implies the shedding of tears, but is probably, like 'sob,' an onomatapoeic word.

3 **Gancha**=" domestic animals." This incident of fighting animals occurs more than once in Lepcha folklore; vide **Lepcha Folklore**, Journ. Asiat. Soc. of Bengal, Vol. XXI, pp. 38, 415.

4 **Jangshiel** the wild mithun or gaur (*bos gaurus*). Solitary bulls of this species frequently associate with **shiel**, the domestic mithun or **gayal** (*bos frontalis*), fighting with and often killing or seriously damaging the bulls and begetting hybrid offspring, which are disliked as they are apt to be troublesome when they come to maturity.

5 **Humpi**—generic. It might be a tiger, a leopard or even one of the smaller felines such as a golden cat.

cock she provided a hawk, for their boar she provided a wild boar. Then they summoned (the King, and the animals) fought in pairs. The mithun fought with the mithun and Manmashi's mithun killed (the other); the dog fought with the dog and Manmashi's dog killed (the other); the cock fought with the cock and Manmashi's cock killed (the other); the boar fought with the boar, and Manmashi's boar killed (the other).

APPENDIX B.

The House of Dongngel.

I add this Dongngel pedigree as there has been so much pother about the illegitimacy of the line that now represents Dongngel. The theory appears to be based on the scandal caused by Neingul's marriage, and perhaps on doubts as to the real parentage of Ngulchin, but it seems really to arise from the arrogance of Khutinthang, who probably really claims precedence rather as the head of the lineal descendant of Thado, which he is, than in any *bona fide* belief that the elder line is extinct. They are far from that, and if the Lhotjim and Gwite are excluded, there are still members of the Thomlhun and Haolai clans with pedigrees every bit as genuine as Khutinthang's, if less distinguished. All these Dongngel clans, however, are smaller numerically and poorer in possessions than their collaterals descended from Thado.

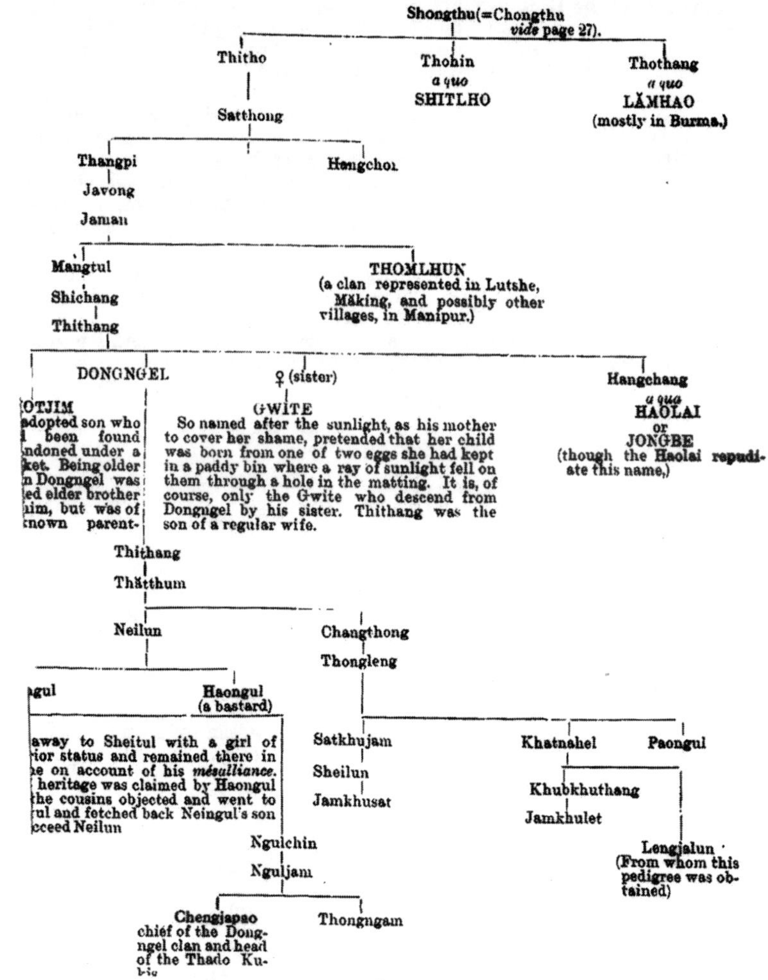

There is also a story that Dongngel had connection with a female serow which he had caught in a snare. He let her go and the boy child seen later with a serow in the jungle and ultimately recovered was beloved by his father and called Lushei (*a-lu, lun*=much cherished), and from him are descended the Lushei tribe.

It will be seen that the line of Dongngel is senior to that of Thado himself, although the latter has given his name to the tribe. Khilkhung (Khutinthang) the head of the Shitlho clan used to pay *satthing* to Chengjapao until the Kuki rebellion, and the ground on which he claims that the line is extinct is presumably that of Neingul's *mésalliance.* Even if this were a legitimate ground, however, Changthong's decendants would have a prior claim to seniority to Thado's, not to mention Chungngul, chief of the Haolai, as well as the head of the Thomlhun clan, if the Gwite can be ruled out. I gather from Mr. Duncan, however, that the allegation that the Dongngel are *ingam* is based on a story that Dongngel died without legitimate issue and had omitted to recognise his illegitimate offspring, and that Thado was entitled to inherit under the circumstances, but refused to claim his inheritance, which passed by default to a slave. As according to the Shitlho genealogy Dongngel was the son of Thitho and Thado was three generations later, the alleged personal quarrel between Dongngel and Thado over the *chontul* at Nanglengbung presents much difficulty; I suspect the *ingam* theory to be a recent invention of the Shitlho. The Lhotjim claimed seniority to the Dongngel clan in court in 1928, on the ground that Dongngel called their ancestor "elder brother," but it is said that all the evidence supported the Dongngel contention.

The following alternative pedigree of Dongngel was given me by Ehpu, a minor chief of the Haolai clan, who was much concerned because he thought other informants had given me an incorrect account. He was, I must admit, very far gone in his cups at the time and I had no opportunity of discovering whether he held to his version when sober.

```
Shongthu
   |
Satthong
   |
Thangpi
   |
Javong
   |
Mangtul
   |
Shingmen
   |
Hangmen
   |
   |------------------------------|
   |                              |
Thitho (of Aishan)*       Thohin (of Jampi)
   |                        (a quo Thado)
   |
Sheichang
   |
   |------------------------------|
   |                              |
Dong-ngel                    Hangchang
                                  |
                               Haolai
```

It will be noticed that the number of generations from Chongthu to Dongngel is the same in each case, and many of the names are identical though not in the same order. The discrepancy is probably such as must inevitably arise between two versions of an account preserved only by oral tradition. Eh'pu's version agrees more closely with that of the Shitlho, who, however, make Hangmen the younger brother of Shingmen and the ancestor of the Kom and the Old Kukis.

APPENDIX C.

THADO TERMS OF RELATIONSHIP.

The terms of relationship that follow are given in the form used in address. Those which are the more honorific begin with **he**—which is replaced, when the relative is spoken of, instead of spoken to, by **ka**=' my,' **na**=' your,' **a**=' his', etc. In the case of terms reference, therefore, I have indicated the use of the possessive pronoun by an apostrophe. In the case of the less honorific term s **ka**,—the possessive of the first personal pronoun, is used in address a s well as in reference, and has accordingly been given here instead of the form in **he**—.

The Thado are patrilineal and exgamous and their terms of relationship are of course classificatory. The proper marriage for a man is with his mother's brother's daughter, while that preferred for a girl is with her father's sister's son. The latter however is much less important. But marriage of a girl to her mothers' brother's son is prohibited, and marriage into the mother's clan is eschewed for women for at least two generations as a rule. The important terms of relationship therefore indicate definite classification for purposes of marriage. Thus **hepu** is used primarily for any man of the speaker's mother's clan, and **hepi** for the wife of such, probably originally the mother's mother (?<**henupi** =' great-mother') and hence applied by courtesy to all women whose husbands are addressed as **hepu**, whence again no doubt **hepu** has been applied conversely to all grandfathers. **Henunga** is used for the women of the speaker's mother's clan, the potential wives of the speaker (if a man), and it may be observed that in the case of a father's brother's wife the implication is avoided by respectfully addressing her as **henu** though referring to her by the classificatorily correct term **'nunga.** Similarly an elder brother's wife is addressed as **he'u**, elder sister,' but likewise referred to as **kanunga**.

Etiquette is less strict with relatives who marry the daughters of the clan than with those whose daughters are married by it. **Hegang** is applied to the former, but only to the senior men of the clan, men of the standing of the speaker's father. For persons outside this marriage scheme personal names are used or honorifics such as **hepa** 'father,' **henu** ' mother,' or **he'u**, ' elder brother' or ' elder sister.' **Hepu** is also commonly used as an honorific form of address to anyone of unusually high social standing.

To elucidate the system a genealogical table is appended to the list of terms, giving the forms of address in lieu of names from the point of view of a man and his two sisters who marry into different clans.

A husband addresses his wife by her name or as **kajinu**=' my wife' but she addresses him by the name of his first child, of whichever sex, to which '**pa**' is suffixed—i.e. ' Father of so and so.' Till he has a child she cannot address him by any name or title.

Hepu =
1. *Grand-Father.*
2. *Mother's Brother* (the personal name may *not* be added in address).
3. *Mother's Brother's Son.*
4. Wife's Father
5. Wife's Brother
6. Wife's Brother's Son

(4–6: when of the same clan as speaker's mother and followed by personal name if necessary.)

Hepi =
1. *Grand-Mother.*
2. *Mother's Brother's Wife.*

3. Wife's Mother
4. Wife's Brother's Wife } (if the speaker's wife is of the same clan as his mother, otherwise **henu** or **he'u** according to age and circumstances.)

Hepa = 1. *Father.*
2. *Father's Brother* (in reference *'pa lɜn*, *'pa neo* according as older or younger).
3. Mother's Sister's Husband, etc. (by courtesy).

Henu = 1. *Mother.*
2. Father's Brother's wife (in address, but **nunga** in reference).
3. Mother's Brother's Wife
4. Wife's Mother } (unless of the speaker's mother's clan— cf. **hepi**
5. Husband's Mother
6. Husband's Father's Mother } (unless of the speaker's own clan, when **heni** is used). } as courtesy titles

Hepanga[1] = *Father's Male Cousin on Father's Side* (or any other patrilinal collateral of that generation).

Henunga[1] = 1. *Mother's Sister.*
2. *Mother's Brother's Daughter.*
3. Wife's Sister
4. Wife's Brother's Daughter } (Followed by personal name if necessary but only used if of the same clan as the speaker's mother. Otherwise personal name alone is used).

Hegång = 1. *Father's Sister's Husband.*
2. Husband's Father (when his mother is of the speaker's clan).

Ḥeni = 1. *Father's Sister.*
2. Husband's Mother
3. Husband's Father's Mother } (if of the same clan as speaker, otherwise **henu**).

He'u[2] = 1. *Elder Brother.*
2. *Elder Sister.*
3. *Father's Brother's Child Older Than Speaker* (followed by personal name).
4. Father's Sister's Child
5. Mother's Sister's Child
6. Husband's Elder Brother
7. Husband's Elder Brother's Wife
8. Elder Sister's Husband
9. Elder Brother's Wife[3]
10. Wife's Sister's Husband } (Probably by courtesy merely *cf.* also *q.v.* **hepi—3, and 4**).

Kanao[2] = 1. *Younger Brother.*
2. *Younger Sister.*

Kacha[2] = 1. *Son.*
2. *Daughter.*

---

[1] The root-*nga* in these two words is apparently the root meaning "watch over," 'tend,' as in *bongnga*="cow-herd." cf. the Sema term of relationship *angu* (*The Sema Nagas*, p. 141).

[2] In the case of these four terms *'nu* is suffixed in reference when it is desired to indicate the female gender.

[3] But **Kanunga** in reference, if of the speaker's mother's clan.

Katu[1]= 1. *Sister's Child.*
2. *Father's Sister's Child.*
3. Grand-Child.

Kajinu= *Wife.*

In other cases, except as already noted in that of 'husband,' the personal name is used, though **hepa, henu, he'u, kanao, gulpa** (=' friend,') and, for important persons **hepu,** are frequently used as merely honorific without any implication of kinship.

---

[1] In the case of these four terms *'nu* is suffixed in reference when it is desired to indicate the female gender.

APPENDIX D.

Thado Warfare.

The Thado is an enemy by no means to be despised when the matter is one of jungle-fighting and guerrilla warfare.[1] Initiative is not his strong point in war, and he will readily admit that his best plans for taking the offensive are conceived in his cups and abandoned with the return of sobriety and consideration. Thus during the Thado rebellion of 1918-19 plans were repeatedly made, and as often abandoned in the morning, for sending parties through Naga country to cut the telegraph wires between Kohima and the plains as well as between Kohima and Manipur. His tactics are mainly defensive and the prevailing note is 'tip and run.' Ambushes are laid, posts or camps are worried by night attacks which there is never any intention of pushing home, and the enemy is generally harrassed, but never engaged in the open. Stockades are built across narrow paths where the turning of them is likely to prove tedious and prolonged, and are defended as long as the defenders can hold on with a reasonable chance of ultimate escape by flight. These stockades are sometimes of remarkable strength, some I have seen having been made of a palisade of upright trees 8 inches or more in diameter backed by a thickness of even larger tree trunks laid horizontally, and this again by another palisade of upright trunks similar to the first, the whole being well over three feet thick, the interstices packed with earth, and loopholed for musket fire. The approaches and sides were well defended by 'panjis' (bamboo spikes stuck into the ground, excessively noxious to a barefooted foe and by no means innocuous to the booted), while deep communication trenches were dug running back from the defenders' position, to enable them to bolt in safety when the flanks of the position were turned.

Ambushes in thick jungle are laid for an approaching enemy whence the Thado warrior will fire and disappear, to lie up again further on if a suitable opportunity is afforded. The same tactics are adopted at fords across rivers or any spot where natural obstacles hamper any rapid approach. Panjis, stone-shoots, and booby traps of all sorts are the defensive weapons used. The offensive weapons are practically confined to powder and shot, the powder home-made, reported slow in ignition but none the less powerful, the shot usually angular or rectangular pieces of metal—hammered lead or filed iron, fired from a flintlock or percussion-cap musket or from one of the hide cannon described below (Apx. E). On one occasion only during the Kuki rebellion did I meet with the use of the bow and arrow, and the dao was never, I think, actually used as a weapon of offence except when dealing with defenceless villagers. For "frightfulness" is a normal policy of Thado warfare. Laruri village was cut up by a party of Thado early in the present century, the somnolent inhabitants being attacked and mostly massacred at early dawn, others being carried off as slaves, and the village has never properly recovered from that decimation. During the Thado rebellion Kasom, to give one instance only, a small Tangkhul village in the north of the Manipur State, professed in 1918 its inablity to produce the

---

[1] For the general fashion of Kuki warfare see Carey and Tuck, *op. cit.*, Ch. xxiv. The Kukis were reputed in Bengal, to drive off their captives strung together by cane thongs threaded through the lobe of the ear. The Arakan pirates used to put thongs of this sort through the palms of their prisoners' hands (Harvey, *op. cit.*, p. 143.)—(Ed.)

further supplies demanded by Chengjapao. The massacre which followed has been already described (*supra* page 23).

The Thado is not without a certain ready resourcefulness and a sense of humour. When the columns operating in Manipur in 1918-19 took a couple of antiquated 7-pounder guns known as "Bubble" and "Squeak" into the field, the Thado at once retorted with his hide cannon, which had not previously been heard of, and these did very little less damage than "Bubble" and "Squeak" and made very near as much noise. During the enquiry after the final surrender of the rebels I was questioning one of their captured leaders Enjakhup, an ex-sepoy of the Naga Hills Military Police and the only Thado from that district who took any prominent part in the rebellion. He had not, he said, taken any active part in the operations, but had merely been present with the rebels under compulsion. "Is it not true, then" I asked, "that you drilled the men of the rebellious chiefs and taught them how to shoot?" "I did," said he with his tongue in his cheek, "and why wouldn't I? It was the best I could do to help you all." "How so?" I asked him. "Why, the more powder and shot they would be wasting on their targets, the less they would have for shooting at your soldiers with." A stout fellow. He escaped the rope he doubtless deserved and was deported temporarily to Sadiya with the rebel chiefs. There he fell sick and died in Kohima on his way back to his home.

A number of Thados are now being enlisted in the Assam Rifles, and the Naga Hills Battalion has already one Thado Kuki platoon, and is recruiting a second.

APPENDIX E.

THADO MANUFACTURES AND WEAPONS.

Mr. Shaw has mentioned several articles of metal formerly manufactured by the Thado. It is true that the art of making them is rarely practised now, but it is not dead. In 1918 during the Kuki rebellion an ingenious follower of Tingtong manufactured a brass muzzle-loading gun, and one or two Thados of Holkang village in the Naga Hills still makes brass tobacco pipes and liquor siphons, while the chief of Chongchin near Saipimol in the Manipur State gave me a bronze mouth-piece, for a pipe, that he had made himself. The craft is usually hereditary and confined to certain clans. The method used is the *cire perdue* process, which I had demonstrated for me by Ngulshi' of Holkang in June 1928.

The crude bees-wax is broken up into a pan of water which is boiled so that the wax forms a thin sheet on the top, the impurities sinking to the bottom or adhering to the under side of the wax sheet. When cooled the water is poured off and the impurities scraped from the wax with a knife. The wax is then heated at the fire, kneaded reheated, kneaded and rolled like dough, a heated glass bottle being used as a roller in this case, until it is all completely soft and fine without a lump of any sort.

If a solid article is to be cast, a wax core is modelled of the shape required, but if hollow, like a pipe or a siphon tube, a solid removeable centre is required. This is made with wire in the case of a straight hole like that of a pipe-stem, or a pipe-bowl; if a curve is required, as in the siphon tube, a piece of pliable bamboo is used. In either case this wire or bamboo is wound closely with thread, as a spindle, the binding being thickened as necessary where a bulge is needed, as in the bowl of a pipe. As this core would be liable to burn when the wax is melted out and the molten metal poured in it is covered with a thin layer of fine blue clay. Strips of the prepared wax are then rolled out thin. and wrapped round the core, and shaved and smoothed with a heated knife-blade till a smooth and symmetrical surface is obtained. The ornamentation is then put on in wax appliqué, lines, coils and spirals being laid on with the fingers using very fine threads of wax, which are produced in various thicknesses by means of bamboo pistons, the wax being forced through a minute hole in the centre of the node at the bottom of the bamboo cylinder by means of a plunger of wood or bamboo; from this hole it comes out in the form of a fine cylindrical thread. The wax model is completed by the addition of a stalk, as it were, of cylindrical wax about 3/16 to ¼ inch in diameter which represents the hole through which the wax will be run out and the metal run in.

For forming the mould round this wax two sorts of clay are required; the very fine blue clay already mentioned is pounded thoroughly to get rid of anything in the nature of grit or lumps. A layer of this is applied well moistened, direct to the wax modelling and rubbed well into the interstices of the ornamentation with the fingers. On the top of this is laid a second layer of the same blue clay which has been thoroughly pounded up with the husks of paddy so as to bind and not crack in the firing. This is allowed to dry and is then covered with a third layer of a coarser red clay obtained from the mounds thrown up by termites and likewise pounded up with paddy husks, and very thoroughly kneaded. Through all these coats of clay the wax end of the "stalk" attached to the core is allowed to protrude, and the clay at the point of emergence is moulded round it into a funnel-shaped hollow. The clay moulds are dried slowly.

The same prepared red clay is used for the manufacture of a crucible into which the metal to be melted is put and which is then closed

Fig. 1.—Thado pipe in brass.

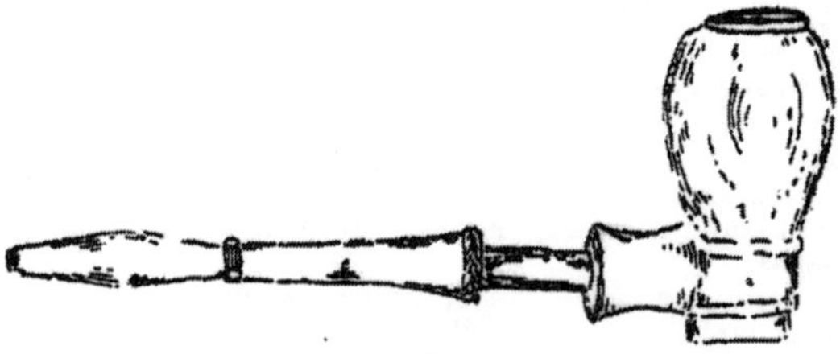

Fig. 2.—Thado pipe in wood with bronze mouth-piece cast by Bapu, Chief of Chongchin.

Fig. 3.—Thado pipe in pipe-stone with brass mouth-piece and mounts.

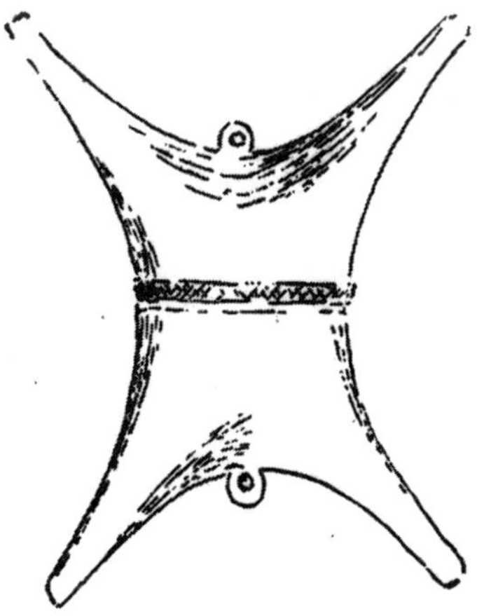

Fig. 4.—Brass box for flint and steel.

Articles cast in metal by *cire perdue* process.

and covered with a turnip-shaped dome having a small aperture at the point. This crucible is heated to a white heat in a fire fanned by the usual upright piston bellows, a process which needs considerable physical exertion and takes at least a couple of hours. Meanwhile the dried moulds are heated, and the wax melted and run out, the emptied moulds being then baked to a red heat while the metal is being melted in the crucible. Both this latter and the moulds are handled with rough bamboo pincers made on the pattern of the bamboo clappers used for bird scaring in various parts of Further India (*vide The Sema Nagas*, p. 66, fig. 3). When the crucible is white-hot the metal is poured into the mould, and as the latter is also heated, to prevent the metal's cooling too rapidly, the metal fills up the hollow evacuated by the wax.

Beautiful work is produced by this process—brass dao-handles, brass gauntlets for women, tobacco-pipes, mouth-pieces, siphon tubes or curved joints for siphon tubes (used in drawing off the liquor from the fermented rice and husks), brass boxes for flint and steel of a curious design with corners prolonged into points, and beautiful metal vases ornamented with designs reproducing the basket work which is used to cover and strengthen the earthenware originals. The most characteristic perhaps are the tobacco pipes and siphon joints ornamented most frequently with hornbills, often with animals such as elephants or mithun, which are sometimes excellently modelled.

Other metal work includes swords, daos, knives, agricultural implements and women's iron walking sticks. Various other forms of manufacture are also practised. Blocked hide is used for making covers to bamboo tubes used for quivers, etc., for pouches carried at a belt like those of sepoys, for ammunition, and for similar articles. The usual method is to soak it in water, mould it and dry it in the form required, after which it is usually treated with *bombalnai* i.e. tree-oil or wood-oil obtained possibly from a *dipterocarpus* (*vide* J.A.S.B., No. 110 of 1841, *visit to Kyok Phyoo*, p. 142) giving the appearance of black lacquer. Coloured lacquer perhaps is also used for covering the stocks of guns, for ornamenting powder horns, some times beautifully inlaid with silver, for covering pocket tinder boxes made of basket work and for similar purposes. Elegant wooden dishes (one in the form of a quaich) are made, mainly with the dao and adze. As by the Konyak Naga, tie-dyeing is practised, the Thado producing spirally striped red and white porcupine quills for use as hairpins, by this process. The Konyaks use a similar process of tying a spiral strip round a javelin shaft and then smoking it so as to leave a spiral white band alternating with a dark one all down the shaft, and Lhota Nagas have a similar method of ornamenting bamboo mugs; the Kacharis use the method also.

Weapons include daos, muskets, bows and arrows and cannon of sorts. The spear is not popular, the non-use of the throwing spear, which is the principal Naga weapon of offence being one of the points that distinguishes Kukis from Nagas. The daos vary in type, the old Thado dao, now obsolete, being a single-handed short-handled weapon with a broad triangular blade well illustrated in Butler's *Travels and Adventures in Assam*. The commoner subsequent form has a narrow blade curved somewhat back towards the point and a single-handed pummel usually mounted in brass. The long bladed two-handed Shan sword is also in use, and now-a-days a short knife with a longish handle, the blade shaped on the lines of a *kukri* but straight, is popular. Its shape is certainly due to the influence of the Gurkha *kukri* used by the Assam Rifles. The old Thado dao used to have a curiously bent handle sometimes covered with blocked hide or with hair bound round and lacquered and mounted with a plume of red or white hair at the tip, rather suggestive of the handle of a *kris*. Soppitt (*op. cit.*, p. 6) mentions "a long sword-like weapon made of iron," which sounds rather like the Khasi or Mikir two handed sword.

Archers' bracers (*ja'shel*) are, or rather, used to be made of brass, ivory, bone or wood. The brass ones were cast and were rather like a

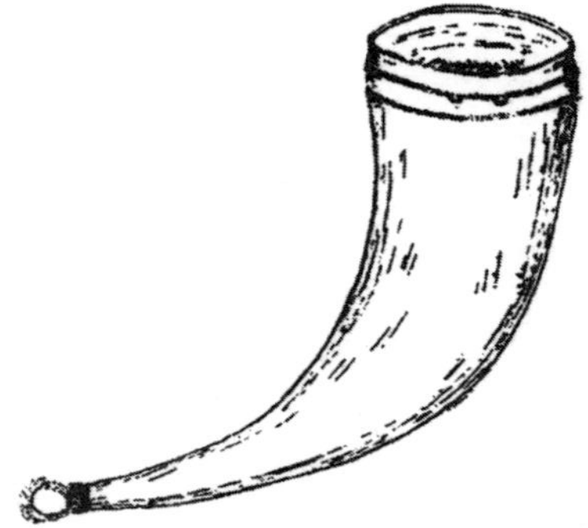

Fig. 2.

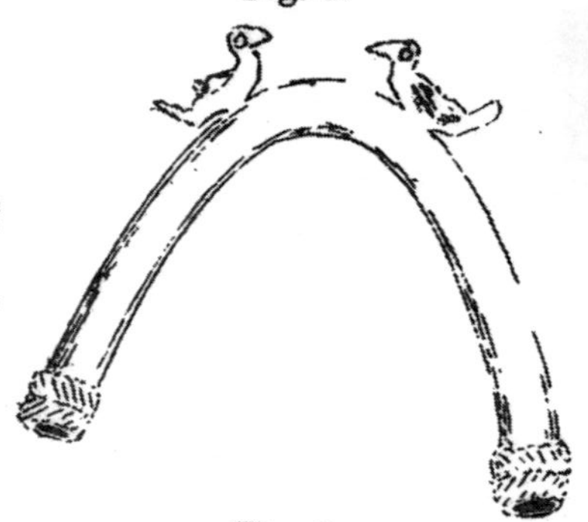

Fig. 3.

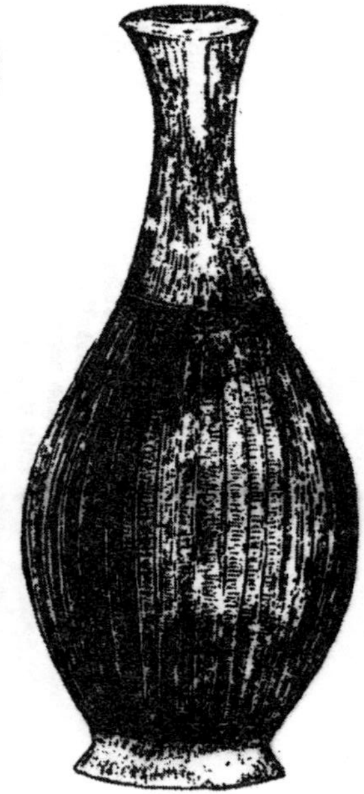

Fig. 4.

Fig. 1.—*Tuidol* belonging to Thangkhumang, Chief of Sangnao. Scale—$\frac{3}{14}$ act. size.

Fig. 2.—*Shumshelki*. Metal drinking horn, the property of Kimkhulum, Chief of Taitah.

Fig. 3.—Brass Siphon Joint for drawing off *ju*. Scale c. $\frac{1}{2}$.

Fig. 4.—*Shumhai* (=" bronze jar.") Scale *c.* $\frac{3}{8}$.

(1 *and* 2 *are after drawings by Mr. S. J. Duncan.* 3 *and* 4 *from specimens in the Editor's possession.*)

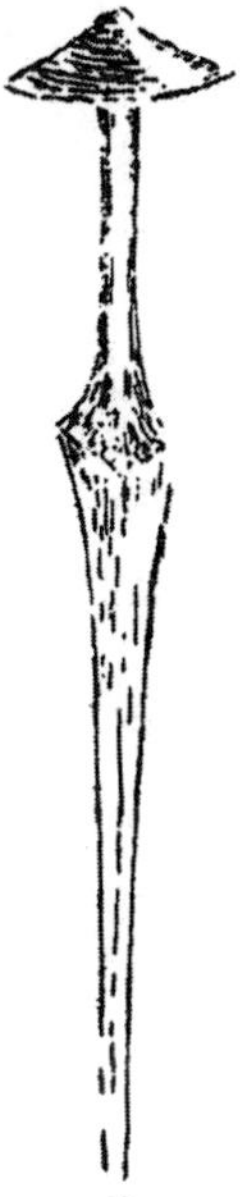

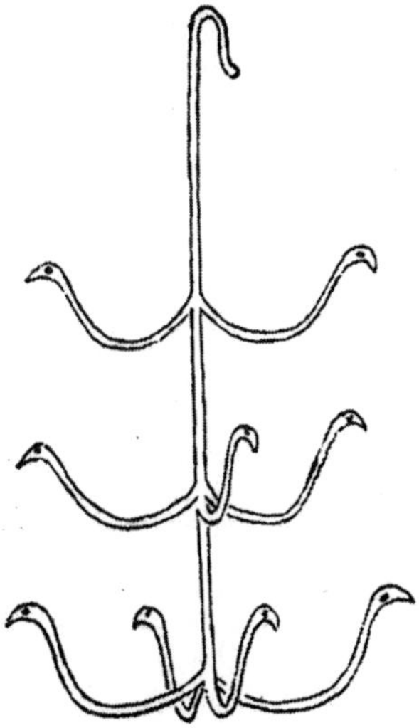

Fig. 2.

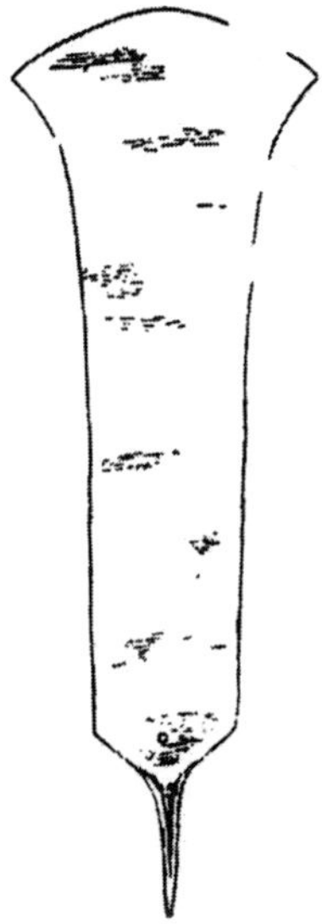

Fig. 3.

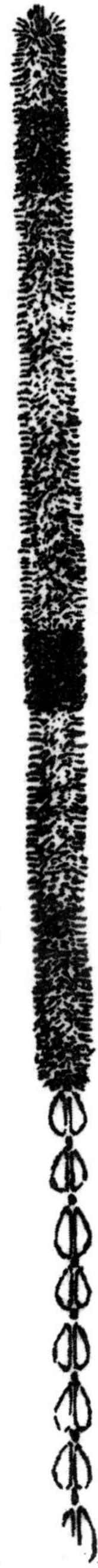

Fig. 1.—Top of iron staff used by Thado women. Scale c. $\frac{1}{8}$.

Fig. 2.—Iron hooks (*chinking*), fo hanging up utensils, etc., the property of Khilkung Chief of Jampi.

Fig. 3.—*Chaldep*. ·ale $\frac{1}{4}$.

Fig. 4.—Portion of *jouchal*. Scale $\frac{1}{2}$.

Fig. 5.—Thado wearing *chaldep*, *jouchal*, *thu'pa* and *vakul-gé*.

(*2 and 3 after drawings by Mr. S. J. Duncan*).

greatly thickened bracelet, and were used also as "knuckle-dusters"; the others were generally something like an enormous clothes-pin with a truncated fork and greatly extended head. The fork was fitted on to the wrist while the head protected the thumb and hand. I am told by Mr. Duncan that the bracers of this type are said to have been used to protect the hand when in conflict with a tiger or leopard, as the ivory made a wedge which prevented the wrist being crushed in the animal's jaws.

Muskets are usually ancient flint-locks or Tower muskets the former of which originally belonged to the Honb'le East India Co. The stocks put on by Thado are thin in the grip and are cut away as fine as possible consistently with the requisite strength so as to throw the weight into the barrel. They are sometimes handsomely ornamented in black and red, with a very pronounced 'bend' to the butt.

Bows[1] now quite obsolete, are of the simple bamboo type about 5 ft. long with a fibre string, arrows are iron-headed with barbs. They used to be poisoned, probably with aconite, and I collected a number of such arrows during the Kuki rebellion, but they were all very old, and it is probably a long time since the Thado have obtained any fresh poison, and they do not apparently recognize the plant but seem generally to have obtained the poison from other tribes by trade. The butts are swelled behind the feathering, which consists of two pieces of feather stripped from the quill and bound to the shaft, which is notched at the end for the bow string; they are drawn and released by the forefinger and thumb, the so-called "primary" method. I have only come across three bows, all old, and only one of these was used. It was held in an oblique almost horizontal plane. A bracer of ivory, bone or brass was worn to protect the left wrist, and resembled a very massive stumpy clothes peg in shape. It is quite obsolete.

Cannons are made of wetted hide, rolled round in several thicknesses with or without a bamboo core and generally bound with coiled wire, cane, or hide strips; the butt is made by bending forward the wetted hide and tying down to the barrel and letting it dry in that position; a short iron tube serves as a nipple or touch-hole. This weapon is loaded with about a quarter of a pound of powder and a handful of slugs made of pieces of iron filed or hammered into a rectangle, fragments of telegraph wire, rough lead bullets, anything handy in fact, even pebbles. They frequently burst at the first discharge and but rarely survive two. The method of using them was sometimes to tie them to a tree and touch them off with a train of powder, sometimes to arrange a musket-lock so as to discharge them by a cap on the end of the touch-hole either by pulling a string, or arranging a trip in the path.

The Kuki method of manufacturing gunpowder has been fully described by Messrs. Carey and Tuck in Vol. I of *The Chin Hills* (page 225), and by Reid in *Chin-Lushai Land* (page 232).

The blow-gun *khuondo'* is used as a toy or as a weapon for killing birds and rats. It consists of a simple bamboo tube of as long a node as can be found locally but of only a single node of bamboo. The dart is of bamboo, of bamboo tipped with iron or of porcupine's quill and is provided with a windage plug by means of cotton thread wound tightly round the projectile or by giving it a conical butt of folded leaf hollowed at the base of the cone. I have described the apparatus in detail in *Man* (77, July, 1924), since when Mr. Mills has come across a harpoon form in the North Cachar

[1] Bullet-bows firing clay pellets and strung with cane are common. The bow is of the simple type the inside of the bamboo forming the convex side of the bow, though the Biete and Sakchip (Tippera) Kukis use a composite bow in which the inside of the bamboo becomes the concave surface of the bow. The Thado call the giant armadillo woodlouse, which curls up into a ball as big as a cherry *Pathen-pa Sailichang* i.e. "God's bow-bullet."

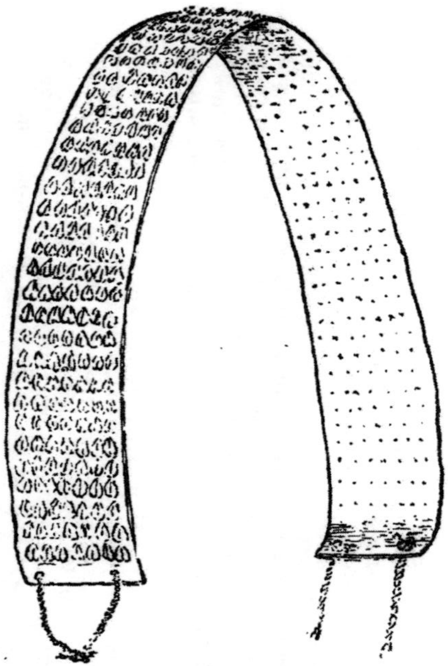

Fig. 1.—Baldrick (*paigen*) worn across one shoulder to support dao sheath (made of hide sewn with cowries). Scale approx. $\frac{1}{12}$.

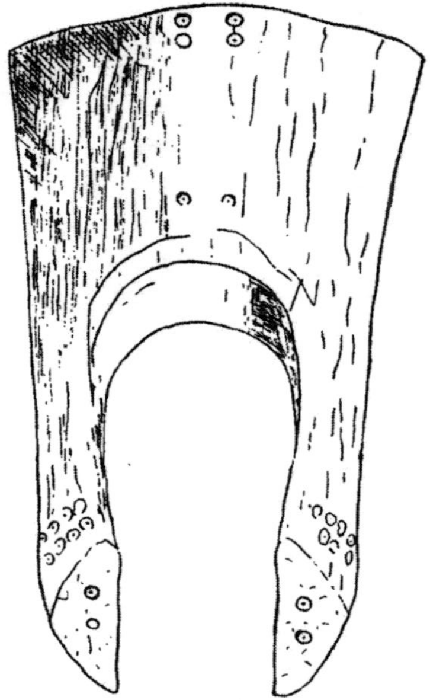

Fig. 2(A).

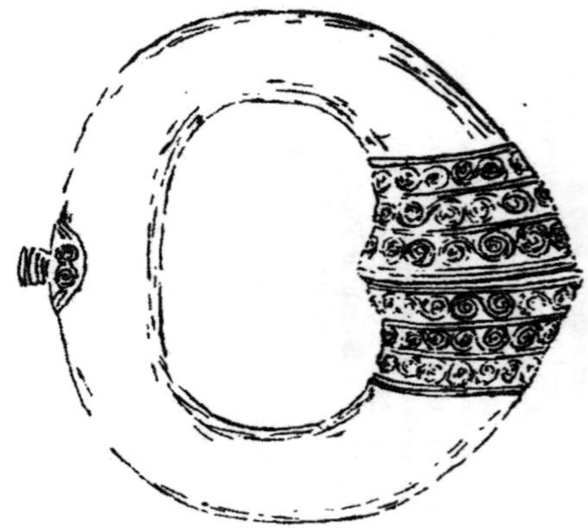

Fig. 2(B).

Archer's bracers (*jahshel*) in ivory (A) and metal (B). Scale approx. $\frac{3}{4}$.

(*After drawings by Mr. S. J. Duncan.*)

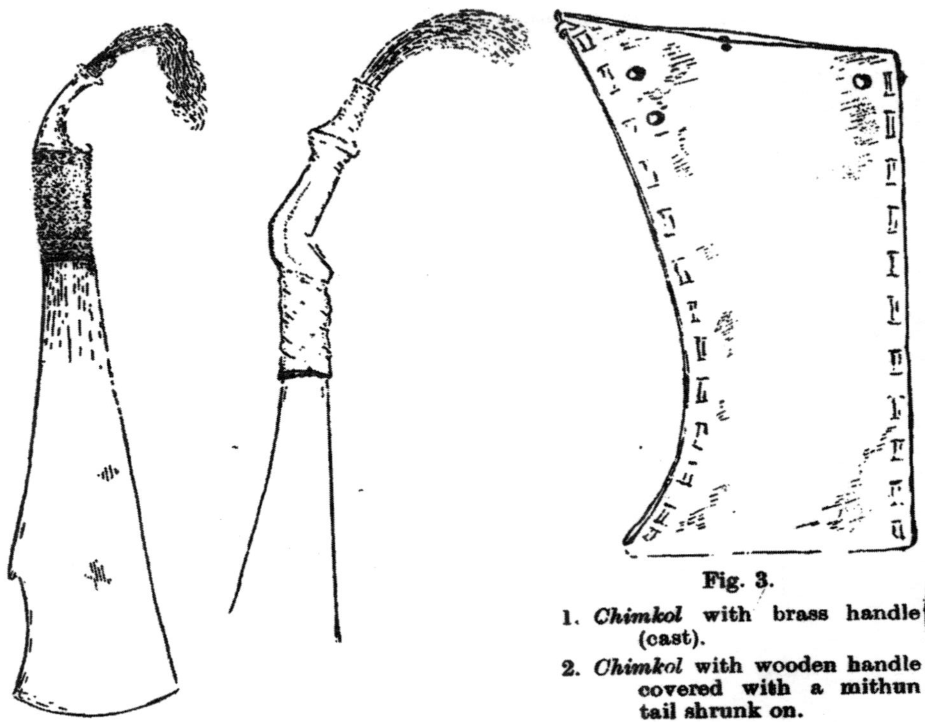

Fig. 3.

1. *Chimkol* with brass handle (cast).
2. *Chimkol* with wooden handle covered with a mithun tail shrunk on.
3. Hide sheath for *chimkol*.

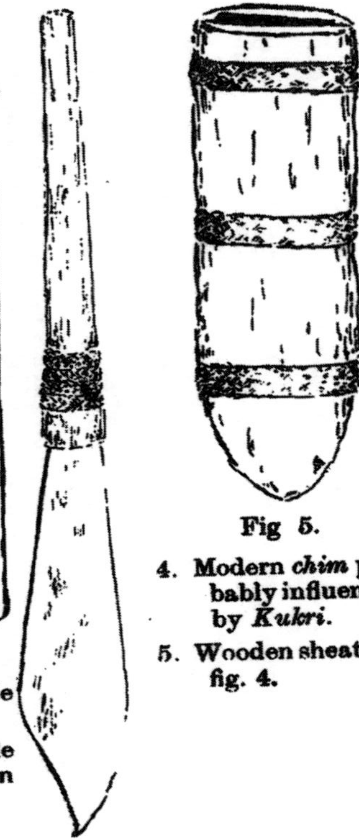

Fig 5.

4. Modern *chim* probably influenced by *Kukri*.
5. Wooden sheath of fig. 4.

Hills in which the projectile is attached by a thread to the tube so that the rat-shooter can haul it in after a miss to save himself the trouble of getting up to fetch it or so that the rat may not run away with the missile sticking into him.

A hide cuirass is reported by Mr. Duncan from Teloulong village, where it belongs to one Mangjalhun of the Phoh-hil clan, formerly chief of a small and now non-existent village. Mangjalhun had it from his grand-father Chongjalhun in the marriage price of one of his sisters. Chongjalhun then lived at Lunglen or Lungthul in what is now the Lushai Hills, and was subsequently chief of Solo in Manipur.

This hide armour covers the back and shoulder blades and fastens down the chest being supported over the shoulders by straps. The Thado call it *Sapho* apparently after the pangolin (scaly ant-eater). This breast plate is similar to the type found in the last century by Peal in the Naga Hills (Konyak), where it has now apparently entirely disappeared, and reported from Formosa, from Borneo, from the hills of Indo-China and elsewhere in the Indonesian area. Mangjalhun's specimen is made of rhinoceros hide, but the Semas use a degenerate form of the same cuirass which consists of little more than a very broad hide belt protecting the abdomen, and made of cow or mithun hide. The Sema article is virtually identical with that of the Ashluslay warrior of S. America (Nordenskiöld, *Les Indiens du Chaco*, pl. xi).

The method of treating hide is to soak it for a long time in the lees of rice wine, and then pound it repeatedly with paddy pestles until quite soft.

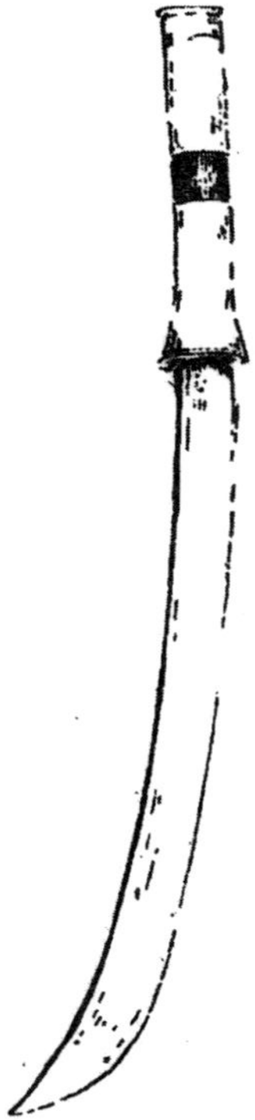

Fig. 1 *Chimjām*.
Scale *c* $\frac{1}{6}$.

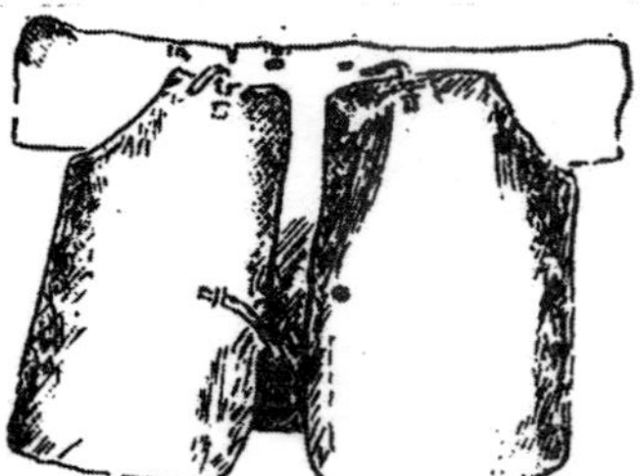

Fig. 2(A).

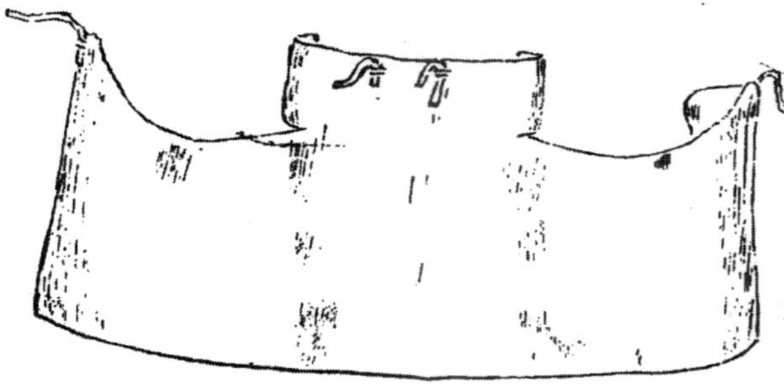

Fig. 2(B).

MANGJALHUN'S RHINOCEROS HIDE "SAPHO."

A. From the front.
B. Seen from behind, opened.

(*From a drawing by Mr. S. J. Duncan.*)

Scale *c.* $\frac{1}{8}$.

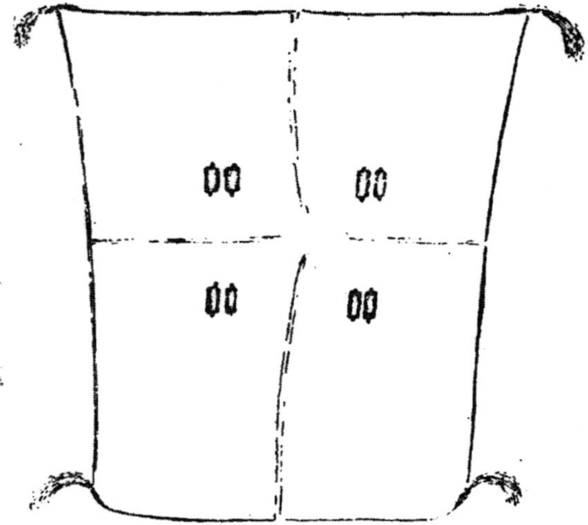

Fig. 3.—Thado shield, *lum*. Usually it is ornamented with a sort of cymbal of bell metal (*lumdal*) borne as a boss in the centre, or with lines of brass discs, either slightly domed or else conical, across the upper half of the shield. From the centres of the discs or of the cymbal is hung a plume of scarlet goat's hair. (*Vide* Tickell, *Notes on the Shendoos; J.A.S.B.*, No. vi of 1852, plate x.)

APPENDIX F.

THADO MUSICAL INSTRUMENTS.

The Thado are more prolific than Nagas in musical instruments and though their singing is not to be compared with good Naga singing they produce far more in the way of instrumental music from a set of instruments mostly rather crude. The music is all in a minor key.

The following instruments are used :—

1. **Dapi**—a large Burmese gong. valued according to the clarity of the note, and its reverberations when the gong is struck on the boss.
2. **dabu**—small Burmese gongs in sets of three, the three gongs being theoretically in tune at equal intervals of about a half tone of western music.
3. **kingkidit**—a wooden gong used in the fields, partly to scare birds, partly also to produce pleasing sounds.
4. **diengdong**—a xylophone consisting of six solid wooden slats laid across two cords which are fastened at one end each to the big toe of the foot on the corresponding side and at the other together behind the player's back, resembling in effect the back-strap of the Indonesian tension loom, the slat with the lowest note being nearest the player's body and the others receding in ascending order. They are played with two miniature wooden clubs held and manipulated as drumsticks are by a kettle-drum player. This instrument is rarely met with. Hlunjangul of Saijang is the only man I could find to make and play one in the Naga Hills.
5. **khoung**—a drum, made from a hollowed section of tree trunk covered at both ends with a hide membrane for which the skin of tho serow (*capricornis sumatrensis rubidus*) is preferred. The two membranes are laced together with a cane lashing which runs backwards and forwards across the barrel of the drum. A small round hole is often made in the centres of the membranes. Some of these drums are of large size, and I sent an outsize specimen to the Oxford University Museum.
6. **gu-shumkol**—a trumpet (**gu**=' bamboo') made of successive sections of nodes of bamboo one fitting inside the next so as to produce a diameter gradually increasing from the mouthpiece onwards. To make the sections hold and fit, water is frequently poured over it before use so that the bamboo swells and each section fits tightly inte the next. The mouthpiece is cut obliquely at the end and placed between the lips so that the edges of this oblique aperture are in the same plane as the lips and the mouth of the trumpet points sideways, for the trumpet is blown with a loose lip, the mouthpiece being kept in position against the lips by holding the right hand round it and as near to the end as possible, the thumb and fore finger keeping contact with the performer's mouth.
7. **kuli**—flute—There are several types of **kuli**. One is the ordinary flute made from an internode of bamboo one node of which is retained. Just below this node is the hole into which the musician blows ; above the open end are four holes, the upper two stopped by the first and second finger of the right hand,

and the lower two by the same fingers of the left hand (thus differing from the Naga type which has two stops for the fingers, and sometimes one for the thumb of the right hand, and has the aperture at the end stopped by the palm of the left hand). The other types of flutes are devised to give extraneous assistance to the player by directing the air currrent for him. I have seen two patterns; in one two internodes are used both ends being open; the musician blows into one and the wind leaves it by a hole just above the dividing node and passes into a conduit made of a small bamboo, split and attached to the instrument by wax; this conduit conducts the wind past the node and redirects it through a second hole back into the lower internode, this artificial redirection performing the same service as that performed by the lips of the flautist when playing on the simple flute; for the rest the instruments are similar having the same four stops. In the other variety an identical effect is obtained by using a single internode, but retaining a narrow projectio n about an inch long above the node which forms the upper end; another piece of bamboo is tied to this leaving a narrow aperture between the two into which the musician blows, this projecting portion going bodily into his mouth; as before the wind is directed into a hole just below the node, and the usual four stops are found lower down.

8. **chapang-kuli**—small boys' flute—is a still more simplified form of **kuli** consisting of two separate sections of bamboo, one which fits inside the other and has a hole at the point of contact and has the node above this hole; by blowing into the upper tube the air is directed by its lower edge at the point of contact with the lower and inner tube into the hole in the latter; there are no stops, so that variation in note can only be obtained by modulation of the lung power, and the instrument is really no more than a whistle.

9. **theili**—a rudimentary flageolet, the flute reversed as it were, and played from the open end, the node of the bamboo being at the lower end with two holes just above it stopped by the first two fingers of the right hand; the mouthpiece is the nodeless end which is cut away so that the upper edge rests just under the edge of the musician's upper lip and the aperture is filled by the lower lip which is flexed to allow the passage of air into the tube; immediately below the upper edge and opposite therefore to the musician's lower lip is a square hole the edge of which divides the blast, part going down the tube and part outside.

10. **gu-chang-pol**—clarinet—is derived from a still more primitive "scrannel pipe" of paddy straw, for the meaning of the word is "bamboo paddy straw," the latter being the original material for the instrument, for which Hlunjangul who made it for me could, indeed, offer no name at all. It consists of a thin bamboo with a node as the mouthpiece, just below which a tongue-shaped cut is made, the cortex of the bamboo being scraped away till it is quite thin, so that the tongue within this cut vibrates as the wind passes through. Below this are four stops modulated by the first two fingers of each hand.

11. **gu-shem**—mouth organ—is a familiar instrument consisting of a gourd the stalk end of which is fitted with a mouthpiece made from a node of small bamboo inserted node downwards and having an aperture cut above the node so that the node itself forms a receptacle for any saliva that may escape from the mouth. The belly of the gourd is fitted with two rows of pipes one row above the other projecting more or less at right-angles from the shell, in which the bases are made fast with wax. In

A & B—*Kuli*.

C—*chapang-kuli*.

D—*theili*.

E—*gu-chang-pol*.

F—*lhemlhai*

THADO MUSICAL INSTRUMENTS I.

Scale *c.* ½ (linear.)

N.B.—All are of bamboo; A & D are shewn with the node to the right, B & E with the node to the left, while C has the node in the middle.

J. H. H.

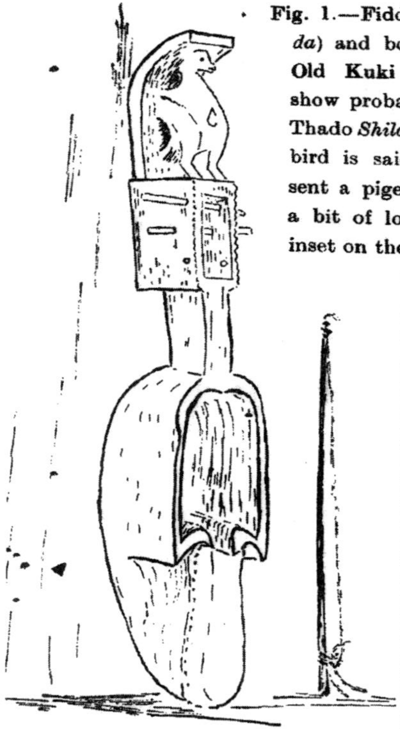

Fig. 1.—Fiddle (*Sarangda*) and bow from an **Old Kuki** village to show probable type of Thado *Shilangda*. The bird is said to represent a pigeon and has a bit of looking glass inset on the breast.

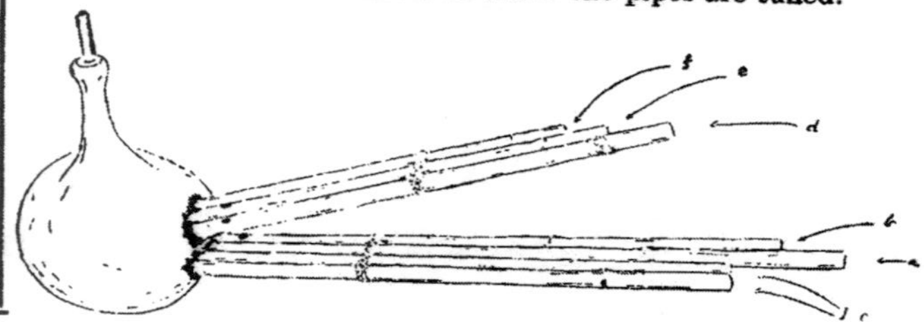

Fig. 2.—Gushem. The letters *a, b, c, d, e, f* indicate in ascending order the different notes to which the pipes are tuned.

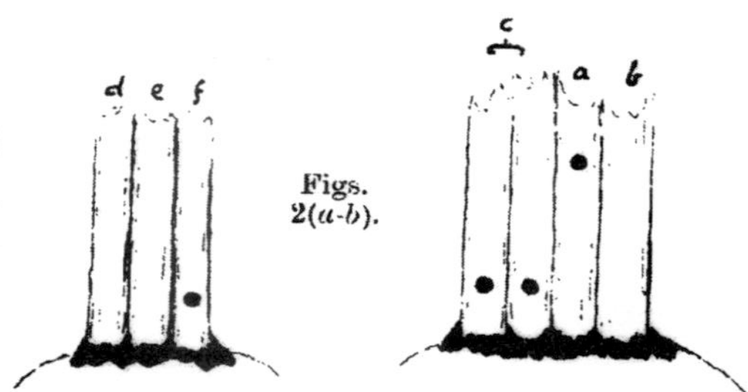

Figs. 2(a-b).

Fig. 2(d).

Fig. 2(*a-b*).—Show the under-side of the two rows of pipes indicating the position of the stops.

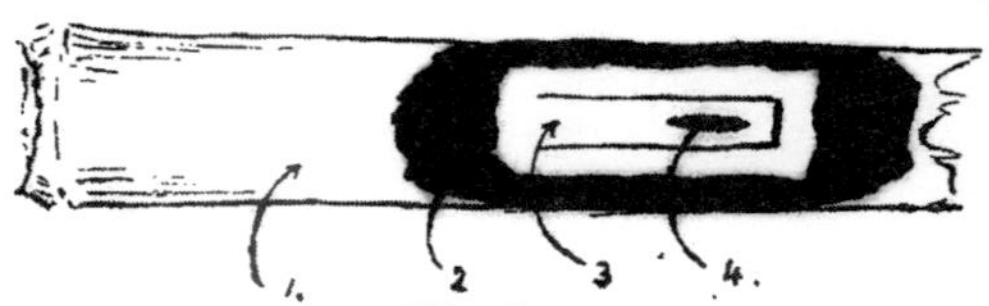

Fig. 2(*c*).

Fig, 2(*c*).—Shows the end of the pipes inside the gourd from the under-side; (1) bamboo, (2) wax, holding the metal reed to the opening cut above the node, (3) the metal reed with a vibrating tongue, (4) the wax weight fastened to the tongue to increase vibration.

Fig. 2(*d*) Shows the mouth-piece.

In large *Gushem* with heavy and long pipes, the base of one in each row is often carried right through the gourd and waxed in to the opposite side to keep the instrument from being too top-heavy.

THADO MUSICAL INSTRUMENTS II.

the Thado instrument there are seven of these bamboo organ-pipes; each ends in a node inside the gourd, and between this node and the shell of the gourd the bamboo is cut away on the under side and the wind allowed to enter the pipe through a metal plate the centre of which is cut into a vibrating tongue which is often weighted with wax to increase the vibration, the whole plate being fastened to the bamboo by a wax setting; the metal used is preferrably bell-metal and sometimes brass; there is a tradition that these reeds used formerly to be made of bamboo. Each pipe has a single stop; there are three pipes in the top row, of which the outside left (the pipes point away from the player's body) has the stop underneath and is controlled by the second finger of the right hand, while the other two have their stops on the upper side and are both controlled by the right thumb. The lower row has four pipes, of which the outside left has the stop on the upper side and controlled by the left thumb; the next pipe to it has the stop below and is controlled by the first finger of the left hand; the remaining two on the right also have the stop below, and are both controlled by the second or third finger of the left hand. These two pipes are tuned to the same note. The lowest pipe is the one next to them, above which comes the outside left hand pipe of that row and then the pair on the right; above this is the top row from right to left in ascending order.

Subdued but harmonious notes are produced, including a fair approximation to the human voice and an excellent imitation of the notes emitted by the wings of the great hornbill when flying overhead.

The legend of the origin of the **gushem** is that a chief had seven musicians who played in harmony on pipes of different pitch. Finding by some misfortune that his musicians were reduced to one he hit on the expedient of combining their instruments into one by means of a gourd. Though this instrument is widely known in south east Asia, being found in the mountains from Tonking to at least as far west as the Dafla country and as far south as Malay, and in the Philippines in the south east, it is, in Assam south of the Brahmaputra, essentially an instrument of the Kuki as distinct from the Naga tribes to whom generally speaking it is unknown.

12. **lhemlhai**—jew's harp—a simple form in which the tongue is made to vibrate by jerking the string tied at its root. The end of the tongue is weighted with wax as by the tribes north of the Brahmaputra, but otherwise it resembles the usual Naga form.

13. **gu-da** [1]—zither—made from an internode of bamboo both nodes of which are retained. Three or more strings are made by incising the outer bark of the bamboo and raising strips of it under which are inserted at each end moveable pegs or bridges of bamboo to make this self-string taut and tunable. The bamboo is cut away on the underside to make the interior act as a sounding board. This instrument, again is not Naga at all, but is common among the Kuki tribes and again extends to Malay and to the Philippines. The Malays call it **gendang batak** associating it with primitive tribes (Balfour, *Fascicul Malayenses*).

14. **Shilangda**—fiddle—Though well known to Thado folk-lore and

[1] **gu**—bamboo, so there is no derivation from "guitar"; the perplexing Khasi **duitara** for a species of guitar may therefore also be entirely fortuitous and **duitara** and "guitar" merely a case of "convergent evolution" from **gu-da** and *κίθαρα*.

tradition this instrument seems to have disappeared among the Thado proper with whom I am in touch. I have, however, obtained an old specimen from a village of Chirus who call the instrument **sarangda**. It is, even in name apparently, identical with the Bengali **sarinda**, a three-stringed fiddle played with a bow strung with horsehair. The resonator has roughly the shape of a flying bird (whence, no doubt, its application in the story—Appendix A, vii) the "tail" only being covered with parchment while the wings make an uncovered hollow resonator. The end above the keys is carved into a sitting bird both in the Chiru specimens I have seen and in all the Bengali specimens in the Indian Museum, but the only other specimens of this type there come from the north-west frontier and have no carved bird above the keys, though otherwise resembling the Bengali instrument. The bird represented was said by the Chirus to be a dove or a pigeon, and it and the whole body of the instrument is carved from one block of wood.

An almost complete set of Thado musical instruments will be found in the Oxford University Museum. It should perhaps be added that to accompany dancing the long bamboo tubes used for water carrying are struck on the ground (node downwards, of course) to produce a musical note, but they are not made for that purpose in sets to produce a specific series of notes as are the "**ding tengkhing**" of the Malay Peninsular, similarly used. The Besisi, by the way, like the Thado, use the **guda** called "**banjeng**" by them, and probably borrowed from Malayan tribes, see Skeat and Blagden, *Pagan Races of the Malay Peninsular*, II, 140 sqq. and 117.

A musical instrument called **pheiphit** is reported by Mr. Duncan, which consists of ten simple bamboo tubes of graduated lengths. He describes it as follows:—

"The notes are produced by blowing at the open end. Generally the notes are only four, viz., G (**Soh**), E (**Me**), D (**Ray**) and low C (**Doh**). Each man holds a tube and blows into it at regular intervals to harmonize with the sympathetic note played by another man. The order of the notes as they are played is more or less as follows :—

M : R I D_1 : S I M : R I D_1

. : S I M : R I D_1 : S I M }

S : M I R : D_1 I S : M I R } Harmonisation

This is the common harmonisation when a tiger or big game is killed. The Kotlhangs use this form of music in dancing too, and it serves as accompaniment to the song."

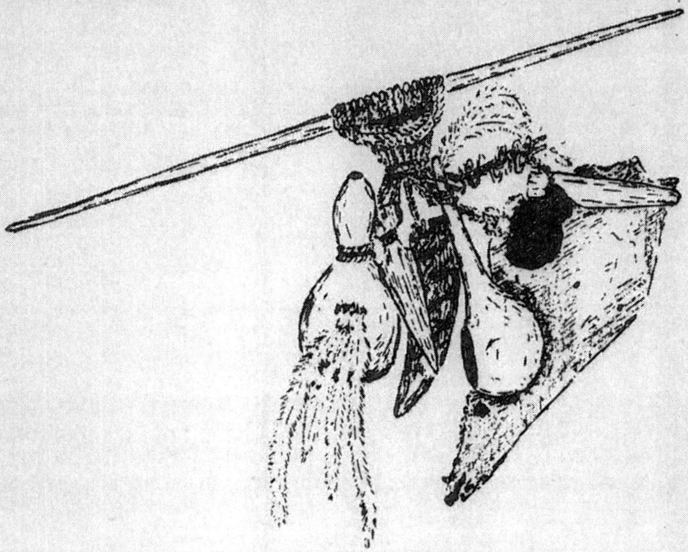

Fig. 1.—*Indoi* as made by most Thado clans.
Scale c. ⅜.

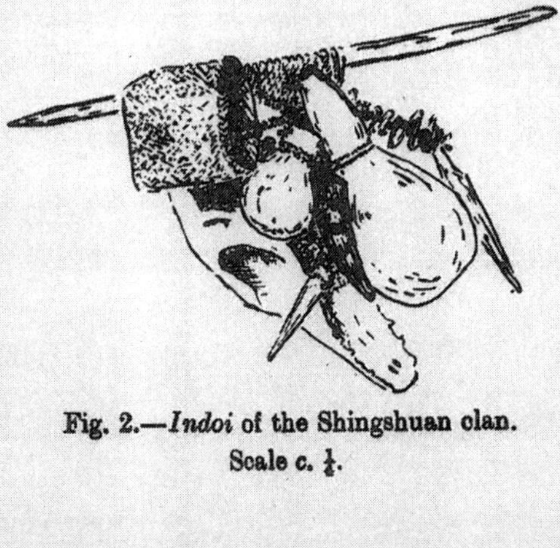

Fig. 2.—*Indoi* of the Shingshuan clan.
Scale c. ½.

APPENDIX G.

MISCELLANEOUS NOTES.

INDOI. The **Indoi** is the "house-magic," a bundle of charms, which is made either by the **thempu** or by any other person who has the requisite knowledge of what is required and of the signification of the objects used and of the formulae used in putting them together. It consists of seven objects bound with a single cord to a bamboo spike, some of the objects being ornamented with feathers from a white cock. The spike is thrust into the thatch in the porch of the house. The component parts and their significance are as follows:—

1. *A pig's skull*, to confer vigour and fertility like that of the fabled sow of Lheival (the place of origin of men), which had ten bonnives at a farrow, and which rooted up and rooted down, overthrowing great trees, even as disease shall be uprooted and cast forth from the bodies of the owner of the house and all that dwell therein.

2. *A goat's horn*, to confer beauty and vigour like that of the goat of Heilhongpi (the rock that 'eats all water' and stands in the sea where the rivers flow into it), with curling horns and long silky hair.

3. *A miniature gourd ladle* to confer plenty in all that can be lifted in a ladle—water, wine (i.e. rice-wine), grain, etc.

4. *A miniature gourd, complete, containing water and seeds*, to confer rapid increase, prosperity and perfection like that of the gourd, and wealth in cattle, crops, and all else, that shall never dry up.

5. *A belval* (that is a circular stand for a jar, but it is represented in a purely conventional manner by a fragment of split stick with a coiled sliver of bamboo peel) to ensure that all wealth acquired by the owner is encircled and bound in as with a **belval**, and cannot escape or be lost.

6. *A minute bamboo dao* (**chimpong**) of **Kol-thi** (i.e. iron of "Alva"—Burma) to ensure that even as such a dao will cut through everything there is high up or low down (**kol-sa kol-lhang**), so all evil spirits that bring disease or misfortune shall be cleft and driven away from the body of the owner of the house and all that dwell therein.

7. *A minute bamboo spear-head* (**theingcha**) to ensure that even as from one horizon to the other (**Kolsa Kollhang**) the spear is used of all men for slaying and killing, and there is nothing that is not pierced by it, so all misfortune and disease and ghosts ("**pughao paghao**" i.e. ghosts of cognates and ghosts of agnates) shall be pierced and driven off.

The above seven are bound together on a single cord fibre made from the fibre of the plant **khaopi** and with the cord bound fast to a bamboo spike. The spear head is at one end of the cord, the 'dao' at the other. On the two gourd articles are feathers from a white cock fastened with wax.

8. *The bamboo spike* is cut from the cultivated bamboo only and confers vitality and straight strong growth like that of the cultivated bamboo and ensures prolific increase like the green shoots which the bamboo puts forth early.

9. *The cord* ensures that as the plant from which it came was produced from the earth and has ten layers of cortex, so shall the owner of the house and all that dwell therein be strong, and that even as it is bound about the bamboo spike, so is all disease, misfortune and evil bound fast and prevented from attacking the owner of the home and its inmates, and that even so also are cattle and crops and all forms of wealth bound so that they cannot escape him.

10. *The white chicken feathers* ensure that as the white cock of Molkoi recalled the sun after the Thimzin and restored the light dispelling the darkness so shall all disease misfortune and evil be cleared away from the persons of the owner of the house and the dwellers therein.

The Shingshuan clan and their offshoots use a slightly different **indoi.** It has no cock's feathers and no gourd ladle, since the **thempu** of the ancestor of the clan had the ill-luck to be "chopped" by enemies during the performance of the ceremony and before its completion. As it could never be finished, the miniature gourd, which he was using, as in all Thado ceremonies, to pour libations to the spirits and which he had left unemptied was added to the **indoi.** Having been killed moreover he was unable to claim the basket of grain which is the recognized **thempu's** fee, and in consequence a miniature basket is attached to the **indoi** and whenever there is a feast day observed in the house this miniature basket is filled up with cooked millet as the **thempu's** share. It must be millet not rice, as the ancestors of the clan used millet, sorghum and coix only, rice being at that time unknown.

(From information supplied by a **thempu** of the Shitnhao clan, which observes the Shingshuan custom, who made me a Shingshuan **indoi.** J. H. H.)

OF SERPENTS. The Thado believe in a serpent with seven nostrils which lives under water and causes men to drown by catching them under water and making them into pillows. This legendary serpent appears to be confused in general thought with the rock python, **gulpi,** which is regarded with great awe. Formerly it was the only poisonous snake, and it bit a man and he died. It asked a little snake whether the man had died or no. The little snake replied "No, Listen how they are beating drums and drinking modhu (referring to the funeral ceremonies); how should he have died?" The big one then said that his poison was of no use, and vomited it all over a plant. The other snakes divided up the poison and became poisonous from that time, and last of all the little red ant got what was left, and the plant had sharp edged leaves, so that they could not get the poison from the edges, and since then the tree-nettle (*Laportea crenulata*) has stung men and the big snake has used magic instead of poison.

The awe of the python is common, but not universal, among the Naga tribes. The Chakroma Angami eat it, but the Ao and the Chang hold it in very great awe, as do most tribes in a lesser degree.

Great fear is felt by the Thado of a black snake called **gulshie,** which I have not been able to identify. The male is said to keep watch in a tree above the female when the latter is guarding her eggs in a nest on the ground. This sounds like the hamadryad, but the snake is reported to be totally black without any transverse bars at all and not to have any hood, and they have another name for the hamadryad. However, so great is the fear of this snake, which is said to be very deadly, that a man who kills one may not enter the village that day. He throws down on the path, as he goes home, quantities of little leaves which the pursuing soul of the vengeful snake must count ere it can catch him. Similarly in the ceremony (ai) performed for killing a tiger a wooden post with many incisions is put up. Above it hangs a rattle made of a gourd and some slats of wood like bull-roarers (v. Shakespear, *Lushei Kuki Clans*, p. 207, illustration). The tiger's ghost cannot pass the post to come to the village where the slayer is till it has counted the cuts on the post, and it can never do this as the gourd swinging in the wind and rattling repeatedly distracts it, making it lose count. The killer of the **gulshie** on reaching the outskirts of his village must split a bamboo placed upright in the ground and scrape through between the split sides closing them quickly and tightly behind him and tying them together.

The names of the following snakes may prove useful to someone :—

Gulpi, rock python.
Gulsho, hamadryad.
Thangchom, Russell's Viper.
Gulngongshan, Common Himalayan Viper.
Gullha, green pit viper.
Gulvankal, green tree-snake.

If a snake be found eating another animal it is wrong to let it go. The snake should be killed.

OF GHOSTS. The Thado believes in certain disembodied spirits or beings of a ghostly nature which are apparently akin to the astral bodies of humans, and are known as **kau**. Thus **in-kau** (='house ghost') is used of the familiar spirit or rather of the astral body of the **kaushi** or vampire (q.v.).

Kau-mei (='ghost-fire') is apparently the Will o' the wisp, as it consists in small pale moving fires and is regarded as harmless to human beings.

Găm-kau (='jungle-ghost') on the other hand is dangerous. It appears in the night in the form of a much more powerful light, single and concentrated, but with some movement, as it swells and subsides. It is often seen by parties fishing; my informant watched one in the jungle near Kohima; one was seen by a woman of Thenjol in 1916 or thereabouts, when she left her house at night. It was in the top of a tree and she ran back to her house in terror, fastened the door and fainted. She recovered enough to tell her husband what she had seen, but was smitten with violent diarrhœa and vomitting and was dead by morning.

In addition to ghosts there are the usual godlings of the jungle—Those that preside over trees **(thingbu nga)** and those that preside over stones **(shoungbu nga)**, etc. Such an one is the **Gămnupi** or 'jungle-wife' of female shape with red teeth and breasts that hang down to her hips.

VAMPIRES. The Thado live in great dread of vampires, **kaushi**, men who can so project their astral bodies as to enter into those they wish to and devour their internal organs, particularly the liver and heart. So great is their fear of persons reputed to have this power that they will not as a rule on any account mention the name of a person as being a **kaushi** for fear that if the vampire came to hear of it he would start to devour the person who had spoken ill of him. The Meithei of Manipur have a similar belief in vampires which they call **hingchabi**, and the Maori also believe in vampires who send their **atua** to enter a man's body and slowly eat away his vitals (*Old New Zealand*, ch. viii). This belief differs from the commoner belief in material vampires which attack persons bodily and suck their blood, much as the Sema Naga belief in wer-leopards who project their souls into the familiar beast differs from the commoner belief in a bodily transformation into a tiger or a wolf.

Some Thado say that if a man is suffering from the attacks of a vampire, and his hair be cut off, it will be found, when he is recovered of the disease, that his hair is intact and that of the vampire has been cut.

THE SOUL. The Thado shares with his Naga neighbours the conception of the soul as a minute replica of the individual, and like them (the Kachha Nagas) stretches a thread along side the plank across a ditch or a ladder up which he may have to climb in order that the soul may cross or climb beside him. This is done by a sick man who goes to the fields to recall the soul which has played truant there. The Khasis also use thread to make a bridge for the soul (Gurdon, *op. cit.*, 141). This use of thread as a path for the soul seems to have been incorporated into Buddhist ritual as a means of bringing the priest into contact with the worshippers and so, no doubt, increasing the efficacy of their worship, *vide* Lewin, *Wild Races of S.E. India*, 105, 114, and *cf.* 173, 197, 209.

There appears to be some idea that the colour red has certain particular property with regard to the soul, as red cloth may not be buried with any person who leaves any surviving relatives. Perhaps the idea is that the souls of the survivors are attracted by the colour to follow the dead to the next world and so cause the death of the survivor also.

THADO MEDICINE. The Thado is more primitive than the Naga in general in the treatment of disease, in that he makes little use of simples, being more single-heartedly devoted to the use of ceremonial for the cure and preventive of illness. No sickness is in his opinion natural, but all is due to the malevolent attacks of evil spirits. These spirits, however, are little removed in conception from the notion of bacilli, and the Thado explains the effectiveness of European medicine, which he readily admits, as due to the fact that Europeans have discovered the particular odours which are noxious to particular spirits, and can thus drive them away by the application, internal or external as the case may be, of the appropriate compound in each case. Precisely the same theory is held by the Tinguian of the Philippines (Cole, *The Tinguian*, 409), and in Sierra Leone in W. Africa (Beatty, *Human Leopards*, 25). The view that illness is due to evil spirits probably still survives in Europe (*v. Folk-lore, XXXVII*, iv, p, 350 sqq.). At any rate it was strong in the XVIIth century. The life of Jon Olafsson affords a case in point, as he and nine other sailors got headaches on account of a "ghostly presence" on their ship (*Life of Jon Olafsson*, I, 54), and the same idea seems to have actuated the famous John Mytton two centuries later when he set fire to his night shirt (and he inside it) "to frighten away the hiccoughs."

Purely magical remedies are also resorted to by the Thado. Thus a remedy for heartburn is to tie round the neck a (?) clavicle bone from a pig's throat. The reasoning is obscure here, but it is clear enough in the practice of tying a bit of polished horn from the tip of the horn of a serow (Capricorn) round a wrist that has been broken in order to strengthen it, for the joints and muscles of this extraodinarily active cliff-dwelling beast are strong and massive out of proportion to its size and weight. The jaw of a monitor lizard (the **guisamp** of Bengal) is used as an antidote for the stings of the tree-nettle (*Laportea crenulata*), the stung spot being scraped with a piece of the jaw. The jaw-bone of a mud turtle is similarly used for stings caused by the hairs of hairy caterpillars, and Thados have asseverated to me that relief is almost immediate. Kachha Nagas (Lyengmai) use the lizard jaw for both purposes.

Simples are used occasionally. One is the yellow berry of the plant **āpilinga** or **lingkang** (*Solanum indicum*) dried and pounded and smoked in a pipe, as if tobacco, to alleviate toothache This berry is used for the same purpose by Khasis who put the seeds of it on a hot dao and inhale the smoke, while some of the Kachha Naga (Nruongmai) put it into hot water and inhale the steam, also to alleviate toothache, the belief being, as among the Thado, that the minute worm which is gnawing the tooth (?=the nerve) will be killed and drop out (*cf.* Cole, *The Tinguian, loc. cit.*, also Burton, *Arabian Nights, IV*, 298n).

FIRE.—New fire is made with flint and steel, and there appears to be no tradition even of the use of any other apparatus in the past. The fire-stick (split 'hearth' and flexible sawing-thong) is hardly ever used and then only by persons who have learnt its use from Nagas.

BULL-ROARER.—The Thado bull-roarer, rarely seen, is tied by a notch, not, apparently, like some Naga ones, by a hole. It is sometimes used to scare birds, but in the Shingshuan clan, at any rate, the old men object to its use on the ground that it calls up the spirits. The same idea is found in other tribes of Assam. Thus the Khasis say the same, and the Southern Sangtams that it attracts tigers. On the other hand the Semas would appear to credit it with the opposite property as imitation bull-roarers are hung up in the door ways of houses in Mishilimi and elsewhere to act as disinfectants in case of illness.

SALAAM.—Old and old-fashioned men among the Thado, when performing ceremonies to propitiate any spirit use an action to express their reverence which consists in placing the palms of the hands together and raising them infront of the face with the thumbs to the forehead.

This action distinctly suggests contact with some Indian culture and is perhaps to be compared with such uses as that of a word (*taima*) for the number 10,000—a lakh, with the practice of singeing a tiger's whiskers (*v.* Appendix A, Folk-tale, No. vi, note 16) and with the introduction of foreign apparatus such as kings and elephants into Thado folk-lore (*v*, Folk-tale, No. vii). Cf. also under Appendix F—*Shilangda.*

BUGS.—(măt) May be got rid of by tying one in a little parcel and putting it into the basket of a visitor at the house. *Cf.* the common Naga method of getting rid of a minor ailment, e.g. Mills, *The Lhota Nagas*, p. 136; Marshall, *Karen People of Burma*, p. 241.

CELTS.—Stone adzes, although called ordinarily by another name (*ke'*), are none the less said to be spirit-hoes. A sky-spirit blacksmith, or, according to other accounts, Pathen himself makes them, but while doing so is sometimes infuriated by the persistent shrilling of the cicada, and throws the hoe he is making at the cicada to make him stop, hence they fall to earth and men find them. A variant version says that they are thrown down because the maker is prodded in his fundament. The belief that they are thunderbolts and that in this capacity they split trees is also held, and an intelligent and literate Thado friend of mine tells me he will believe that it is otherwise when I can show him what does split the tree, if the "thunder-bolt" does not.

NATURAL HISTORY.—The Thado, though an accurate and generally reliable observer of animals wherever such observation is of direct and appreciable benefit to him, as in the case of the habits of animals that he wants for food, is no less capable of naturalistic fantasies than Pliny the Elder in matters that concern him less nearly. Thus a large and fleshy caterpillar called tangngol is said to turn into a small field mouse instead of into a moth. The bone from a bear's penis, if dropped into the village well, will cause the damsels of the village to become pregnant by drinking the water. The slow loris (*Nycticebus coucang*) is the priest of the gibbon (*Hylobates hooluck*). It is a rare beast and a Thado will not willingly harm it, as a rule. *cf.* Lewin *Hill Tracts of Chittagong and the Dwellers Therein*, p. 95. His "sloth" must be the slow loris.

DREAMS.—To dream of a wedding, according to the Thado, portends a death; to dream of the death of a man foretells success in hunting; the familiar falling dream is significant of the growth of the body. The first and last of these interpretations are common in the British Isles, at any rate in Ireland, and the first of the three is shared also by the Sema Naga. Another dream, that of the loss of a tooth, is held to portend the death of a near relative particularly, say the Thado, on the mother's side. The Angami go further and say it is actually the mother's brother's death which is foretold. The Memi and the Lhota, however, seem to see in this dream merely a presage of a death in the family, and the death of a friend or of a relative is its significance in Europe as well.

ASINUS IN TEGULIS.—For a dog or a goat to climb on to the roof of a house is an omen of terrible misfortune to its inhabitants.

INCEST.—This crime, when it occurs, which is very rarely, is punished by expulsion from the village. The only case I ever heard of was that of a man of Thengbung by whom his own mother had a child. Both were turned out of Thengbung.

STONES.—Stones are used as substitutes when a man wishes to break a tabu on leaving home. A small oblong stone is taken and set upright in the ground. A little food and drink is supplied for it and it remains and observes the tabu while the man himself goes abroad. Stones are so often set up by Nagas as abodes for souls that one is tempted to suggest that the Thado leaves his, or one of his, at home in the stone when he goes out.

GAMES.—Games played by children include a game with peg-tops, and a game in which two boys amuse themselves by dressing up as a man and his wife and successfully taking in strangers. The Thado, however, and I have made many enquiries, seem to have no trace, unless this game is such, of the custom common to so many tribes of Malay affinities, including the Lushei, whereby some males dress as females and follow female occupations. Mr. Shaw, however, states that impotence is common among the Thado, and it may be that this is a symptom of the same physical tendency.

Cat's cradles are another Thado game, and one of the first I saw was called "duck's foot," and is made by the Kabui also. In Samoa likewise, this same figure is called "the three toed duck" (Hornell, "Cat's cradles" in *Discovery*, April 1928, p. 112).

A form of dance, somewhat on the lines of a sword dance, has been described to me by Mr. Duncan (I have not yet seen it myself), called *su'talăm*, in which the dancer dances between four men who face each other from opposite sides of a square, each pair holding two bamboos one end in each hand. As the one pair closes their bamboos together, the other pair parts theirs at right angles, and so alternately in varying time, while the dancer has to skip from the spaces formed by the closing bamboos into those formed by the parting bamboos in time to the singing and with enough agility to save his ankles from severe contusion.

APPENDIX H.

ANTHROPOMETRY.

The measurements given below are those taken by me from sixty male and fifteen female Thado in 1927. The averages work out as follows :—

Height	♂	1608·7
	♀	1466·6
Length of head	♂	190·4
	♀	184·1
Breadth of head	♂	147·8
	♀	141
Nasal length	♂	47·7
	♀	44
Nasal breadth	♂	38·5
	♀	35·7
Cephalic index	♂	76·5
	♀	76·6
Nasal index	♂	80·7
	♀	81·1

These figures agree pretty closely with those given for Kukis by Waddell in *Tribes of the Brahmaputra Valley* (J. A. S. B., XIX, iii, 1900), except in the matter of nasal width for which Waddell's figure is distinctly higher on the whole. Waddell, however, took all his measurements but one from members of the Lakher tribe in the South Lushai Hills, and there were even fewer subjects measured by him than by me.

(Ed.)

Name.	Sex.	Clan.	Height.	Cephalic length.	Cephalic breadth.	Cephalic index.	Nasal length.	Nasal breadth.	Nasal index.	REMARKS.
Sheikhup ..	♂	Biete ..	1573	193	152	78·8	45	36	80·0	
Nguljapao ..	♂	Changsen ..	1698	193	148	76·7	51	37	72·5	Straight nose; glabial depression slight or absent.
Laikhulet	♂	Chonglui ..	1662	185	140	75·7	43	37	86·0	
Pacheng	♂	Do. ..	1597	197	143	72·6	48	39	81·2	
Helbel	♂	Do. ..	1690	182	152	83·5	52	35	67·3	
Lamngul	♂	Do. ..	1542	187	147	78·6	53	37	69·8	
Khupcha ..	♂	Gamlhou ..	1594	195	148	75·9	52	39	75	Straight nose; (i.e. glabial depression absent or only slight).
Sehlam	♂	Hangshing	1607	193	144	74·6	42	37	88·1	
Seilam	♂	Do. ..	1601	187	147	78·6	48	43	89·6	Slightly prognathous, thick lips, coarse nose, negroid appearance.
Seilun	♂	Do. ..	1565	191	146	76·4	44	42	95·5	Slightly prognathous, thick lips coarse nose. (head lopsided.)
Sonlam	♂	Do. ..	1620	198	147	74·2	48	39	81·2	
Thangjahao	♂	Do. ..	1541	175	138	78·9	44	36	81·8	
Lamkhotung	♂	Do. ..	1602	192	142	73·9	43	38	88·4	
Lalthing	♀	Do. ..	1427	182	140	76·9	38	34	89·5	Slightly prognathous; negroid appearance.
Lhaineng	♀	Do. ..	1552	176	138	78·4	44	35	79·5	
Hemkholet	♂	Haokip ..	1640	194	144	74·2	47	37	78·7	
Kimpao	♂	Hengna ..	1537	188	149	79·3	52	37	71·2	
Paoshei	♂	Jate' ..	1633	186	148	79·6	46	42	91·3	The Jate' is an offshoot of the Gwite clan.
Khubshe	♂	Jongbe' ..	1643	189	141	74·6	44	37	84·0	
Pasem	♂	Khulhou ..	1670	197	154	78·2	49	39	79·6	

Name.	Sex.	Clan.	Height.	Cephalic length.	Cephalic breadth.	Cephalic index.	Nasal length.	Nasal breadth.	Nasal index.	Remarks.
Lengjang *	♂	Khulhou	1602	189	149	79·3	51	41	80·4	
Helkhushei	♂	Kipgen	1673	188	147	78·2	52	39	75	
Hoikhunem	♀	Do.	1593	181	137	75·7	45	37	82·2	
Lhaijakim	♀	Do.	1456	191	144	75·4	48	38	79·2	
Thangkhonem	♀	Do.	1432	184	143	77·7	45	37	82·2	
Ngullhun	♂	Kolhang	1732	191	142	74·3	49	39	79·6	
Hilshe	♂	Do.	1609	193	154	79·8	51	39	76·4	
Sheithang	♂	Do.	1586	192	143	74·5	45	40	88·8	
Khuplal	♂	Do.	1560	187	144	77·0	48	37	72·9	
Selkhup	♂	Do.	1574	187	135	72·2	43	36	83·7	
Arui	♂	Do.	1482	192	145	75·5	48	35	72·9	Very like a Kachari in appearance.
Kimhat	♀	Do.	1553	185	140	75·7	44	38	86·3	Slightly prognathous and negroid in appearance.
Nguljalam	♂	Lenthang	1540	189	143	75·7	50	37	74	Overhanging brows.
Lunglen	♂	Do.	1623	185	151	81·6	50	38	76	
Khaine'	♂	Leite	1603	189	141	74·6	42	40	95·2	
Thanglet	♂	Do.	1594	191	142	74·3	44	37	84·0	
Nguljapao	♂	Lhangal	1595	202	147	72·8	42	38	90·5	
Hatdem	♀	Lhoutong	1436	183	135	73·8	43	35	81·4	
Lhingkho	♀	Do.	1412	171	134	78·3	45	35	77·7	
Lunkhujang	♂	Lhouvum	1559	185	137	74·0	46	34	73·9	
Lamkhutong	♂	Mangjel	1565	194	137	70·6	50	37	74	
Khotinpao	♂	Do.	1497	182	139	76·4	50	37	74	Chief of Shongsang. Nose straight (no glabial depression).
Ngulshei	♂	[Milong]	1690	192	145	75·5	52	41	78·8	Mixed origin, Father Nzemi (Naga), mother Hôlthang (Thado).
Khupjahel	♂	Misao	1721	197	152	77·2	52	35	67·3	

* See plate 5

Name.	Sex.	Clan.	Height.	Cephalic length.	Cephalic breadth.	Cephalic index.	Nasal length.	Nasal breadth.	Nasal index.	Remarks.
Khupni	♂	Sanchoung ..	1527	185	150	81·1	42	41	97·6	
Kheipao	♂	Sa'um ..	1634	200	140	70·0	46	38	82·7	
Paokhutong	♂	Do. ..	1661	194	144	74·3	45	38	84·4	
Jamlet	♂	Shingshuan ..	1581	188	150	79·8	47	40	85·1	
Thangkhupao ..	♂	Do. ..	1672	194	143	73·7	47	41	87·2	Markedly Prognathous.
Lhunjahel	♂	Do. ..	1520	187	151	80·7	48	40	83·3	
Nguljalen	♂	Do. ..	1644	188	153	81·4	51	42	82·3	Chief of Kanjang.
Shongkhulal	♂	Do. ..	1592	190	146	76·8	56	42	75	
Sutmang (" Pasut ")* ..	♂	Do. ..	1602	197	151	76·6	57	39	68·4	} his brothers.
Thanglet	♂	Do. ..	1620	193	144	74·6	44	41	93·2	
Nemlhing	♀	Do. ..	1488	186	150	80·6	45	38	84·4	
Chongthem	♀	Do. ..	1479	186	140	75·3	49	39	79·6	
Nengnu	♀	Do. ..	1420	186	144	77·4	44	35	79·5	
Nengjanem	♀	Do. ..	1454	188	143	76·1	42	34	81	
Valhai	♀	Do. ..	1532	195	146	75	45	36	80	
Panei	♀	Do. ..	1468	186	141	75·8	41	32	78·0	
Jahao	♂	Shingvung ..	1567	190	144	75·8	50	40	80	
Paothang	♂	Shitlho ..	1676	187	147	78·6	49	40	81·6	
Lunkhulet	♂	Do. ..	1622	192	147	76·6	50	42	84	
Kaikhu	♂	Do. ..	1611	193	145	75·1	50	43	86	
Sheivom	♂	Do. ..	1557	184	143	77·7	47	42	89·4	
Mangkhukai	♂	Do. ..	1591	183	147	80·3	43	37	86·0	Brother of Khutintong, Chief of Jampi. Somewhat overhanging brow.
Lashu	♂	Telshing ..	1502	193	142	73·6	49	34	69·4	
Haokhokhai	♂	Do. ..	1674	202	143	70·8	50	39	78	
Thoukholet	♂	Do. ..	1636	187	155	82·9	53	37	69·8	
Nguljathong	♂	Do. ..	1524	194	145	74·7	46	36	78·3	
Hoikhunem†	♀	Do. ..	1298	182	140	77	42	33	78·6	Exceptionally small, but fully adult.
Khaikhup	♂	Thanggen ..	1620	196	149	76·0	46	34	73·9	
Lamjakhup	♂	Thomsong ..	1566	189	141	74·6	45	38	84·4	Prognathous; negroid appearance.
Thangkhup	♂	Do. ..	1592	188	154	81·9	44	42	95·5	
Haothang	♂	Vaiphe ..	1636	185	141	76·2	45	39	86.6	Markedly overhanging brows.

* See plate 3.

† See plate 7

APPENDIX J.

BIBLIOGRAPHY OF THE THADO.

In an Appendix to Mr. Mills' *The Ao Nagas*, I have given a bibliography of the Naga Hills down to 1925 which includes a number of books dealing with the Thado in particular and the Kuki race in general. T. C. Hodson has given a good bibliography in his *Thado Grammar*, and Colonel J. Shakespear has also given a Lushei-Thado bibliography in his *The Lushei Kuki Clans*. I give here, therefore, only such references as either bear on the Kukis as a whole, irrespective of individual tribes, or on the Thado in particular, and include nothing which relates exclusively to some other branch of Kukis. Works marked with an asterisk contain at least one illustration of a Thado.

1. 1840. Fisher, Capt., *Memoir of Sylhet Cachar and the Adjacent Districts*. *J.A.S.B.*, IX. pp. 836, 837.

2. 1854. Jenkins, Col., *An Account of the Assam Tribes* in Mills' *Report on the Province of Assam*.

3. 1855. Butler, Major J., *Travels and Adventures in Assam** (Smith Elder, London) pp. 80-101.

4. 1855. Stewart, Lt. R., *Notes on Northern Cachar*; *J.A.S.B.*, XXIV, pp. 617-649; 656-675; 685-691.

5. 1857. Stewart, Lt. R., *Slight notice of the Grammar of the Thadou or New Kookie Language*, *J.A.S.B.*, XXV, pp. 178 sqq.

6. 1859. McCulloch, Major W., *Account of the Valley of Munnipore*, (Calcutta); pp. 55-64, Appendix II, and Vocabulary pp. xi to xliii.

7. 1872. Dalton, E. T., *Ethnography of Bengal** (Calcutta) pp. 44-48 and 75.

8. 1873. Butler, Capt. J., *Vocabulary of some of the Dialects spoken in the Naga Hills*, *J.A.S.B.*, XLII, pt. I, Appendix.

9. 1874. Brown, R., *Account of Manipur and the Hill Territory, 1873*, pp. 47-53.

10. 1874. Campbell, Sir G. *Specimens of Languages of India* (Calcutta), pp. 204-217.

11. 1875. Damant, G. H., *The North Cachar Hills and their Inhabitants*, in the *Calcutta Review*, vol. LXI, pp. 97-99.

12. 1876. Damant, G. H., *Report on a Tour in the North Cachar Hills*.

13. 1879. Hunter, W. W., *Statistical Account of Assam*, (London), II, 186 to 188, and 384 to 387, and elsewhere (v. index *s. v.* "Kuki").

14. 1880. Damant, G. H., *Notes on the Locality and Population of the Tribes dwelling between the Brahmaputra and Ningthi Rivers*, *J.R.A.S.*, XII, 228-231, 237-239, 252-255.

15. 1884 Mackenzie, A., *History of the Relations of Government with the Hill Tribes of the N. E. Frontier of Bengal* (Calcutta), Ch. xv and parts of xvi and xxi and some passages in the "appendixes" (*sic*).

16. 1884. Soppitt, C. A., *Short Account of the Kuki and Lushai Tribes on the N. E. Frontier* (Shillong).

17. 1886. Hunter, W. W., *Imperial Gazetteer of India*, (London), vol. X, pp. 150-151.

18. 1886. Dun, E. W., *Gazetteer of Manipur* (Calcutta), pp. 32-36.

19. 1887. Watt, D. G., *The Aboriginal Tribes of Manipur, J.R.A.I.*, XVI, pp. 349-350.

20. 1892. Gait, E. A., *Census of India, Assam*, vol. I, pp. 181, 182 and 251, 252.

21. 1893. Elles, Col. E. R., *Military Report on the Chin Lushei Country* (Simla), (Shillong), p. 16.

22. 1894. Davis, A. W., *Gazetteer of the North Lushai Hills* (Shillong), pp. 3 sq.

23. 1896. Johnstone, Genl. Sir J., *My Experiences in Manipur and the Naga Hills*, pp. 25-27 and elsewhere, *e.g.* in ch. xx (London).

24. 1896. Carey, B. S., and Tuck, H. N., *The Chin Hills*, vol. 1, ch. xii and pt. II passim.

25. 1900 Scott, J. and Hardiman, J. P., *Gazetteer of Upper Burma and the Shan States* (Rangoon), vol. 1, part i, page 437.

26. 1901. Waddell, L. A., *Tribes of the Brahmaputra Valley, J.A.S.B.*, LXIX, 50-52.

27. 1902. Allen B. C., Assam Census Report, pt. i, page 90.

28. 1902. Allen, B. C., *Assam District Gazetteers*, vol. I, *Cachar* (Shillong) pp. 51 and 52.

29. 1903-'27. Grierson, Sir G., *Linguistic Survey of India*, (Calcutta), III, iii, 1-19, 59-71 and 88-105, I, i, 40-49 and 71 to 77 and maps.

30. 1906. Shakespear, Major L. W., *Military Report on the Naga Hills* (Simla), page 19.

31. 1906. Hodson, T. C., *Thado Grammar* (Shillong).

32. 1912. Shakespear, Lt.-Col. J., *The Lushei Kuki Clans* (London), pt. II, ch. iv and vi.

33. 1913. Shakespear, Lt.-Col. L. W., *Military Report on the Naga Hills*, 2nd Edition, (Simla), pp. 38, 39.

34. 1924. Hutton, J. H., *Occurrence of the Blow-gun in Assam*,* Man, XXIV, viii, 77.

35. 1927. Vickers, Col. A., *Among the Kukis*, Blackwood's Magazine.

36. 1927. Crawford, C. G., *Handbook of Kuki Custom* (Manipur).

37. 1928. Mills, J. P., *The Hill Tribes of Assam, IV, The Kuki Clans*,* Assam Review I, iv, (June 1928), pp. 9-11.

Of the above references Nos. 27 and 29, Hodson and Grierson, are important for the language, and No. 15 is important for the early history of the relations of the Thado with Government. For Ethnology the following are important :—

No. 4—Stewart (*Notes on North Cachar*), now unobtainable, but largely reproduced in

No. 7—Dalton (*Ethnography of Bengal*), which, as reproducing Stewart in a concise form, is the most valuable early authority with the possible exception of

No. 6—McCulloch (*Valley of Munnipore*) and

No. 9—Brown (*Account of Manipur*) both of whom give short but as far as they go accurate accounts of the Thado of the Manipur State sixty to seventy years ago, and

No. 16 Soppitt (*Account of the Kuki and Lushai Tribes*), which, like No. 4, is now unobtainable. There is a copy in the library of the Deputy Commissioner's Office at Kohima, and another is possessed by the Catholic Mission in Shillong. He gives some interesting and remarkable details, elsewhere unrecorded, but dealing with the Sakchip (*i.e.* 'Tippera') and Biete sub-tribes, as well as with the Thado, does not always clearly distinguish between the customs of the Thado and of these Old Kuki tribes, while the section on language is based on Hrangkol and Biete.

No. 24 Carey and Tuck (*The Chin Hills*) deals primarily with Chins, of whom it has excellent illustrations, but Part II relates generally to the Chin Kuki Tribes as a whole.

No. 30 Shakespear (*Lushei Kuki Clans*) though primarily concerned with the Lushei deals (in part II) with the non-Lushei Clans including the Thado, on whom it is the best recent authority.

No. 34 Crawford (*Kuki Custom*) deals with Thado custom, not Kuki custom in general, and is valuable, but contains little, if anything, that is not included in this volume.

APPENDIX K.

TYPES

Plates 1–7.

PLATE I.

GROUP OF THADO MEN.

LHUNVOM of Chongjang (Dongngel clan.)

PAOMINTHANG of Aishan (Gangte clan.)

THONGNGAM of Aishan (Dongngel clan.)

LENGJANG of Taning (Khulhou clan.)

DOUKHULET of Thenjol (Lenthang clan.)

PA-SUT of Kanjang (Shingshuan clan.)

SHEIKENG (Chonglui clan.)

THOSHEI of Paona (Hangshing clan.)

PLATE 2.

Fig. 1.—Chengjapo, Chief of Aishān, Head of the Dongngel clan.

Fig. 2.—Lhokhumang commonly known by his nickname Pachei, Chief of Chahsat, Head of the Haokip clan.

Fig. 3.—Khutinthang (or Khilkung Chief of Jāmpi, and Head of the Shitlho clan.

Fig. 1.—Enjakhup of Thenjol (the rebel leader).

Fig. 2.—Tintong, Chief of Laijang.

Fig 3.—Sutmang (commonly known as Pa-Sūt) brother of the Chief of Kanjang; Shingshuan clan; wearing *vakul* and *thu'pa*.

Plate 4.

Fig. 1.—A boy (Lalkhulet) of Dulen village. He belongs to the Chonglui clan.

Fig. 2.—Two girls of Dulen village.

Fig. 3.—A matron of Dulen village, smoking a woman's pipe.

Fig. 1(a).

Fig. 1(b).

Thado dressed for war or hunting (*a*) with flintlock gun, and (*b*) in ceremonial cloth (*thangnang*) and headgear (*jouchal*—hair and cowrie band: *vakul*—feather plume). (Lengjang of Taning, Khulhou clan.)

Fig. 2.—Heads (crania) of Tangkhuls of Kasom impaled outside Chengjapao's village near Vahong, 1918-19.

Vajanem of Kanjang village—(Haokip clan).

Hoikhunem of Kanjang village—(Telshing clan).

APPENDIX L.

INDEX.

In the following index Thado words other than the names of persons or places are shown in italics.

The Index serves also as a bibliography of books, other than those given in Appendix J., to which reference is made in the course of the preceding pages, names of authors being given as they occur alphabetically, and against each work separately the pages of the passages in which the reference occurs.
